BELGIAN ADVENTURES

Derk-Jan Eppink

BELGIAN ADVENTURES

A European discovers Belgium

lannoo

www.lannoo.com

This book is also published in Dutch under the title
Avonturen van een Nederbelg. Een Nederlander ontdekt België

English translation Ian Connerty
Layout cover Gert Dooreman
Illustration cover Ever Meulen
© 2004 Lannoo Publishers, Tielt, Belgium
D/2004/45/170 – ISBN 90 209 5625 6

All rights reserved. No part of this book may be reproduced, stored in a retrieval system, or transmitted in any form or by any means, electronic, electrostatic, magnetic tape, mechanical, photocopying, recording or otherwise, without the prior permission in writing of the publisher.

CONTENTS

Introduction 7
All change 11
What on earth are you doing here? 45
A desirable residence, with inconveniences 81
Brussels by night – and day 103
A Burgundian gentleman 125
Reconciliation lunches 145
The cobble eaters 187
The powers that be 199
The holy cross 219
Belgification 249
Photo credits 264

INTRODUCTION

Brussels is the capital of Europe and Belgium is the country that surrounds it. However, like so many other Europeans, I knew little or nothing of Belgium until I came to live and work here. As a child, I scarcely knew that such a country existed. I was born and brought up in the Dutch countryside, a green and brown chequerboard of remote meadows and protective woods. We had seen and heard a lot about Germany, our largest and most powerful neighbour, but Belgium...?

The very name sounded so distant and so alien, partly because 'the Catholics' lived there. 'The nearer you are to the Pope, the nearer you are to trouble', my father used to say. My brother-in-law, a fervent anti-papist, was even worse. He flatly refused ever to cross the border into Belgium. 'Far too many Catholics.' He preferred to go on holiday to northern provinces. 'Reliable people', he said knowingly.

As a result of this family prejudice, the only mental picture I gained of Belgium and Flanders during my youth was from television, with its regular diet of programmes about monks in black robes, the confessional box and the Pope. I sat before the screen with a mixture of amusement and disgust. It seemed so mystical and so horrible all at the same time. I asked myself how the Catholics, with their sordid little lives around the church tower, failed to realise that they were being oppressed. As for Flanders, with its cycling classics, its chip shops and its cafes which opened on Sunday, it seemed like something from another planet.

Nothing in my early years suggested that I would ever become closely associated with Belgium. My first step into the big wide world took me to Amsterdam for my studies.

I was familiar with Germans although they lack a sense of humour. A trip to London taught me that the British don't know how to make coffee. A trip to Paris taught me that the French don't know how to stop talking. Travelling any further south seemed out of the question – it was much too risky, much too different. And what of Belgium? It was a country which simply did not feature in my vision of the world.

Yet it was precisely in this country that I would spend so much of my working life. A country which in many respects is not a country at all, inhabited by a people I had been taught to distrust since birth. I arrived in Brussels with a single suitcase and made straight for the European quarter. Here I occupied a damp and smelly basement in the Stevinstraat. Each morning I watched the feet of the passers-by through my one small, pavement-level window. Of the bodies attached to these feet, I knew nothing. Nor did I wish to know anything. I wanted to learn about Europe, not about Brussels (a city of organised chaos) and certainly not about Belgium. In short, the country and its people left me cold.

Yet after many detours and diversions, I was destined to return to both Brussels and Belgium. As a parliamentary journalist, I found a place in the political heart of the Belgian capital – probably the first Dutchman to do so since 1830. As a European outsider, I discovered the secrets of the inner circles of Belgian society. I met the people and came to know both their good side and their bad side: the curious inhabitants of a curious land, where fact is often stranger than fiction. A land of politicians and prophets, of saints and sinners, of farmers and fraudsters, of bakers and bourgeois. More by accident than design, I was to become involved in a series of adventures with many of these typical Belgian characters: adventures which would alter my view of the country, its capital and its people for ever. In short, I was destined to change from a Netherlander into some sort of a Belgian.

ALL CHANGE

When I told my colleagues that I was planning to move to Belgium, I saw a look of sadness creep into their eyes. They stared at each other in amazement, shaking their heads in disbelief. Surprise quickly turned to sympathy for one so obviously misguided as myself.

'You're going to Belgium? What on earth are you going to do in Belgium?'

A journalist who works for the NRC *Handelsblad* has reached the very top of his profession. There simply isn't a better newspaper in the Netherlands. The NRC has style, the NRC has quality, the NRC has popular respect and political influence. A reporter on the NRC can take pride in all these praiseworthy qualities, even if he does not actually possess them himself. If a NRC editor telephones a Dutch Member of Parliament, he can be certain that he will be called back. In fact, in many cases he will probably be 'called back' before he has even made the first call himself! The paper is especially popular in the government and bureaucratic circles of The Hague, in the ethereal world of official memoranda and policy notes. Ambitious civil servants will do just about anything to get an article published on the NRC's opinion page – for them, this represents a brief moment of fame and recognition in an otherwise dull existence of endless meetings around oval-shaped tables, drinking plastic cups of plastic coffee. Some of these officials seem to think that getting an article in the NRC is the quickest way to scale the slippery ladder of promotion. However, this is by no means certain. The major players in the corridors of power are not always impressed by the public musings of their more junior pen pushers, particularly if they fail to toe the official line.

Having dropped my bombshell, I felt that some kind of explanation was owed to my colleagues in the Parkstraat (where the NRC editorial offices are sandwiched between a software company and the more luxurious premises of the *Algemeen Dagblad* newspaper).

'Why now, for God's sake?', asked one of them in a surprised voice. 'A Purple Coalition has finally got into power, and so you choose this moment to flee the country... Explain it to me...' For many journalists, the Purple Coalition (between 'blue' liberals and 'red' socialists) seemed to symbolise the dawn of a new and more truly 'democratic' society in the Netherlands. The Christian-Democrats had at last come to the end of the road and had finally been thrown onto the scrap heap of history – or so we thought. Many reporters had already developed a kind of lapdog mentality towards the new regime. The corruption and abuses of the 'old guard' would become a thing of the past. From now on, everything in the Dutch political garden would be rosy. And just as things were starting to get better, I wanted to emigrate to Belgium! If it had been London or New York, people would have understood. These are cosmopolitan cities, where major news stories are breaking every day: in short, a professional step in the right direction for any self-respecting journalist. But Belgium, the land of provincial tittle-tattle? To many, my decision seemed almost to be a kind of desertion: Eppink letting the side down again. Either that, or the first sign of an impending midlife crisis.

'Are you really sure?' asked my boss, with genuine concern in his voice.

He was a good and well-meaning man, with whom I had always got on well. Sometimes a bit indecisive, perhaps, and a little too scared of the senior management, but always friendly and accommodating. He also understood and appreciated my rebellious nature, my need to express opinions which went contrary to the popular and accepted view. Although we were more or less the same age, he had an almost fatherly attitude towards me. 'You know as well as I do that Belgium is a funny place – more a kind of hornet's nest, really. None of us Hollanders can ever hope to understand it – and this is the place you want to go to! ... As I said, I hope you're sure.'

The general amazement at my decision became all the greater when I further announced that I was going to work for a Flemish newspaper, which still had the old Flemish battle cry 'All for Flanders, Flanders for Christ' (AVV-VVK) as part of its daily title page. The sympathy that I had previously enjoyed now turned to mild disgust. 'Far too nationalistic' and 'far too Catholic' were amongst the most common reactions. 'Quite spooky, in fact', said one colleague.

The newspaper in question – *De Standaard* – was one of a collection of foreign newspapers which were circulated daily in our editorial room, although few of my colleagues had ever bothered to look at it. Dutch journalists read Dutch newspapers. In the rarefied atmosphere of the Binnenhof (the Dutch parliament) there is little place for the outside world, and almost none for what is happening abroad. One of the exceptions was columnist and ex-editor-in-chief J.L.Heldring, who regularly leafed through *De Standaard* because, as he put it, 'there are no decent Catholic newspapers left in the Netherlands.' The last Catholic daily – De Volkskrant – had severed its links with Rome at the beginning of the 1970's and had since become a mouthpiece for the political left. It had exchanged the world of bishops and mitres for the red scarves of the socialist PvdA – the Dutch Labour Party.

Gradually, I came to accept the fact that my colleagues all thought that I had gone mad. To an extent, I could understand their point of view. The country (Belgium) and the paper (De Standaard) I had chosen were not exactly calculated to appeal to your average career journalist. It all smacked a bit too much of 'Alice in Wonderland': Eppink in search of exotic adventures in foreign parts. And for most Dutchmen Belgium is still the nearest country which can be described as both 'foreign' and 'exotic'.

The reactions from journalists outside my own paper were even more cynical.

'Have you won the lottery, or something? Or is this just some kind of smart tax move?'

A lot of people clearly seemed to think that I had decided to join the growing colony of tax exiles in Brasschaat, where many Dutch industrialists had already transferred both their homes and their fortunes. They were surprised when I answered that I was going to live in Leuven, the city of the Red Baron, Louis Tobback – a man whose small stature belies the size of his mouth. Tobback was reasonably well-known in Dutch press circles, since he had recently won a prize in The Hague for political eloquence. This was hardly a major achievement, since the majority of Dutch politicians are so poor at public speaking that even your average stutterer would give them a good run for their money. Tobback at least had a certain style, albeit a somewhat exaggerated one. He could speak for hours, apparently without notes, and had a penchant for livening up his speeches with a liberal use of spicy invective. Several of his socialist colleagues had felt the sharp edge of his tongue, being described severally as 'a waste of space' or 'ready for the knacker's yard', for their failure to make regular enough visits to the party faithful in the council estates of downtown Leuven. In short, 'Tobbackgrad', as Leuven was already coming to be known, was not the ideal place for someone planning to retire on his ill-gotten capitalist gains.

After a while, people stopped talking about my move. My decision seemed so strange, so incomprehensible, that it was easier not to ask. They wished me luck, of course, with *'les Belges'* but I could see in their eyes that they all expected me to be back within a couple of months, tail firmly between my legs. Perhaps this is why they never bothered to organise a farewell party.

In retrospect, their scepticism was not unreasonable. I was sometimes still sceptical myself. What could a native of the Achterhoek – a Protestant heartland of the Netherlands – possibly find to interest him in Belgium? If it was someone from south of the Great Rivers – the Maas and the Rhine – this might have been more understandable. The average Limburger or North Brabanter has always been spiritually far closer to Rome than to the Reformation. North of the Great Rivers these two provinces are viewed with suspicion, even today, as being too overtly 'papist'. Hardly surprising, then, that there is a strong body of opinion amongst the mandarins in The Hague that the Limburg and North Brabant should be merged to form a single new province, already known disparagingly as 'Limbabwe'. Many government politicians regard North and South Holland as the core of the Netherlands, with the outlying provinces just making up the numbers. For these men, the North and the East are parochial backwaters, but just about acceptable. The South, however, is beyond the political pale – almost like having a 19th century colony on your own backdoor step.

I had a different view of the Netherlands from the gentlemen in The Hague. If you grow up in the Achterhoek (like I did) and if you move to Amsterdam in the hope of discovering something of the world (as I did), you are quickly – and sometimes painfully – confronted with the fact that you are little more than a second class citizen in your own country. As soon as you arrive in 'Holland', the Hollanders make it perfectly clear that you are just another ignorant yokel from the sticks. Your accent is normally the most frequent target of abuse: the soft 'g' of the provinces is regarded as a sign of stupidity by the cityslickers of the West Coast, whereas the guttural sounds of North and South Holland (which have more in common with Arabic than any Germanic language) are supposed to be a mark of cultural sophistication. This kind of self-deception is typical of the Hollanders: they take what everyone else regards as a defect and try to turn it into a virtue. 'A Hollander looking into a mirror sees just what he wants to see – himself.'

The rest of the Netherlands – to which in my youth I was more mentally attuned – looks somewhat differently at Holland and the Hollanders: for most Dutchmen and women 'The West' is the land of big heads and even bigger mouths. Nowhere is this more in evidence than when they are trying to speak a foreign language. Never conscious of their limitations, most Hollanders think that they are born linguists. Sadly, they are mistaken. Ex-premier Joop den Uyl once began a speech to a conference of entrepreneurs in Davos (Switzerland) with the words 'Dear Undertakers', thinking that this meant 'someone who undertakes something', a businessman. Little did he realise that in English it actually means 'someone who buries someone', a funeral director. Not surprisingly, the reaction of his audience was mixed. One of the ministers in the den Uyl government was

Irene Vorrink, who held the Environment portfolio. After a meeting of the European Council of Ministers in Strasbourg, she announced to the press in her best French: 'Je suis ministre Vorrink, je suis ministre du milieu'. She seemed unaware that milieu does not mean 'environment' in French, but 'middle'. One of the puzzled French journalists asked her in perfect English what 'the Minister of the Middle' actually did! Perhaps best of all is the story of a Dutch deputy Minister of Finance, who went to the airport to pick up the chairman of the German Central Bank. As they were driving through Wassenaar, one of the poshest suburbs of The Hague, the German commented 'Schöne Hauser hier', meaning 'nice houses here.' His Dutch colleague replied: 'Ja, aber die Huren sind teuer'. He thought he had said: 'Yes, but the rents are expensive.' In fact, he had said: 'Yes, but the whores are expensive!' No wonder the German looked 'puzzled'!

East of Amersfoort the general view of the Hollanders and of the Randstad – the sprawling urban conurbation along the western Dutch seaboard – is not very complimentary. The Rotterdammers can usually count on a degree of sympathy. They are hard workers and run one of the world's greatest ports. Practical and unpretentious, they are also more willing than most Hollanders to accept outsiders. The Hague has a much less enviable reputation. As the seat of government in an over-centralised land, the city has an exaggerated influence over the lives of the entire Dutch population. 'The country waits, while The Hague debates' is a complaint frequently heard in Dutch town halls from Apeldoorn to Zutphen. Every matter, however trivial, seems destined to pass through the Binnenhof (the Dutch parliament) and the rights and opinions of ordinary citizens are continually being stifled by the long arm of bureaucracy. Little wonder that The Hague is seen as the home of toffee-nosed pen pushers and busybodies. And then there is Amsterdam – the city which likes to see itself as the cosmopolitan centre of Northern Europe, but which is, in fact, more internationally famous as a centre for sex, drugs and crime. The Amsterdammers – with their sing-song nasal accent – always have the answer to everybody's problems – apart from their own. The city has a rich past but a poor present, and can only survive thanks to financial subsidies from the outlying provinces – the very provinces which the Amsterdammers are always so keen to insult and belittle. But that is how the Amsterdammers are: insular, insensitive and always ready to bite the hand that feeds them. Or at least that's how the majority of Dutchmen view the inhabitants of their own capital city. And true or not, it was also my view – at least before I actually went there.

When I broke the news that I wanted to go to Amsterdam to study, my father was strongly against the idea. 'Amsterdam – in all that filth and misery. Over my dead body!' Nijmegen was also dismissed: 'too Catholic' (this, however, was no longer true: by the 1970's Nijmegen was more left-wing than the Kremlin, being full of students who had all discovered Chairman Mao as the new Jesus). Groningen was an option, but was too far north for comfort: 'provincial, a backwater.'

I decided to ask our local priest to mediate with my father. He was a philosophical soul, who specialised in practical wisdom and very long sermons: 'two peppermint sermons' as I used to call them (based on the length of time it took me to suck my way through the sweets in my jacket pocket). He knew, of course, that his sermons were too long, but he refused to do anything about it: he seemed to think that after six days of sinning, a little suffering on Sunday – even if it was only our backsides that suffered – was good for the soul.

Fortunately for me, he quickly came up with an answer to my problem: 'Why not study at the Free University in Amsterdam?' As a Protestant university, this would offer the necessary degree of guidance to protect me from the corrupt outside world. What's more, it would give me the opportunity to study law under the famous Professor I.A. Diepenhorst. Professor Diepenhorst was a regular contributor to programmes on the NCRV television channel and was renowned for the length and grammatical complexity of his sentences. My father was one of his biggest fans. If I was going to get the chance to be taught by Professor Diepenhorst, then perhaps Amsterdam was not such a bad choice after all.

Diepenhorst was an almost legendary figure in academic circles. Although nearing retirement age, he still lived at home with his mother in Zeist. Rumour also had it that he conducted examinations in his car, whilst on his way to his holidays in Germany. The candidates had to report to Zeist and were driven off in a southerly direction, with Ma Diepenhorst at the wheel and the professor firing off a whole barrage of testing questions. The candidates were always dropped off at Arnhem and consequently had just 60 kilometres to prove their satisfactory knowledge of the Dutch legal system. Happily, for most of them, Ma Diepenhorst drove very slowly.

At long last, I arrived in Amsterdam and soon found myself struggling to adjust from life in a small village to life in one of Europe's major cities. It wasn't easy. People from the Achterhoek are quiet, calm and sober. They are country people, cautious and careful. A city-dweller is none of these things. He is usually quick-tongued, impulsive and volatile. A countryman always has space around him; a city-dweller sees space as something to be occupied. Perhaps this explains why, in spite of all my efforts, I never really became a true Amsterdammer. I never even bothered registering as an official resident! The city had too many moods, too much tinsel and glitter and too few people who did any real work. There was lots of talk, lots of coffee, lots of shopping, lots of missed appointments and lots of broken promises. In short, Amsterdam was a city for the tourists and the lotus-eaters. From outside it all looked slick and glossy, but the closer you got the more you saw the pain and the dirt.

I found myself living in a third storey back apartment in the district known as 'De Pijp'. I rented my room from a local Dutch woman, whose husband spent all day in his dressing gown, slumped in front of the television. The Dutch colony of Surinam had just become independent and many of the Surinamers had exercised their right to come and live in the Netherlands. Large numbers of them had made their new homes in 'De Pijp', with far-reaching consequences for the character of the district. What had once been a traditional and authentically 'Dutch' community was transformed in a matter of months into what sociologists are now pleased to call a multi-cultural society. The old cafés and the old shops gradually began to disappear, to be replaced by coffee houses and all-night stores. Not everyone was happy with the change. My landlord for one. 'Just give me three months', he foamed angrily, 'and I'll sort the whole bloody lot of them out. No questions asked.' I never troubled to enquire just how he planned to do this (although I think I could guess) and instead concentrated on trying to keep him sweet, by bringing him a regular supply of fresh eggs from the Achterhoek.

Amsterdam might not have been my favourite city, but my time spent there was important in helping me to make my way in the world. Amsterdammers were different. Their way of life was different: very verbal and very direct. I missed the warmth of the social contact in our village, where everyone knew everyone else. The city was anonymous: not like a real community but more a collection of individuals, of whom I knew only a few. People seemed to have no time for each other, and what was important for one person was totally irrelevant to the next. There was no fellow feeling, no appreciation of the other man's point of view. And worst of all was the Amsterdammer's built-in belief that Amsterdam is the best and most important city in the world. If it hadn't happened in Amsterdam, it hadn't happened at all. It was a kind of urban provincialism gone wild.

Yet for all its shortcomings, Amsterdam gave me two important things: it showed me the way I wanted to go in my life and it taught me how best to follow that way. The move from village to city had given me a new kind of mental flexibility, a flexibility that allowed me to mix with people from many different backgrounds, without ever revealing my true self. I was like a chameleon, who could change on the outside, whilst always remaining the same on the inside. Consequently, I was able to more than hold my own in my seminars with the illustrious Professor Diepenhorst, but was equally at home chatting to my unemployed landlord about his dubious racial theories. It was as if I had developed some kind of internal compass, a sixth sense which allowed me to cross over social and cultural divides with ease. And so it was, with a wink and a joke, that I finally learnt to live with the Hollanders, without ever becoming one of them.

After five years, my studies in Amsterdam came to an end. 'What now?' I asked myself. Initially, the diplomatic service had a certain appeal, but after a few student visits to Dutch embassies abroad I quickly dropped the idea. The life was too structured, too conformist, too rootless. Did I really want to become one of these jet-set nomads? No, I didn't. But while it's one thing to know what you don't want to do, it's an altogether different matter to know what you actually *do* want to do. I was running out of time and options, when a friend suggested I might try the training programme at the European Commission in Brussels. My first reaction was sceptical, but as the weeks passed the idea grew on me, until I thought it might actually be fun. But Europe meant living in Brussels. In Belgium.

Both the city and the country were totally unknown to me and, in spite of their relative nearness, I had the feeling that they were a long way away from home. I was convinced that the people of Brussels only spoke French – the solitary piece of information (wrong, as it turned out) that I remembered from my only visit to Brussels, as a student on a day-trip to NATO.

My general impressions of the country at that time were not favourable. In my personal atlas I had catalogued Belgium as the 'messy' bit on the map between the Netherlands and France. Unknown, unloved and preferably to be avoided. My arrival in the Stevinstraat in Brussels (just around the corner from the headquarters of the European Commission and next to the star-shaped Berlaymont Building, where I was to work on the 11th floor) did little to alter these preconceptions. Dilapidated houses in all shapes and sizes, ugly blind walls covered with insulation panels, potholes in the road, loose paving slabs which slopped water into your shoes. The planning madness, which began the moment you crossed the Dutch border at Roosendaal, seemed to have reached its highpoint in central Brussels. In short, the place was a dump. A concrete monster, a festering eyesore, a Third World enclave in the middle of Europe. A bastard city in a bastard land, that had only come into being by political chance. A city and a land, moreover, populated by a people who seemed to have elevated lawlessness into a kind of civic virtue. Even the newspapers were strange, as if they had been made on another planet: grey, boring and full of stories I did not understand about governments, crises, strikes and budget cuts. It seemed to me that the political superstructure of Belgium was as rotten as its social and cultural foundations.

After one week, I had already drawn my conclusions: 'I want nothing to do with this country!'

As a result, I spent nearly all my time in the European complex, a world of office blocks and different nationalities, where I was safe from the mad country outside. My initial training programme quickly passed, but I was able to stay on as an assistant in the European Parliament in the Belliardstraat. With the extra money I now earned, I was even able to move out of my damp basement in the Stevinstaat and into a more spacious room on the second floor of the same building. I now actually had a window I could look out of! It seemed like the height of luxury.

It was in the European Parliament that I met my first Flemings. I was certain that any Dutch-speaker had to be unhappy living in such a disordered society as Belgium. 'It was bad luck to be born in a dump like this, eh', I said in a cheery voice that was intended to convey sympathetic understanding. To my amazement, they reacted with something very close to indignation. 'We're very happy, thank you very much. At least we don't all live in identical boxes, like your lot. And we eat better. And we have more fun....' It was clear from their tone that I had insulted them. This set me to thinking: if the Flemish like living here, maybe the country outside Brussels is not so bad after all. It seemed a possibility that was worth exploring further.

Surrendering my hitherto self-imposed isolation, I decided to go in search of more Flemings. One place I knew where I could find them was on the sixth floor of the European Parliament building. The sixth floor housed the parliament's bar, and wherever there's a bar you will usually find the Flemish. 'Permanent dry throat is a century's old problem in Flanders', I was told by my new friends. The Flemish dialect might not have been recognised as one of the European Community's official languages, but it was certainly one of the official languages in the Community's bar!

Yet even here, in my new Flemish environment, the wider question of 'Belgium' was never far away. The most frequent topic of conversation was the so-called *Bende van Nijvel*, a gang of bandits who had carried out several violent robberies at supermarkets in and around Brussels. Dozens of innocent shoppers had already been gunned down, so that the whole country was scared to go and pick up its groceries on a Friday evening. The streets were full of armoured cars and policemen patrolling with machine guns. There were even stories that the police might be involved in some of the attacks themselves and that a coup d'état was being planned by the extreme right. It all seemed more reminiscent of Latin America than Northern Europe and my feeling of insecurity in this strange country grew to new heights. At the same time, I also began to get my first insights into how the Belgian system actually works – or doesn't. If there had been thirty innocent deaths in the Netherlands, the country would have been torn apart until the guilty were found. In Belgium not a single arrest was ever made but the activities of the *'Bende'* suddenly and mysteriously stopped. It was clear that in Belgium there was a hidden agenda, an unseen world just below the surface, so close that you could almost touch it – almost, but not quite.

On the sixth floor, the talk was mostly of politics. Belgian politics, not the European variety. Many of the Flemings were involved in politics at a local level, most of them as members of town councils. 'Politics begins at home', they informed me. 'Or 'next to the church tower', as we say in Flanders.' Every day they were sucked into the vortex of Brussels, but every night they went back to their church towers, to discuss the boring minutiae of local issues with little old ladies in cold parish halls. Apparently, this was the only way to make a political career in Flanders.

One of these political commuters was Rudy from Ghent. He was a talkative thirty-something, with a happy smile and a mild tendency toward cynicism. He was ambitious to rise to the top with what he called 'The Blues'. To me, blue was just a colour. To him, 'blue' was a political concept: blue is the colour of the Flemish Liberal Party. Rudy eventually hoped to make it into parliament with 'The Blues', but for the time being he was still working hard at a local level in Ghent.

'Rudy', I asked him, 'how is it possible that the *"Bende van Nijvel"* is massacring people left, right and centre, while the government does nothing and not a single arrest is made?' Rudy looked into his glass. 'You don't really understand much about it, do you?' he replied softly. 'In Belgium there are sometimes things you don't see and sometimes you see things that aren't there.' I took another sip of my cheap fizzy wine masquerading as champagne and thought about this. 'There are sometimes things that you don't see.' Well, this at least sounded logical enough: nobody can possibly see everything. But what about 'sometimes you see things that aren't there'? I had seen the pictures of the attacks and knew beyond doubt that they had actually taken place. I had also seen a government that looked as if it wanted to act. 'No, not really', said Rudy. 'And that is what I mean. You see a government, but in Belgium there is no government. It's all a show. There are just different political parties. They are the real bosses. They decide where the subsidies go. They decide who gets honey and who gets jam. They have their own clients and their own circle of favoured friends.' The implications of all this were not pleasant. The government was not acting, for the simple reason that there was no real government. There was no public interest, just party interest. As if reading my mind, Rudy's next statement confirmed my worst fears: 'If this coalition falls, it won't be because of thirty dead people in supermarket car parks – it will be because of the language question in Voeren.'

I looked sharply at Rudy, who wore a cynical smile on his lips. A crude and unnecessary comment, I thought. But what if it was true? What if thirty innocent victims meant less than the wild ravings of José Happard, a failed apple farmer from a small Limburg village in the middle of nowhere. This needed further investigation: perhaps it was finally time that I made an effort to learn more about 'Belgium'.

My first step was to buy a television, so that I could watch the daily news. I had already tried the Flemish newspapers, but they were almost unreadable: full of strange names, odd abbreviations and a plethora of political parties which I had never heard of. True, it was all written in what was supposed to be Dutch but to a Dutchman (as opposed to a Fleming) it was a code language of another solar system.

Not that the television news was much better. The BRT approach was wooden, to say the least. A dusty set, newsreaders in handled with a lighter touch but the moment the news turned toward the home front the reports became more and more cautious. The tone was respectful, almost humble. The leader of the government was always referred to as 'Mr.Prime-Minister', 'Mr.' being a general term of submission in Belgium. As a result of this obedient attitude – an attitude common to most Belgian journalists at that time – items referring to the government or to the parties were so formal as to be almost meaningless.

It looked like Rudy was right, after all: the broadcasting services were clearly in the pocket of the party bosses. Once, in a rare outburst of journalistic independence, the news department of the BRT went on strike. A reporter had been sacked for asking the Prime Minister an 'impolite question'. The strikers demanded reinstatement for their colleague, otherwise there would be no news. And so for days, there was simply 'no news'. After a decent interval, the strikers went tamely back to work. The journalist was never reinstated. His lack of 'obedience' had proved fatal.

The television news at least made me more familiar with the faces of the Belgian politicians. As far as I was concerned, most of them looked as though they would have been more at home in The Muppet Show than in the Wetstraat, the seat of the Belgian government. The Prime Minister was Wilfred Martens, with his chubby, slightly effeminate face and his expressionless look. No doubt he was a good and sincere man, but at first glance he was not the kind of person from whom you could expect great deeds. Masterly inactivity was more his style: he was the type who would sweat his problems out, not take them by the scruff of the neck.

Then there was the extraordinary Minister of Transport, a busy and excitable little man with a fluffy beard – a certain De Croo.

And what of that angry young man who was endlessly talking of budgets and money – Guy Verhofstadt. Somehow he always seemed irritable, a look emphasised by an uncontrollable lock of hair and a set of front teeth you could park your bike between. He had the air of an agitated Bugs Bunny: energetic, restless and jumpy. Clearly, he was the joker in the pack.

Equally volatile was Jean Gol, an explosive man with a bald head and a high-flown manner of speaking. His mission in life was to stop immigration into Belgium and he had even passed a law bearing his name to prove it.

By contrast, the Minister of Social Affairs had the appearance of a scoutmaster, dressed as he invariably was in a polo-neck sweater which pushed up too far under his chin. In addition, he combined the pear-shaped frame of a walrus with the barking voice of a sea lion. His name was Jean-Luc Dehaene.

Last in the line-up was another noisy man, who seemed to spend all his time shouting and screaming at others: our old friend, Louis Tobback.

These Belgian Muppets were a remarkable group: mean, moody but not – at least in my eyes – very magnificent. With the exception of the impassive Martens, they all seemed to be one-man volcanoes. I wondered how they ever hoped to run a country together.

Gradually, Rudy began to fill me in on the backgrounds of these colourful characters, their strengths and weaknesses, their likes and dislikes. They each had their own cabinet of ten or so staff, all recruited (for preference) from their own home district. Protection and promotion of this home district was their main political concern. To obtain a solid electoral base with the voters, they made sure that 'their people' were appointed in large numbers to government industries such as Sabena, the post office and the railways. These favours would then be repaid in the form of preferential votes at election time. In a similar way, they used all kinds of inside manoeuvres to ensure that the 'right men' were appointed as judges, public prosecutors and police officers. It short, they seemed to have a finger in every political pie.

'Looks can be deceptive, though', said Rudy. 'These ministers seem powerful, but they're not. The real power is in the hands of the party chairman. And together, these chairmen form a kind of junta, which runs the country.' This, at least, was language I could understand, even if I was more used to hearing it applied to General Pinochet's Chile! 'The chairmen tell the ministers what they have to do. And if they don't do it, they get kicked out.' But how had the chairmen come to acquire such influence, I asked? 'That's easy', continued Rudy. 'They're the ones who control the really important political power blocks: the unions, the pension funds and the trade confederations.'

At last, I was beginning to see the light. The party chairmen were powerful because, in the final analysis, they were the supreme defenders of sectional interest, be it Catholic or socialist or liberal. In short, Belgium was a land with no guiding national principles. Instead, it was a country in the grip of sectarianism, a sectarianism oiled and promoted by the various party machines and by their appointees throughout the system. Politics in Belgium had been reduced to a question of 'jobs for the boys': who got them and who gave them. Some of the practices (to my innocent Dutch mind) seemed almost to border on the illegal. It was not uncommon for party members to be appointed to the cabinet office of a national minister, only to be sent back to the same party on 'detached duty' at the ministry's expense! In other words, the central government ended up paying for the political staffs of the individual parties! They were labelled 'submarines'.

It was a system that reminded me of one of those Russian dolls, a Matrjoska: inside every doll, there was another smaller doll waiting to get out. I thought it was corrupt and said as much to Rudy. 'The Belgian way is not such a bad way', he replied coolly. 'It works as long as everyone can be kept happy. And up to now, that's always been possible.'

This equal distribution of the political spoils also applied to scandal and failure. If there were shady goings-on in the Catholic or liberal party, the news was certain to be announced in the socialist *De Morgen* newspaper. By the same token, if the socialists were once again discovered with their hands in the till, the story would break in one of the Catholic or liberal dailies. Thus the Belgian 'balance' was maintained, even in shame, and the junta made sure that everybody got a piece of the cake – and a share of the blame!

Just as I was beginning to get the hang of things in Belgium, my time with the European Parliament came to an end. My job as an assistant had been little more than another subsidised training course, not a permanent position. I wasn't really sorry. During my time in Brussels I had gained insight and I had learnt how the system worked. But a career as a parliamentary assistant ultimately meant being dependent on the politicians, with all their whims and fancies, and I didn't think I was really cut out for that. There had already been a few problems in this respect. From my 'office' in the Stevinstraat, I had written several articles for Belgian and Dutch newspapers, including interviews with

Jacques Delors, the Chairman of the European Commission, and Lord Carrington, the Secretary-General of NATO. This had not always been well received by my political masters. 'It's my name I'm supposed to see in the papers, Eppink – not yours!' one of my bosses had told me testily. I took this to be a hint and applied for a job as a reporter on the NRC *Handelsblad*.

Even so, I still have fond memories of my time with the European Parliament. I did a lot of fun things and met a lot of fun people – some of them a bit too 'funny', as subsequent events would prove.

In an office just down the corridor from mine sat a group of assistants from the German SPD (Social Democrat) delegation. Some of these were active in the young socialist movement of the SPD, known as the Juso's, and one day they asked me if I would like to become their new treasurer. I readily agreed but soon discovered that the Juso account was almost empty. To correct this sorry state of affairs, I decided to increase membership contributions by 300% and put a block on all unnecessary expenditure. The result was uproar. The Juso's were horrified that they would no longer be able to carry out their radical '*linke Aktionen*' – such as organising photographic exhibitions or issuing pamphlets! The Juso's fell under the jurisdiction of the Brussels district of the SPD, which in turn was responsible to the SPD regional office in Aachen, just across the German border. The strong man in Aachen was a European MP, known to all as 'Comrade' Dieter. He quickly reversed my block on expenditure, with the comment: 'money is meant to be used, sonny!' It was a subject he seemed to know a lot about. Flamboyant and inevitably accompanied by expensive-looking ladies in fur coats, Comrade Dieter had acquired a reputation for being very generous with other people's cash. He drove fast cars and led a fast life. As a member of the European-Arab Dialogue Group, he made regular visits to Colonel Gadhaffi in Libya. For all that, he had the air of a parvenu about him – a man who was out of his class and out of his depth. Years later I read in *Der Spiegel* that he had been picked up by the German police with a suitcase full of forged Swiss francs. He went to jail, of course, and his brother gave the whole story an interesting twist by chaining himself naked to the prison gates in protest.

Another curious figure I met was Ad, a fellow Dutchman. Ad was a tall, curly-haired Adonis of great charm and good humour. He used to work for the VPRO – one of the Dutch broadcasting services – but had recently been engaged as a spokesman for the socialist group in Brussels. I liked listening to Ad and I thought that he was a decent enough bloke. He had the ability to make you feel that you belonged, whatever your political persuasion or national background – a rare gift in a world usually dominated by rivalry and hate. In short, Ad was the kind of man to whom little old ladies would willingly entrust their life's savings. Or so it seemed.

It was not long before the first stories began to circulate. Ad was always 'out of the office'. Ad was always at a conference in some strange and exotic destination that seemed to have little to do with European politics. Ad's expenses claims never quite added up. In a cloud of suspicion, Ad resigned and went into business for himself. With predictable results.

The *Vrij Nederland* weekly of 18 April 1998 gave full details of Ad's sorry demise. Pretending to be a famous surgeon and accompanied by his stunning female accomplice, he had gone 'shopping' at a number of Holland's most famous jewellers. He pointed to the Rolex on his wrist, to his flashy Jaguar car outside the door and promised that he would return next week to settle his bill. He never did, of course. And it all worked perfectly, until the day when a suspicious jeweller tipped off the police. Poor old Ad was caught red-handed and was sent to prison for a whole string of frauds and bad debts. Knowing Ad, he probably now spends his time conning the cons.

Having arrived in Belgium with just a suitcase, I left three years later with a whole vanload of stuff and went off to work for the NRC *Handelsblad*. I felt that I had learned a lot about Europe and a lot about politics, but the country itself, with its secret rooms and closed doors, remained something of a mystery to me. As I drove away, I remember saying to myself: 'One day I'll come back and really find out what makes this place tick.' I had no idea when this 'one day' would be, but it was an idea that never left me.

I worked for a total of seven years for the NRC *Handelsblad*, first in Africa, later as a correspondent in Warsaw and finally at the political desk in The Hague. In the beginning, Poland was an interesting assignment, but after the fall of the Berlin Wall the attention of the world moved on to the crisis in the Balkans and the disintegration of the Soviet Union. Some days I had almost nothing to do. My articles remained firmly lost at the bottom of the foreign editor's in-tray and it seemed that all the real news was passing me by. To break the boredom, I went swimming every day at the Victoria International Hotel, not far from the Monument of the Unknown Soldier, where the German Chancellor Willy Brandt made his famous plea for reconciliation and forgiveness. As a result of these daily visits, I became quite a well-known figure in local hotel society, so much so that I was even once asked to take part as a judge in a beauty competition. The Poles have a keen eye for beautiful women and they wanted to see how the local product stood up to foreign examination. I was happy to offer my 'expertise' on the subject and it turned out to be the high spot of my stay in Warsaw!

From Poland it was back to The Hague, and the political desk. For someone used to foreign assignments (as I was), life in the Binnenhof seemed dull and parochial. The world was big, whereas the activities of the government and the Second Chamber seemed small – and small-minded – by comparison. 'A glorified anthill', as one of my colleagues once put it. The eccentric Professor Pim Fortuyn was still relatively unknown, little more than an insignificant provider of unasked for advice. At that time, the concept of a political murder was a purely historical one (which, as the parliamentary experts will tell you, was last put into practice in 1672 on the unfortunate De Witt brothers). The idea that such a thing might happen in this day and age was almost laughable. When MP Theo Joekes wrote a novel called 'Murder in the Binnenhof', most bookstores catalogued it under the heading 'science fiction'.

I arrived back in The Hague full of enthusiasm and good intentions, but I soon found the whole atmosphere stifling and restrictive, almost as if someone had thrown a woollen blanket over my head. A broad view of the world seemed a matter of irrelevance to most of The Hague's official residents, whereas small and seemingly trivial matters could sometimes be blown up out of all proportion. One Friday night I was left in charge of the weekend desk as 'night watchman'. This sounded impressive but simply meant I had to be on hand in case any major news stories broke. However, things all seemed very quiet and, as the weather was nice, I telephoned a friend and asked if he fancied a bike ride out to the beach at Katwijk, where I knew a really good mussel restaurant. We set off half an hour later, little knowing that the Chairman of the PvdA – a lady with the misleading name of Sint (Saint) – had chosen that evening to announce her surprise resignation. When I arrived back in the office at 10 o'clock there was widespread panic that the 'night watchman' could not be found and that the competition were already well ahead with the story. Teams of nervous looking news editors – all hastily summoned from their homes – were running round like headless chickens, desperately trying to make up the lost ground. Personally, I couldn't see what all the fuss was about – after all, it was only some politician who had resigned: it wasn't as if anyone had died. However, I knew enough to recognise that I had made a mistake and so I decided to confess before someone else started looking for the guilty party. 'Guilt' is a strange concept in the Netherlands. If you freely admit your guilt, then you can quite often get away with a light slap on the wrist. If, on the other hand, you wait until somebody else decides you are guilty, then you can normally expect to have the book thrown at you. I thought it best to go for the first option and so I rang the sub-editor in charge and apologised with the innocence of a well-meaning but slightly clumsy beginner. Luckily, it worked. The matter would be taken no further, but I was left in no doubt that I wouldn't be quite so fortunate should I fail to resist the mussels of Katwijk a second time.

To break the monotony of the political desk, I began to look for politically related themes which might touch a nerve with a seemingly indifferent Dutch public. Third World aid seemed one such possibility. The Hollanders are very proud of their record in this area and are convinced that they do 'a lot of good'. What would they think if they really knew what happened to all their money?

I discussed the idea with a friend of mine from the foreign desk. He had worked in India and I had covered Africa for three years, so between us we had considerable experience of the aid circus. Above all, we both knew that a large percentage of all aid money went on maintaining the life styles of senior aid managers – the 'Lords of Poverty', as they are sometimes known. The more we talked about it, the more my friend and I were convinced that we were onto a winner. It offered the possibility of a fruitful collaboration between the political and foreign desks on a matter of broad public interest, with plenty of juicy details and scandalous revelations. One Sunday afternoon we worked our way through several thick government files on the subject and spoke to various ex-aid workers, all of whom had begun with good intentions and all of whom now had nothing but contempt for what they called the 'aid-mafia'. Everything we heard simply confirmed our own first impressions: this was a story that needed to be told.

Unfortunately, it wasn't quite as a simple as that.

First of all, the subject of Third World aid did not fall under the jurisdiction of either the political or the foreign desk. To get our article published, we would therefore have to try and bypass the responsible editor. At that time, he was trying to get into the good books of the then Minister for Overseas Development, Jan Pronk. As a result, he was very keen to distance himself from anything that might seem critical of government policy – after all, he didn't want to lose all those nice, free trips abroad. A negative article such as ours wouldn't suit him at all.

In addition, it quickly became clear that Third World aid is a 'sensitive' subject in Dutch journalistic circles. Your average Dutchman gives money to aid charities for reasons which he thinks of as 'noble'. In short, he does it because it makes him feel good. We ran the risk of making ourselves – and our paper – very unpopular if we suddenly decided to shatter this cherished illusion.

Finally, we seriously underestimated the size and strength of the aid lobby. In fact, it would probably be more accurate to speak of an industry than a lobby – an industry devoted to the protection of its own interests and not those of the Third World. In this day and age, aid has less to do with the homeless, the hungry and the sick, and more to do with the financial interests of the donor cartels. It is a world of 'you scratch my back and I'll scratch yours', dressed up in emotional rhetoric, designed solely to mislead a too-trusting public.

We intended to expose all these matters: the shortcomings, the scandals, the well-intentioned but often misguided pet projects of certain Dutch pressure groups, such as the millions wasted on promoting theatre productions in Africa or the sponsoring of radical women's rights movements in Islamic lands (which often result in the women in question being ostracised from their own community, or even worse).

Once our plans became known, there was considerable opposition. Even many of our own editorial colleagues found the article too right wing. 'How dare you attack all those well-meaning people?' we were asked repeatedly. Several attempts were made both inside and outside the newspaper to have the article blocked. On the night before publication was due, I had to stay in the office until the small hours, in order to prevent a 'colleague' from having the piece scrapped at the last minute.

When the article finally appeared, there was a storm of reaction. Some of it was positive, some of it was negative, some of it was downright threatening and obscene. We had wanted to touch a nerve and it looked like we had succeeded. Maybe behind the facade the world was not such a nice place? Perhaps aid didn't always help? These were messages that many people found difficult to take – particularly as it struck at the average Dutchman's own image of himself. Not surprisingly, the aid lobby was furious, but that was the least of our worries.

The only person who really had a right to be angry was the editor on development issues. It was his portfolio after all. A few days earlier, he had set off on yet another 'study visit' with Minister Pronk to the Dutch West Indies, knowing nothing of our plans. When the story broke, the Ministry faxed a copy direct to their boss's hotel. Pronk's reaction gave a whole new meaning to the phrase 'Caribbean storm'. Our poor, unsuspecting editorial colleague never knew what hit him. His visit was ruined and his relations with the Minister were in tatters. It was hardly surprising, perhaps, that upon his return to Schiphol he had little sympathy for our arguments that our deception had all been in 'a good cause'.

After a while, my work in The Hague became increasingly monotonous. I began to get tired of wandering through the corridors of the Binnenhof, chasing after politicians in the vain hope of getting an interesting or provocative comment. Some politicians didn't require much chasing. One day I was phoned by Frans Weisglas, an MP for the VVD Party (who would later become Chairman of the Lower House): 'I'm out of the country for the next few days', he informed me, 'and I just wondered if you wanted my opinion on world matters before I left!' This was boring work – few politicians dared to say anything that was controversial enough to be worth printing – and the result was a stream of boring articles which somehow had to be made 'interesting', or rather sexed up.

One of the few genuinely 'interesting' developments at this time was the advance of new technology in the newspaper business. During the 1994 election campaign I was issued with my first mobile phone. By present-day standards, it was a large and clumsy affair but I thought it was great. I could go wherever I wanted, but still remain in constant touch with the office. This was to have unexpected benefits during the long hot summer of 1994, whilst the negotiations to form the Purple Coalition dragged endlessly on.

Instead of hanging around the Binnenhof, waiting for the latest snippets of irrelevant news, I decided to move my centre of operations to what I called the 'quiet beach', an unspoilt stretch of sand between Scheveningen (so beloved of Dutch day-trippers) and Kijkduin (so beloved of German tourists). I have always been fascinated by the seashore: the timeless views across the waves, the cry of the gulls, the silent passing of distant ships. On the beach, I can find true peace, a peace which helps me to put things in proper perspective, to decide what is really important and what only seems so.

And thanks to the mobile phone, I could now make this delightful spot my temporary place of work. I dialled the number for the RVD, the all-knowing Government Information Office, and asked for the latest update on the situation. 'The discussions are continuing and we have no further comment at this stage.' This suited me fine. Whether I phoned for such useless information from behind a desk or from on top of a sand dune made absolutely no difference. I chose for the sand dune and decided to catch up on some lost reading. Henry Kissinger's 'Diplomacy' had just been published and I spent several pleasant summer days engrossed in the history of the European balance of power through the centuries. And between the machinations of Metternich and Bismarck, I also had time for some serious thinking.

Did I really want to stay in The Hague, chasing quotes? No, I did not. Could I do something else and, if so, what? In the Netherlands, there didn't seem to be a lot of choice. There was little chance of a chief editor's job and my work was being increasingly labelled as too outspoken and too rightist, following several articles on controversial subjects such as immigration. Did I want to spend my remaining years fighting this stereotyped view, a lone crusader against the prevailing climate of political correctness? Again, I did not. What about a complete change of direction, then? The idea certainly appealed to me, but I kept coming back to the same question: what? what? what?

In the calm of the 'quiet beach', my thoughts often returned to my time in Belgium, now more than a decade before. I had always promised myself that I would go back one day. Had that moment now come? Perhaps it had.

I telephoned an old friend, who was a reporter for *De Standaard*, one of Flanders' leading quality papers. He was a bright and cheerful man, with a big, bushy beard, whom I had first met during a trip in Africa. He was an expert on the Congo, or Zaire as it was now known, and had even interviewed that county's menacing (if slightly ludicrous) president, Mobutu Sese Seko. We had kept in touch since we both returned to Europe and I had visited him recently in Belgium. Even so, I was almost too embarrassed to call him. 'A Dutchman who wants to work for a Flemish newspaper: it's a pretty weird idea', I told myself. What would he think of it? What did I really think of it? I dialled anyway. 'Could I come and work for you?' I asked hesitantly. 'Perhaps on the foreign desk to begin with, and then maybe later on the political desk?'

My friend listened politely. I had no idea what he was thinking, but at least he wasn't laughing. 'I'll ask the senior editor and get back to you as soon as I can.' For a while I heard nothing and I began to imagine that my suggestion really was as crazy as I still sometimes thought. Several days later, my phone rang. 'The senior editor thinks it's a good idea and sees no reason why you shouldn't start on the political desk straight away. Someone has just left, so it would be useful if you could start as soon as possible.'

I was taken completely by surprise, shocked even. To start right away and in the political arena. Doubts began to surface in my mind. 'Would I be accepted?' 'Would it not be a total disaster?' I had an instinctive feeling that a Dutchman would not be welcomed with open arms in Flanders. The Flemish are friendly on the outside, but inside I had the feeling that they view most Dutchmen as being loudmouthed, arrogant gits. A bit like the Dutch view the Germans. The only way for a German to succeed in the Netherlands is to become the Prince Consort – and even then he is still likely to get a bumpy ride. But a Dutchman with no experience of Belgian politics as a political editor on a Flemish newspaper? This was stretching things a bit too far.

The senior editor of *De Standaard* called me the next day. I was sitting in the middle of the NRC editorial office at the time, and so I had to answer his questions with a series of whispered and non-committal replies. The idea that what I was planning might become common knowledge amongst my Dutch colleagues made me break out in a cold sweat. 'Why don't you come and talk it over?' he suggested.

A week or so later, on a boiling hot summer's day, I sat across the table from my prospective new employer in a Thai restaurant on the Karel de Grotelaan in Brussels. For a Fleming, the senior editor was very direct and businesslike, with a serious (to my mind, almost Calvinist) look. He had obviously thought the matter through and he had a clear plan of action.

'Look, if we're going to do it, it's best that we do it quickly', he said. 'It's surprising and it's new – I think it will work.' 'But will they accept me', I whined. 'I really don't know', he answered honestly. 'It's a risk. I would guess that 50% are against it and that the other 50% have no real opinion one way or the other. Nobody is actually for you, but I think that most of them will give you the benefit of the doubt. Why not take a chance? Try it and see.'

And after much further soul-searching, I did. A future with the NRC meant more of the same dreary routine, with which I was already so mind-numbingly familiar. It was a safe option, but it was hardly inspiring. By contrast, a move to Belgium would represent a kind of journalistic leap into the dark: scary, risky but undeniably a challenge. My path would not be an easy one. On the contrary, it would be long, hard and full of potholes. There was a chance that I would stumble and fall, that each new step might be my last. I knew that all eyes would be on me and that one wrong word might bring half of Flanders down on my neck. But I felt it was worth the gamble: wisdom and insight in the long term is often only to be gained at the expense of struggle and suffering in the short term. Or as the Americans put it: 'no pain, no gain'.

I remembered the cryptic remark from my old friend Rudy. 'In Belgium there are sometimes things you don't see and sometimes you see things that aren't there.' I was taking a voyage into the unknown. My destination seemed so near, yet so far away. I knew that I would have to get my feet wet in the murky waters of Belgian politics and I knew that I would have to do it fast. There was no time to test the water with my toe – if I wanted to keep my head above the surface, there was only one option: total immersion, as quickly as possible.

It had to be all or nothing – there was no way back.

WHAT ON EARTH ARE YOU DOING HERE?

Before I arrived for my first day in my new editorial office, I knew that I was unlikely to be welcomed with open arms. My new editor-in-chief had told me as much some months before. At best, I would be given the benefit of the doubt by a minority. The majority would be more openly hostile.

The newspaper premises themselves seemed equally unwelcoming: an ugly, angular building on a nondescript industrial estate in Groot Bijgaarden, just outside Brussels. Like most of the major dailies, *De Standaard* had moved out from the centre of the city, for what were euphemistically referred to as 'organisational' reasons. In reality, it just cost too much. As a result, instead of being located in the vibrant heart of a major city, with all its political intrigues, we were now isolated in a barren industrial wasteland, sandwiched between various motorways and surrounded by companies specialising in nothing more exciting than forklift trucks and car repairs.

However, our new home was not completely without sensation. One of the nearby metal-processing companies had manufactured parts for the notorious 'Super-cannon', which threatened to fall into the hands of Saddam Hussein. This undesirable possibility was nipped in the bud when the director of the company, John Bull, was shot dead on his front doorstep. The killers disappeared without trace, suggesting a professional 'hit'. Those in the know were convinced that the Mossad – the Israeli secret service – was behind the whole operation. It was the only interesting thing to happen in Groot Bijgaarden during all my time there.

As I opened the door to the editorial office on my first day, I could almost feel the scepticism of my new colleagues move across the room to greet me. In most cases, their suspicions were masked behind what seemed to be a friendly smile, but I could still read the disbelief in their eyes.

'What's this bloody Dutchman doing here?', I could see them thinking. 'Come to tell us how to do our jobs, has he?'

In typically Belgian fashion, nobody said this straight to my face, but it didn't require paranormal powers to sense that my arrival was not universally popular. After an initial greeting, the others just carried on as if I wasn't there. Not even the tea-lady spoke to me.

I found myself at the centre of a verbal void, a disturbing situation for someone whose career is largely concerned with expression and communication.

I wasn't even told exactly what I was supposed to do. During our conversation some months previously, the chief editor – a hard-working and agreeable man, who seemed to live on coffee and cigarettes – had been suitably vague on this point. 'Oh, we'll just see how things develop', was all that he had said.

It had all been very different eight years before, when I first started work on the foreign desk of the NRC in the Netherlands. Then, I was very specifically given 'Africa' as my responsibility – largely because nobody else wanted it. With my recent background in European Community affairs, it was not what I had been expecting. Africa? It was a continent about which I knew nothing – and that was how I wanted to keep it. Like most people, I saw Africa as one great cesspool of human misery: all very sad, but a situation which I was powerless to influence or change.

In desperation, I went to the local bookstore and bought a map. Some of the names brought back memories of schooldays, when we had had to learn these countries and their capitals by heart. Niger, Botswana, Gambia, Mauritania. For the first time in years, I remembered that Mali and Malawi were thousands of kilometres apart, even though their names are so similar. As I continued to study my map, my spirits brightened. It all sounded so different, so exotic. Perhaps my new job wouldn't be so bad, after all.

Armed with this somewhat limited background information, I presented myself at the NRC offices and was shown to the desk of my predecessor, who had escaped to a 'cushier' job with *De Volkskrant*. In the meantime, his desk had become a dumping ground for every unread magazine and every unwanted memo in the entire foreign section. I sat down behind a veritable mountain of paper, wondering where I should begin.

I was still wondering, when an angry-looking lady emerged from behind my mountain. She announced that she was the Middle East editor and that she had been assigned to 'look after' me. It was a prospect which didn't seem to fill either of us with enthusiasm.

'You're doing Africa', she said curtly. 'Not all of Africa, of course. I do North Africa. And Sudan and Mauritania. And anywhere else where there are Muslims. The rest is for you. Good luck and get on with it.'

I meekly agreed to this journalistic division of a continent which had long become used to being divided. I tried to count the countries where no Muslims lived. There didn't seem to be very many. However, as a 'new boy', I dared not risk intruding onto the territory of my 'imperialist' colleague. If I did, she would no doubt retaliate with some fiendish Islamic punishment. And I had no desire to become the victim of a 'jihad' or a 'fatwah'.

As a result, I was forced to concentrate my attentions on southern Africa. It seemed both far away and relatively safe. Here I would get into trouble with nobody. There were no Muslims – or, at least, not many – and there were still white rulers in South Africa, which provided a supply of newsworthy stories on an almost daily basis. It seemed that I would have plenty to do, after all.

The situation following my arrival in Groot Bijgaarden was far less clear-cut. Instead of Dutch plain-speaking, I was confronted by two-faced smiles and meaningless pleasantries, which gave the misleading impression that everything was 'O.K.', whilst beneath the surface everything was very far from being 'O.K.'.

Eventually, I was placed under the charge of Ludo, a former priest. It was the first time that I had ever received any kind of instruction from a monk, and I wasn't sure that I was going to like it. As a child, the very thought of such a thing would have given me nightmares and my family would have seen it as the ultimate surrender to the forces of 'Popery'.

Happily, Ludo was a calm man with wavy grey hair, whose pipe contributed to his general air of quiet meditation. Ludo radiated trust and fatherly protection. He also had a sympathetic understanding for the fears and uncertainties of a newcomer: it probably reminded him of his years as a young novice in the monastery.

In my case, I had the added advantage that Ludo saw me as a potential ally. His job in the newspaper was that of 'linguistics expert'. In other words, he had to check each article to make sure that the use of language was correct. Spelling mistakes were an anathema to him, but his pet hate was the increasing use of Flemish regional phrases in everyday Dutch. He was a great believer in the purity of ABN (*'Algemeen Beschaafd Nederlands'* – the Dutch equivalent of the 'King's English') and he thought that I, as a Hollander, would join him in his fight against split infinitives and false subjunctives. 'The well of our language is being permanently defiled by local Flemish usage', he told me one day. A quick look at the newspaper showed me what he meant. Most of the headlines seemed to make no sense at all!

Ludo – who regarded the *Van Dale* dictionary as a kind of second Bible – saw it as his mission in life to ban all regional expressions from the columns of 'his' newspaper.

The problem was that many of these expressions had become so widely used that they were already regarded by most Flemish people as being a part of ABN, even though a 'real' Dutchman like myself had no idea what these expressions meant. One of the first such expressions I came across was: 'The Minister has cancelled his planned trip because he has other cats to whip.' I couldn't imagine what this was supposed to mean, except perhaps that the minister was some kind of sadistic animalhater, who should be forced to resign immediately. Ludo explained patiently that in Flemish 'other cats to whip' was the same as 'other fish to fry' in English – other and more important things to do. After a while, I began to think that the Flemish were obsessed with cats – many of their regional phrases have something to do with them. A colleague once complained to me that he had turned up for a meeting with his ex-wife, only to find that she had 'sent her cat'. Why should she send her cat? In the circumstances, it would seem more appropriate to send her dog. At least a dog can bite. It took me a while to realise that 'sent her cat' simply meant that she hadn't bothered to come herself. 'An expression borrowed directly from the French', Ludo informed me. 'But then what would a North Hollander know about the language of Molière', he added wistfully.

Ludo showed me off around all the various editorial offices, warning my colleagues that their use of language would have to improve, 'now that we have a North Hollander to check up on us.' I remained silent in the corner. Although he didn't realise it, Ludo was doing my reputation no good at all. For most of my colleagues, it was already bad enough that I was a Dutchman, without them thinking that I was also a member of the newspaper's language Gestapo!

I decided that my only chance was to adopt a low profile. Anything I said was guaranteed to be taken the wrong way and would be used to confirm the suspicion of most Flemings that the Dutch are a bunch of arrogant plonkers (which many of them are, of course). The chameleon in me said that if I wanted to keep the 'benefit of the doubt', I would have to sit tight and keep my mouth shut.

Which is what I did. I waited to see which way the proverbial Flemish cat jumped 'Another phrase of French origin', said Ludo, 'meaning to sit on the fence, to wait and see how things develop.' The situation in which I found myself was highly fluid, with no clear structures to which I could cling for security. It was a situation where 'yes' didn't necessarily mean 'yes', and 'no' could mean just about anything. It was like working in a hall of mirrors, where nothing is quite what it seems. Now you see it, now you don't.

The organisation – or lack of it – in the newspaper was equally mind-boggling. Everything was in a constant state of change. Editorial teams were moved from one side of the office to the other, or from one floor to the other. Sometimes teams were split and sometimes teams were merged, or even abolished. New editors arrived and others went. Nobody ever seemed to be consulted and nothing ever seemed to be planned. These things just happened.

Even the editorial offices themselves lacked uniformity. Some offices were partitioned off with glass walls, some with plants and some with wooden panels, like some kind of up-market Gaza strip. Once again, this layout seemed to be changed every five minutes. Whenever you came back from holiday, you were lucky if your desk was still in the same place.

I quickly learnt that this is the Flemish way and just let it all wash over me. It would have been pointless to resist or to complain. If you work in Flanders, you have to be able to improvise. The worst thing that a Dutchman – or any other foreigner – can do is to openly start telling the Flemish how things should be done. A quiet suggestion over a beer is always going to have more effect than a public intervention in a meeting.

To be fair, this organised chaos had much to do with the fact that two newspapers – De Standaard and Het Nieuwsblad – were being run from the same building, often by the same editorial staff. At first, I found this a strange idea: something that would be unthinkable in the Netherlands. The NRC and the Algemeen Dagblad are both run by the same company in Holland, but the two editorial staffs are completely separate entities, both physically and mentally. Each wanted nothing to do with the other, to such an extent that there was even hostility between them. The editors of the NRC saw the AD people as a bunch of half-educated yobs who produced a rag that scarcely deserved the name of 'newspaper'. Most of the NRC staff refused their free subscription to the AD, on the grounds that it produced too much waste paper. In return, the journalists at the AD saw their colleagues at the NRC as arrogant snobs and intellectual dilettantes with an over-inflated opinion of their own importance. Both these images were exaggerated but they both nonetheless contained a degree of truth. The net result was to ensure that both editorial teams kept a safe distance from each other.

This even extended to the car-parking facilities, where the NRC and the AD had their own separate areas. One day, when I was late and in a bit of a hurry, I took the liberty of parking my car in one of the spaces reserved for AD personnel. 'What does it matter?', I thought to myself. 'The lazy AD bum probably won't bother coming in today.' When I returned to my car that evening, not only did I find that the 'lazy AD bum' had indeed come into work, but also that he had phoned the police and had them put a wheel clamp on my car! I was furious and rushed into the AD offices, where I had never been before.

'Which idiot had my car clamped?' I shouted.

A small, balding man stepped forward and answered, 'I did.' The 'idiot' in question turned out to be the editor-in-chief of the AD office in The Hague. He clearly seemed to be enjoying the whole situation. 'You were in my place', he laughed. My anger was not to be cooled. 'Typical for an 'AD-er' like you', I snarled. 'All you lot can do is write sensational headlines and photo captions. And none of you can bloody spell!' The editor seemed unconcerned by this slur on his journalistic prowess. On the contrary, he and his AD colleagues were laughing even more. I could see them thinking: 'we got you this time, you smug NRC bastard.' And they had. I went back to the car park and called the police to come and remove the clamp, which they did, at a cost of several hundred euros. After that, the gulf between the NRC and the AD couldn't be wide enough, as far as I was concerned.

In sharp contrast, the relationship between *De Standaard* and *Het Nieuwsblad* was very close. Each day the same broad editorial team was responsible for making two totally different newspapers. This was a task made easier by the modern technology which was introduced during my time in Groot Bijgaarden. The editors of *De Standaard* could scan through the articles in *Het Nieuwsblad*, extract anything that seemed interesting and then re-write it in their own style for their own public. The editors of *Het Nieuwsblad* did exactly the same. This was the journalistic equivalent of 'borrowing a cup of sugar from the neighbours' and most articles in both papers were the product of this 'cut and paste' philosophy. In particular, the 'serious' *De Standaard* got most of its regional and sport coverage from the 'popular' *Het Nieuwsblad*, which in turn took most of its political and foreign articles from its more illustrious partner.

The results were sometimes strange, and some of the pieces I had written for *De Standaard* were hardly recognisable by the time they appeared in *Het Nieuwsblad*. Yet the system seemed to work. By some invisible process, we managed to produce two very different but complementary newspapers each day, both of which sold well in their respective markets. The fact that this process was invisible – and unexplainable – did not seem to bother my Flemish colleagues, since in Flanders transparency is seldom a requirement. It worked, so it must be good. Eventually, I decided to adopt the same approach. As they say in Flanders, 'it doesn't matter how you make the mayonnaise, what matters is how it tastes.' Or to put it another way: 'if you can't beat them, join them.'

Before my arrival in Flanders, I had promised myself that I would have nothing to do with hierarchy and power. A Dutchman who gets involved in such matters in Belgium is skating on very thin ice and will almost certainly be labelled as a know-it-all 'cheese-head' (the term used by most Belgians to describe the Hollanders). As a result, I preferred to remain a spectator of office politics rather than a participant, quietly watching developments from the sidelines but without risking my chances in the arena itself. In retrospect, this was one of the best decisions I ever made. Power politics in Belgium – whether in government or in the workplace – is an absolute minefield. The Flemish are a cautious people, who seldom say what they think or think what they say. They are like two-legged tortoises, protected by a shell that is impenetrable to outsiders. They never lay all their cards on the table and always try to keep an ace up their sleeve. Most of them behave as though they have got something to hide – which many of them do. In their work environment, most Flemings expect to be 'rewarded' with a number of 'extra benefits', which are known to the 'powers that be' but not to their colleagues: a free holiday here, the use of a lease-car there, the occasional under-the-table tax-free bonus. The existence of these 'benefits' tends to make most Flemish employees careful and non-committal. Like the famous three wise monkeys, they see nothing, say nothing and hear nothing.

This same secrecy is also applied to the question of political affiliation. After elections in the Netherlands, we used to play a kind of party game in the NRC editorial office, trying to work out who had voted for whom. Those who had voted for the winners used to treat the rest of us to coffee and cakes, whilst the losers tried to convince us that they had voted 'on principle'. In general, the socialist PvdA was the most popular party with our journalists, followed by libertarian D66. There were also a limited number of idealists who voted for the orthodox protestant GPV, but the liberal-conservative VVD and the christian democratic CDA hardly got any support at all.

When I tried to introduce the same kind of game in *De Standaard*, I was met by a wall of silence. Voting behaviour is not a matter for public discussion in Belgium. On the contrary, it is something akin to a state secret. I worked closely with colleagues for years, without ever having the faintest idea of their political preferences. When I asked one of my editors openly who he had voted for, he replied indignantly: 'I'm not telling you that – I don't even tell my wife!' For many Flemings, their voting habits and the level of their salaries are more intimate than sex.

Journalists who came to *De Standaard* having first practised a political career were forced to undergo a period of 'de-lousing'. This meant that they were not allowed to write on political matters, but had to devote their talents to issues such as cooking, gardening, pets, etc. One of my colleagues was a well-known political editor, who left the paper to take up an appointment as head of the Study Group for the Christian CVP party. After a couple of years, he had had enough of this boring work and decided to come back to the newspaper. Yet even with his famous background, he was kept well away from political matters following his return: I seem to recall that one of his most memorable pieces was about a Dutch farmer who was breeding pigs as pets. Eventually, he was allowed back onto the political desk, but he never really adjusted to his new situation and soon returned to politics, this time as a member of the Prime Minister's private staff. A final return to journalism towards the end of his career required a further period of 'de-lousing': talk about a glutton for punishment!

After a while, I began to enjoy the intricacies of Flemish office politics, although I always managed to stay on the outside. As in most walks of life, it was the wheeling and dealing at the top of the hierarchical tree which provided the greatest interest.

General editors came and general editors went. Special advisers were appointed to 'save' the paper, only to be quietly shown the backdoor when salvation proved hard to find. Expert reports were commissioned to confirm the findings of the management, only to be buried when the findings unexpectedly confirmed exactly the opposite. And behind all these goings-on lay the unseen but ever-present hand of the Leysen family, which had saved the paper from financial disaster in 1976 but now regarded it as their personal property. I watched all these developments in amused silence. The way to the top seemed full of pitfalls, far too many for a straight-forward Protestant lad like me ever to fully comprehend. I just let the others get on with it and tried to give the impression that I was an enthusiastic but not very knowledgeable beginner in such matters.

As I watched and learnt, it became apparent that many of my colleagues were angry with the newspaper in general and with the Director-General in particular. This is not unusual and probably happens in even the best companies. In the Netherlands, dissatisfaction of this kind is expressed openly in one or another of the 'consultative bodies', where the director is often treated to a public dressing-down by his staff. In Flanders protests against the management are more subdued. For much of my time with *De Standaard*, the Director-General was a wise, old gentleman, who knew little about newspapers and had been directly appointed from the chemical sector, because he was a friend of 'Mr. Leysen'. Every lunchtime the staff restaurant was alive with complaints about this amiable man: 'He doesn't know anything, but what can you expect? He's only here on Leysen's orders.' Just then the Director-General himself entered the restaurant, for his daily steak and chips. The atmosphere changed in a flash. 'And how are we today, Mr. Director-

General? Well, I hope. Enjoy your meal.' The stream of complaints dried up instantly, only to be resumed the moment he left. I pointed out to my colleagues that they had just missed their chance to discuss their grievances face to face with the big chief. 'Are you mad?' they replied in chorus. 'We can't attack the boss in public. What do you think we've got unions for?!'

Gradually, I began to understand the Flemish way of dealing with authority. Criticism was fine, but only if it could be made indirectly or anonymously. Open criticism was dangerous and was likely to rebound on the complainer. As such, it was to be avoided at all costs. It was all very well to call the boss a 'bastard' after a few beers at the bar, but it was a very different matter to call him a 'bastard' when he is standing right in front of you. Better to be an employed coward than an unemployed hero. Perhaps not the most courageous attitude to life but certainly an understandable one, particularly in a country whose motto is 'live and let live'. After all, the world is a small place and there may come a moment when you desperately need the help of a 'bastard' or two. In life, yesterday's enemy can often turn out to be tomorrow's friend.

This was also in keeping with the philosophy of 'Mr. Leysen' or 'Mr. André' as he was known. Throughout his life he had close associations with Germany which was not always popular in the second half of the 20th century. It was by virtue of his marriage to the daughter of a rich German industrial family – the Ahlers – that he came to be a central figure in the economic life of Flanders after the Second World War.

Leysen was born into a pro-German family in Antwerp in the 1930's and during the Second World War he joined the Hitler Youth. In his memoirs – *Behind the Mirror* – he described his activities in the Nazi youth movement in some detail. Originally, he was convinced that the Germans were right and it was only during the last weeks of the war that he came to realise that he was on the wrong side. After this timely – if somewhat late – discovery he left Berlin by one of the very last trains and so avoided falling into the hands of the Russians.

Following his marriage, Leysen assumed an increasingly important role in trade and industry in Flanders, thanks largely to his major shareholding in Agfa-Gevaert. In the 1970's, he financed the re-launching of *De Standaard* (after it had first gone bankrupt) and he continued to manage the business affairs of the larger newsgroup of which *De Standaard* was a part. He was eventually appointed chairman of the Belgian Employers Federation (the VBO) but unlike his predecessors in this job he did not receive a peerage or any other state honour, almost certainly because of his dubious war record.

Even so, his international reputation was considerable. Thanks to his good relations with Germany, he was the only non-German citizen appointed to the board of directors of Treuhand, an organisation set up after the fall of the Berlin Wall to assist the privatisation of industry in the old German Democratic Republic. Following the assassination of the chairman of the board by the Red Army Faction, he was forced to drive everywhere in an armoured Mercedes and it was in this half-tank that he came to the fortnightly meetings of the newspaper group in Groot Bijgaarden.

Happily, he interfered little in the day-to-day running of the newspapers he owned although he was known to dislike 'vulgar' articles or attacks on the royal house. Successive senior editors told me: 'If Mr. Leysen telephones, it is not the boss who is phoning, it is just one of our readers. That's all he is – a reader, like any other.' Well, almost like any other. The German correspondent of *De Standaard* once wrote a critical piece about the activities of Treuhand. The following day the 'reader like any other' phoned the senior editor from his château in France. I only heard one side of this conversation, but it was clear that the *ordinary reader's* German sympathies had been offended. The editor turned bright red and stammered out a stream of apologies. 'Yes, Mr.Leysen... Of course, Mr Leysen... I'll look into it right away, Mr.Leysen....' Two days later, a full-page interview with Leysen himself was published, which pointed out 'certain errors' in the original article. The boss had spoken and the matter was closed.

'I'm not sure any other "reader" could have managed to arrange all that', I said tongue in cheek at the beginning of the next day's editorial meeting. The senior editor surrendered with good grace. 'True', he replied. 'All readers are equal, but some readers are more equal than others.'

Little by little, I began to get used to working in Flanders. It is more relaxing than working in Holland. There is much more humour and an easier acceptance of life's ups and downs. By the same token, there is much less system and almost no planning.

This is not necessarily a bad thing. A Dutchman will make a plan for everything and will then regard this plan as sacred. Anyone who is not willing or able to conform to the plan is instantly labelled as a troublemaker and excluded. The Flemish are much more flexible and can adapt quickly to changing situations. For a Dutchman, an agreement is inviolable, something written in stone. For a Fleming, an agreement is merely a temporary arrangement. If the circumstances change, the agreement can also be changed.

However, you need to be careful when playing this game. A Fleming will not easily show when he is unhappy with something. Instead he will keep quiet and let you find out for yourself what the problem is. A Dutchman will always demand a forum in which to voice his grievances. A Fleming will withdraw into his shell and pull up his defences. He will not openly complain but will express his displeasure by a policy of delay and non-co-operation. Nothing gets done and, before you know it, everything has ground to a halt. If you have a problem with a Hollander, it will quickly become visible. If a problem with a Fleming becomes visible, it is already too late.

I quickly saw the advantages of this good-natured and uncomplicated way of working. It was a system which allowed bygones to be bygones and where the past was quickly forgotten. This was one of the first lessons I ever learnt with *De Standaard*. Almost my very first assignment was to write a summary of the CVP programme for the 1995 elections. Not really knowing where to start, I telephoned the CVP party spokesman, a bearded man who was almost permanently to be found in the pub. Perhaps not surprisingly, he was well-known for his use of bar-room language and one of his more famous comments was that any party wanting to work with the CVP 'should first get a penis extension'.

My colleagues warned me that I should never phone him after lunch. 'He's always as drunk as a skunk after two o'clock.' I found this hard to believe. The official party spokesman for the Christian CVP as drunk as a skunk? Surely not! I rang him in the middle of the afternoon and asked him for a copy of the programme. 'I'll send one straight away', he promised. Within the hour his fax arrived and later the same day my summary was completed. I couldn't understand what all the fuss was about.

Or at least I couldn't until the following day, when I took a closer look at the document he had faxed me. Instead of sending me the 1995 programme, he had sent me a copy of the old 1991 programme! And this is what had been printed in this morning's newspaper!

I resigned myself to the inevitable and drove into Groot-Bijgaarden, where I fully expected to be given the sack. 'What a pity my Belgian adventure is already over', I sighed to myself in the car. 'Almost before it had really got started.' I entered the editorial office, expecting a barrage of catcalls and black looks, but to my amazement everything seemed normal. Nobody said a word, other than the usual 'good morning'. 'Perhaps they haven't noticed', I began to hope. 'Maybe they don't read their own newspaper. Or perhaps the CVP programme has a timeless quality which goes beyond mere years.' All day I waited for someone to discover my blunder – but nobody did! Finally, I decided that I had better go and confess to the chief editor myself – before some irate CVP reader did it for me. He seemed unconcerned by what I regarded as a major professional error. 'Nobody noticed, so what's the problem?'

I was pleasantly surprised (and relieved) by this reaction, which would have been unthinkable in the Netherlands. There a meeting would have been called, where the 'fault' would have been discussed at great length and where the 'guilt' would have been publicly attributed to the unfortunate reporter. This could have serious consequences, particularly in a country where the concept of guilt is a permanent one and where the allocation of blame is more important than putting matters to rights. Not only would the reporter in question slip down the internal pecking order in the office, but he would often find his number of interesting foreign assignments suddenly reduced or his promotion chances seriously damaged. In extreme cases (as I had been expecting myself), instant dismissal was also a possibility.

This was not the way that things were done at *De Standaard*. The newspaper was Flemish and social, and the sack was only used as a last resort. One of the few instances I can remember concerned a young journalist who was responsible for compiling the weather reports for ski stations in Switzerland and Austria. This was a boring job, which involved listing all the ski resorts and the depth of their snow: 'Obersdorf – 15 cm, Kielsdorf – 20 cm, etc., etc.'. One day he decided to brighten things up by creating a new ski village of his own. Next morning, our paper reported that the depth of snow in 'Wankersdorf' was 25 cm. As with my CVP gaff, none of the editors spotted this latest addition to the list of Alpine holiday destinations. Unfortunately, our readers had. There was a storm of protest – mainly from old ladies who had never been skiing in their life – and the reporter was shown the door.

Less drastic was the case of Fientje – a young lady with a rebellious nature – who got into trouble during the Pope's visit to Belgium in 1985. She had put a poster in the window of her office in Ghent, which showed the Holy Father kissing the tarmac on arrival at some foreign airport. The text under the picture read: 'The Pope can kiss my .....' Not surprisingly, Fientje was called to see the senior editor, who gave her a fatherly lecture about 'responsibility' and the 'newspaper's image'. There was no sacking on this occasion, but Fientje soon left the paper and went on to make a career in politics, eventually becoming Minister for Economic Affairs.

My policy of not getting involved in controversies of this type (or of any other type) gradually began to pay off. My colleagues came to realise that I was not a know-it-all Hollander, who poked his nose in everywhere. The numbers of those who had been against my appointment began to diminish, whilst those who had had their doubts also slowly came around to my side. The suspicion and the scepticism disappeared – at last, I felt accepted.

Even so, I continued to play the role of the bemused and amused foreigner, who was constantly surprised by the strange twists and turns of the news in Flanders. At the same time, I pressed on with my self-imposed programme of 're-education', absorbing all that I could of my new home. As the months passed, my more obviously 'Dutch' characteristics began to fade and were replaced by more Flemish traits: quiet good humour, a sense of balance, modest self-mockery. My chameleon-like transformation was complete.

But while I was now accepted by my colleagues at *De Standaard*, the same could not be said of the politicians in the Wetstraat. I was the first Hollander to reappear on the Belgian political scene since 1830 (when King William I and his Dutch army were kicked out of Brussels) and my arrival was not wholly welcome.

The faces which I had vaguely seen on television during my stay in Brussels ten years earlier were now to become as familiar to me as those of my own family. Most of them had survived the intervening period and most of them were still the colourful caricatures that I remembered.

Dehaene had exchanged his polo-neck sweater for a made-to-measure suit and was now Prime-Minister.

Martens had sat out – perhaps 'sweated out' might be a more appropriate expression – several terms as premier but had now been exiled to the European Parliament.

Verhofstadt still led the opposition with anger and energy, fuelled by his own personal vision of a liberal blue heaven.

De Croo was still as busy and as tireless as ever. His vision was more limited than that of his younger colleagues, but even so he still saw a promising political future for himself. As he once said: 'They only make handbags from young crocodiles.' The old crocodile of the VLD would still be going strong, when many of his younger rivals had fallen by the wayside.

Since I had last seen him, Louis Tobback still lashed out ferociously and he was now the undisputed king of the Flemish Socialist Party.

Jean Gol was also still on the political scene, although I only ever met him once – at a reception held by the Walloon Regional Community in Namur. He died the very next day.

In general, the politicians were even more surprised at my arrival than the journalists had been. Once again, I was confronted by the same question: 'What on earth are you doing here?' 'I've come to see how the Belgian political system works', I replied. Their scepticism grew. 'To see how it works? Or to see how it doesn't work?'

This suspicion lasted a number of years – far longer than with my newspaper colleagues. Politicians like to categorise people neatly into little boxes. The problem was that I was impossible to categorise! I wasn't a Fleming, a Walloon or a Brusseler. Nor was I a Christian-Democrat, a socialist or a liberal. I wasn't even a freemason, a free-thinker or a clerical reactionary. In short, I defied classification. This confused the local politicos and led them to see hidden motives in everything that I did. 'A Hollander come to look at our political system? It must be some kind of conspiracy.'

I quickly acquired a reputation as a journalistic 'ugly duckling', a maverick outsider with a high risk factor. I was given access to the corridors of power but I retained the stigma of being a foreigner. 'Be careful – he's a Hollander. Not one of us!'

If I wrote a positive article, the most common comment from the politicians was a condescending one: 'I see you're beginning to learn something, at last.' If I wrote a negative article, the reaction was openly hostile: 'You're a Dutchman. What do you know about it?' Louis Tobback was once furious when I suggested that some of his throw-away remarks about asylum seekers ('seagulls come to scavenge on our Belgian beaches') played straight into the hands of the Flemish Nationalist Party, Vlaams Blok. Not only did he telephone the senior editor to complain, he also got one of his journalistic friends to launch a personal attack on me in *Humo* Magazine, where (in one of the politer comments) I was described as a 'Dutch reject'.

In the 165 years since Belgian independence, it seemed that the gulf between the old provinces of the United Kingdom of the Netherlands had grown too wide for me ever to be fully accepted in Brussels. Suspicion and distrust followed me wherever I went in the Wetstraat and I found myself enmeshed in a world where a high price is set on principles, but only because this makes them easier and more lucrative to sell.

The prevailing atmosphere in the Wetstraat was a curious mixture of political toughness and compassionate understanding for human frailty. For years, there was a high-class brothel behind the Belgian parliament building in the Drukpersstraat, appropriately named 'The Assembly'. I was at a loss to understand how something so shamefaced could possibly be allowed. In The Hague, such a situation would have led to a public uproar. More than once I was tempted to visit 'The Assembly', just to see who actually attended its nightly 'meetings'. Sadly, I never dared: after all, I was the representative of a newspaper whose motto was still 'All for Christ', which was hardly compatible with late-night visits to houses of ill repute. That being said, in all my years in the Wetstraat I never heard a bad word said about 'The Assembly'. But I never found out which 'members' made use of its 'chambers'. It was simply something that was accepted, but never talked about. In some areas, Belgium is capable of 'conspiracies of silence' of which even the Mafia would be proud.

One of my earliest guides through the Belgian political maze was Marc Eyskens. He is a distinguished politician (although not without a streak of vanity), a renowned professor, a visionary writer and a more than competent painter. He has the rare gift of speaking well, exudes sophistication and possesses sufficient cunning to have survived in the Wetstraat for more than 40 years.

He was once prime-minister, but his administration only lasted six months, as a result of difficulties with his Walloon ministers. They simply went on strike. He had also held posts as Minister of Finance and Minister for Foreign Affairs. Nevertheless, he remained constantly in the shadow of his father, Gaston – known generally as Daddy Eyskens – who had guided the country through several difficult years after the Second World War.

Daddy Eyskens was one of the reasons why I first tried to get into conversation with his son. I remembered from old television interviews that Gaston had a strong Dutch accent when he spoke. In fact, Old Man Eyskens spoke Dutch better than most Dutchmen. 'He lived as a refugee with a family in Breda during the First World War', Eyskens Junior told me one day, when I finally cornered him in the parliament building.

We began to talk and I was fascinated by Eyskens' stories, his deep knowledge and his graceful powers of expression, which were both sharp and critical. I told him that I was fascinated by the opaqueness and unpredictability of Belgian politics, by the fact that there was always a snake in the grass somewhere, even though you couldn't always see it. He smiled and gave me some fatherly (and prophetic) advice. 'Mr.Eppink, in the beginning you will write much, because you know little. Later on, you will write little, because you will know too much!'

He went on to reveal to me what he saw as the three golden rules of Belgian politics:

'In the first place, trust nobody – not even your wife. Above all, watch out for journalists – they are 'insects', who take comfort from the fact that every politician will be betrayed sooner or later, usually by someone from his own party. Finally, if you get caught, always confess. If you confess, you will almost certainly be forgiven, and then you can go and start sinning again. It is one of the advantages of a Catholic country.'

Little did I know that within a few years I would be applying these rules to Eyskens himself, when I visited him at his summer villa in 't Zwin, just down the coast from Knokke-Heist.

Summer time is always a difficult time for the newspapers. Parliament is in recess, the politicians are all on holiday and there is almost nothing of importance to report. At the NRC, we used this quiet period to write obituaries for older politicians who we didn't think would make it through the next 12 months. This saved time when the grim reaper finally came to call. As a result, I passed my summers in The Hague browsing through old party lists and phoning around to check on the health of Holland's senior political citizens. My boss and I then sat down to draw up our own personal 'death list'. 'Do you think the old boy who looks quite pale lately will last until Christmas?' he would ask me. If I didn't, we would write an obituary – just in case.

Of course, things didn't always turn out the way we planned. Some apparently healthy politicos dropped dead unexpectedly, before we had had time to do their 'ob.', while many of their more sickly colleagues went on for years and years. Some of the people I wrote pieces for are still alive, even today! Be that as it may, my obituaries for them are still filed away in a cabinet in the NRC, waiting patiently 'for when the time comes…'

When I moved to Flanders, I decided to stop this slightly ghoulish practice, largely because the Flemish regard this type of forward planning as totally unnecessary. 'Why do you want to write about something that hasn't even happened?' was the most frequent comment. Facts should only be dealt with when they present themselves – and not before.

This meant that I had to find some other way to occupy my time during the long summer months. I thought it might be a good idea to do a number of holiday pieces about some of Belgium's more influential political figures. I would visit them at their holiday homes along the Belgian coast (or 'Flemish coast', as all my colleagues called it) and see how they spent their leisure weeks. A glass of wine, a view over the sea, a relaxing chat about the world and its problems – it sounded like it might be fun. It would also give me a chance to continue my Flemish 're-education', since during the months of July and August all the different segments of Belgian society descend on the 60 kilometre stretch of sand between De Panne and 't Zwin.

Knokke-Heist is the most elegant and 'refined' of the coastal resorts and has a strong French-speaking tint. The Burgomaster is Count Leopold Lippens, whose family has owned large parts of Knokke since Napoleonic times. The count regards the town as a kind of personal fiefdom and that is the way he runs it. During local elections, he does not represent a political party – he represents his own party, the Party of the Burgomaster. If any of the more established parties dare to stand against him, they are immediately accused of putting party interests before local interests. It is a tactic that has worked well up to now. Lippens is proud of his town's chic reputation and that is the way he wants to keep it. One of his most famous comments concerned his desire to keep away 'ice-box tourists', meaning less well-off day-trippers who bring their own picnics with them.

The plebs gather 20 kilometres further down the coast at Blankenberge, which is run by the socialists. The Socialist Medical Insurance Fund has even built a holiday centre there – the Floreal: a concrete monstrosity where sick members of the fund can come to convalesce, surrounded by Socialist Party workers, all attending the latest party conference or seminar.

Ostend was originally a liberal stronghold, but in recent years the 'Blues' have been replaced by the 'Reds', under front man Johan Vande Lanotte. This bearded minister started his political career in Ghent, but later switched to the so-called 'Queen of Resorts', which he has now turned into one of the strongest left-wing bastions in all Flanders. It is rumoured that on 1 May there are more socialists marching through the streets of Ostend than through the Red Square in Moscow!

The Christian-Democrats have been wiped out along the coast during the past two decades, although they still control a village here and there. This is a result of the general secularisation of society in Flanders, which along the coast reached its high water mark with the opening of a nudist beach in Bredene – a 100 metre stretch of sand, ringed by security guards to keep away the peeping Toms.

Such goings-on would be unthinkable in Knokke-Heist, where only the 'better class of person' comes to stay. It was here that I found Marc Eyskens, one of the first subjects for my series of summer interviews. As I arrived, he was waiting to meet me in the hall. 'Your editor has just phoned', he said. 'It sounded like it was urgent. He would like you to call back straight away.'

My heart skipped a beat. What on earth could have happened? My home burnt down? Some terrible accident in the family? With trembling fingers, I dialled the office number and was put through to my boss.

'Have you seen today's edition of *De Morgen*', he screamed. I told him that I hadn't seen a newspaper all day and that I never read *De Morgen* anyway. 'They have a lead article which claims that an ex-CVP prime minister had a secret account with the Credit Bank in Luxembourg. Eyskens is one of those named as a possible suspect. Check it out with him.'

I put down the phone and sighed. It seemed as though my 're-laxing holiday chat' was about to turn into something less pleasant. Initially, however, things went well. Eyskens was in a good mood and it was soon clear that he, too, had not yet seen a copy of today's papers. His wife made coffee and my host asked me to stay to lunch. He'd even got the Chablis out. It somehow didn't seem the right moment to interrogate him about illegal bank accounts in Luxembourg!

We moved into his study, an elegant room whose walls were lined with paintings and books – most of them by Eyskens himself. 'I only do landscapes', he commented modestly, 'although I can't paint leaves.' The atmosphere was warm and friendly and it was getting more difficult by the minute to pop the fatal question. His wife poured a second cup of coffee and we began to talk about history, politics, international relations – about everything other than the thing I wanted to talk about!

Suddenly, the telephone rang. Eyskens rose from his chair and went out into the hall. He closed the adjoining door, but I could still hear him, talking in his polished and cultivated French: 'No, I am telling you formally that I do not have a bank account in Luxembourg.'

It was obvious that one of my journalistic colleagues had found the number of his holiday home and had asked him the question that I had been trying to ask for the past half hour. When he came back into the room, I acted as though I knew nothing and carried on with the interview. Five minutes later the phone rang again. 'No, I have not got a bank account in Luxembourg. Goodbye.'

This time he was less good-humoured when he returned to the study. 'What kind of a country is this?' he asked. Once, in private, he had compared Belgium to 'the planet of the apes'. He thought it wisest not to repeat this phrase in the presence of a journalist, but I could see clearly what he was thinking. I continued to play the innocent and asked him some innocuous question about European milk subsidies. Before he could answer, the phone rang again. This time it was the Flemish radio, the VRT, who wanted a statement for their news broadcast. Eyskens could no longer restrain himself. His pent-up anger burst free and he sent a stream of molten lava over the entire press landscape of Flanders:

'It's scandalous. They write whatever they like, without checking to see if it's true. *De Morgen* is just a rag, the gutter press at its worst. Journalists are insects, pathetic and inadequate little men with no talent of their own...'

The conversation went on like this for some time, until Eyskens finally brought it to an abrupt close. He was still plainly irritated when he returned for a third time to his study. I tried to pour oil on troubled waters: 'Yes, Mr.Eyskens, what you say is true. *De Morgen* is just a scandal sheet. It's not the first time that they have printed false accusations against an innocent person. It shouldn't be allowed. It certainly wouldn't happen in the Netherlands.' I hoped that in this way I might at least manage to make it through lunch, but it was obvious that the friendly atmosphere was gone for good. Throughout the meal, I could see the ex-premier struggling to control his emotions, which were in danger of bubbling over, just like the pot on his wife's stove. It was only after his second glass of Chablis that he finally cooled down. Even so, I left as soon as possible after the dessert. I had the impression that he had a number of telephone calls of his own to make and I didn't want to overstay my welcome.

Back in the office, I was greeted by a smiling editor. 'And how was it then with Mr.Eyskens?', he asked sarcastically. 'I've had more comfortable mornings', I confessed. In the meantime, the whole editorial office had enjoyed his outburst about 'journalistic insects', which the VRT had not surprisingly broadcast in full.

In fact, there was general enjoyment at Eyskens' discomfort. Laughing at your neighbour's misfortune is a popular pastime in Flanders. Almost every Fleming is a fixer of one kind or another, but he thinks that the biggest and most corrupt fixers of all are the politicians, making vast quantities of money from the sale of jobs, building permits, contracts, etc., etc. When one of these big fish is actually caught with his hand in the till – or even suspected of it, as in the case of Eyskens – all the little fish close in for the kill. The truth is almost irrelevant. It is enough to say that 'it is known that...' or 'sources had revealed...' It is like some sort of strange confirmation that the system works. 'You see, everyone is doing it. So why shouldn't I?' It also allows the smaller fish the chance to join in an enjoyable bout of righteous indignation, whilst at the same time whispering a silent prayer: 'Thank God it wasn't me that got found out.'

The fact that I understood all this showed that I was finally coming to terms with the Flemish mentality and with the Flemish way of doing things. On the other hand, I was beginning to experience more and more embarrassment with the increasing numbers of Dutchmen coming to Flanders to do business. They knew nothing of the country or its people and seemed totally insensitive to local sensibilities.

A classic example of this phenomenon was the attempt by the Dutch ABN-AMRO Bank to take over the General Bank, one of Belgium's largest financial institutions. I watched on television with a mixture of amusement and distaste as the two Dutch negotiators, Jan Kalf and Rijkman Groenink, arrived at Zaventem Airport. They stepped off their private jet, each carrying a large and expensive briefcase, and were whisked off by luxury limousine to the Hilton Hotel, where they held a press conference to inform the world how they planned to 'save' the General Bank.

Nobody in our office said a word, but I could sense that they all regarded the arrogant and over-confident performance of the Dutch bankers as some kind of attack, an assault on Belgian economic sovereignty and independence. I knew instantly that this was also how Kalf and Rijkman would be viewed by the politicians in Brussels. I could see them getting bogged down in the endless marshland of Belgian bureaucracy. They had come to 'save' the General Bank, had they? They would soon need saving themselves!

The duo went to visit Premier Dehaene, whose welcome was not as warm as they had hoped. It quickly became clear that the Belgian political top, encouraged by signals from the Royal

Palace, wanted to keep the General Bank in Belgian hands. When they realised that there was royal opposition, they asked if it was possible to meet with the King to discuss the matter. This was another big mistake. Audiences with the King are not requested: they are granted. The King's private secretary, Jacques van Ypersele de Strihou, didn't even bother to see them.

In the meantime, the rest of the political and economic establishment was also being mobilised against the invaders from Amsterdam. Maurice Lippens, the top man in the powerful Fortis Group and a key figure in the Belgian financial world, persuaded his colleagues in the General Bank to issue a capital increase, which the Fortis Group then subscribed in full. As a result, it was Fortis that acquired the real power in the General Bank, not ABN-AMRO. Kalf and Rijkman went home with their tails between their legs.

The Belgian elite has always had a strong sense of symbolism. Lippens was able to secure the future of the General Bank on the very same day as King Albert's birthday. 'You could not have given me a better present', said the grateful king to his financial hit-man. Soon afterwards Maurice Lippens was elevated to the peerage and like his brother Leopold – the semi-feudal Burgomaster of Knokke – became a count.

The two bankers are not the only Dutchmen to have met their Waterloo in Belgium. The difference in mentality can often lead to difficulties and misunderstanding. As I was now beginning to realise, work in Flanders is governed by a whole different set of rules – some of them official, most of them not. Dozens of Dutch businessmen have arrived in Belgium full of confidence, only to return home months later, confused and angry. 'It's impossible to work with those Belgians. They called me arrogant and they tried to block me at every turn.'

I heard the same complaints from my fellow-countrymen time and time again, but there was little I could do about it. Or at least there was, until one day I got a telephone call from a female research assistant at the Tropical Institute in Amsterdam.

'Mr. Eppink, we are thinking about giving a course on Belgium. Would you like to help us?'

I was intrigued. The Tropical Institute was well-known for giving background and training to businessmen and diplomats who were being posted to exotic locations such as Brazil, Indonesia, Singapore, etc. But Belgium? It hardly came into the category of tropical. As if reading my mind, the voice on the telephone continued: 'We know that the Belgian climate is not very tropical, but their way of working is very different to ours. We've had lots of requests to do something about Belgium.' I thought about what she had said and began to realise that perhaps it was not such a silly idea after all. 'Yes, you're probably right', I said. 'Belgium is not tropical on the outside, but it is on the inside!'

A couple of weeks later I drove up to Amsterdam and reported to the Institute. I was welcomed by a young lady at the reception desk. 'Good morning, Mr.Eppink', she said in a business-like tone. 'Which country have you come for?' I showed her the map I held in my hand. 'Belgium', I replied. 'Belgium? Are you sure?' I confirmed that I was sure and she led me to a waiting room, barely able to conceal her amusement. The room was full of other teachers, who at least looked as though they belonged in a Tropical Institute. One had come to talk about Surinam, another about Kenya. I waited with growing discomfort for the obvious question. 'And what's your country?'

'Belgium', I mumbled.

'Sorry?'

'Belgium!' I roared in a voice that was probably audible in Brussels. 'What's wrong with that? It's a little bit tropical. Well, they have some quite warm days in the summer.'

My first student was a Dutchman, who ran a metal processing company near Mechelen. He had come to Amsterdam to learn about the country where he lived and worked, but about which he understood nothing. In particular, he was having trouble communicating with his staff. 'I've tried to encourage more worker participation', he told me. 'I've said to them all: "my door is always open; if you think there is a better way of doing things, just come and tell me."' Unfortunately, this openness had met with a zero response. Not a single member of his Flemish staff had been to see him. Worse still, a number of them had actually resigned. 'How is that possible?', he asked me. 'I only meant it for the best.'

I tried to explain to him that a Fleming is much happier with a dominating boss than with a boss who is always asking him to express an opinion. In Flanders the boss is called 'sir' or 'Mr. Director' – and he is expected to act like a boss. 'Look', I said. 'If you are always asking your worker's advice, sooner or later they are going to feel unsure. They won't say anything, but they will be thinking: "the boss doesn't know what to do anymore; he's even asking me for help." This thinking will then go a stage further: "things must be going badly; maybe its time I got another job."' Instead of helping to promote greater team spirit, the well-meaning Dutch manager had actually been responsible for forcing some of his best people to look for other work! I hoped that by showing him how the Flemish mind works, he would have more success in the future. 'Remember', I said to him at the end of the lesson, 'you can't beat them, so you might as well join them…'

In addition to Hollanders, I also had pupils from the United States, Canada and Singapore. I tried to show them all what Belgium is like and how it had become that way. It was not an easy task. How do you explain a country with six governments, six parliaments and almost 60 ministers? If China had the same number of ministers per head of population as Belgium, there would be more than 10,000! I soon noticed that the people who best understood the Belgian system were the people who came from countries which were also 'divided'. The students who came from more unified countries – such as the Americans and Dutch – had much greater difficulty in coming to terms with the complexities of Belgian society. Students from Canada (with its large French-speaking minority in Quebec) and Singapore (with its delicate balance of ethnic groups) seemed to catch on much quicker. The Americans and the Dutch saw the Belgian system as being over-complicated and corrupt. The Canadians and the Singaporeans realised that this diversity and flexibility were necessary evils for the country's survival.

After I had been at the Institute for some time, I could tell within half an hour which of my pupils would do well in Belgium and which would not. I remember one couple in particular, a husband and wife from 'de Veluwe' (the Dutch Bible Belt region), who were being sent to work in a steel plant between Brussels and Charleroi. They were quiet, decent people, who hardly said two words, other than to say prayers before we went in for lunch. They were pure and innocent in a world of deceit and corruption. I had never had such hardworking and attentive students, but I knew that they didn't stand a chance in Belgium. They just didn't have the necessary adaptability – and certainly not for the area they were being sent to. Charleroi is an epicentre of modern industrial misery, a wasteland of decaying factories, surrounded by a moonscape of slag heaps and disused pits. It is a centre for corrupt politicians and the home of the Belgian mafia, with its strong Italian mining connections. It is also one of the last bastions of old-fashioned trade unionism, where the union bosses are even bigger gangsters than their mafia counterparts. In Wallonia it is not unusual for managers to be taken hostage during industrial disputes. This is a situation which would lead to the use of riot police in France or to a major parliamentary debate in Germany. In French-speaking Belgium it is just accepted as part of the industrial way of life. And it was into this maelstrom that my mild-mannered, bible-reading students were to be sent!

I thought of them again a couple of months later, when I saw a news report about a strike at the steel plant for which they had been destined. The Walloon unions were quick to blame the dispute on 'the stubbornness of the Dutch mother company' and 'their failure to find new funding for modernisation and further pay increases.' Union boss Robert D'Orazio – whose office is decorated with portraits of Mao, Lenin and Ché Guevara – went to 'negotiate' with the curator. He banged his fist on the table and then, when he failed to get what he wanted, he banged it into the face of the curator – apparently because of the latter's 'asocial behaviour'.

The curator – the liberal politician Alfred Zenner – staggered out of the meeting, covered in bruises and dripping blood. He appeared later on television with his head wrapped in bandages. The Minister of Home Affairs sent in the police to try and control the strikers, but D'Orazio's troops just rode over their vehicles in bulldozers. At this, the police beat a sensible and hasty retreat, leaving the strike to burn itself out. The Dutch mother company had also had enough – they withdrew all their staff and investments from what they described as a 'war zone'.

I wondered what my religious couple had made of it all and hoped that they had found something safer back in their home town. Perhaps they would believe me now, when I said that Belgium can sometimes be a bit too tropical.

A DESIRABLE RESIDENCE, WITH INCONVENIENCES

My return to Belgium brought with it the prospect of more spacious, one might even say more luxurious, living. In the Netherlands I had become used to small, hutch-like houses, where the use of every square centimetre of room is minutely planned. Space is always at a premium. Often there isn't even a hall – you just walk straight off the street into the living room. By the same token, bathrooms are often replaced by shower cabinets hidden away somewhere in a cupboard. Everything has to be practical. Aesthetics hardly come into it and even differences in taste are regulated by a thick book of administrative rules and regulations. An Englishman's home might be his castle, but a Dutchman's home is subject to the intervention of a thousand and one local government officials.

In my early years, I knew no better and found it perfectly normal that people all lived in the same type of house, preferably arranged in neat, straight rows. The same design, the same streets, the same gardens. Brick elevated to the highest expression of an ordered – perhaps even regimented – society: clean, tidy and egalitarian. A Dutch version of the American dream.

However, I then met someone who had experience of living in Flanders. This friend – a fellow Hollander – had no intention of returning to his monotonous homeland: he had tasted the pleasures of a more individual lifestyle. Flanders is full of houses in all shapes and sizes, built to no particular scheme or plan and all designed in accordance with personal preferences and tastes. In general, the houses are bigger, more comfortable and more spacious. Sometimes they are like little palaces, surrounded by Roman statues, luxurious gardens and baroque follies. The opinion of the neighbours or the neighbourhood is of no consequence. For the Fleming, his home is the outward expression of his personality, his life, his social status.

I had already noticed early on in my career how some Dutch politicians had similarly tried to make a statement with their homes – but a statement of a different kind. Most politicians in the Netherlands live in ordinary houses, and those who move into large villas are immediately suspected of being on the fiddle. The small terraced house of former prime minister Willem Drees Sr. in The Hague was legendary in this respect. After the war, he received a United States minister at his home in the Beeklaan and the American was so impressed with the modesty and simplicity of this humble dwelling that he reported back to Washington that the Marshall Aid funding in the Netherlands was clearly in good hands!

In Belgium, the opposite is true. If a politician lives in a terrace, people are inclined to think: 'Clearly, the man doesn't know what he is doing. He can't even arrange a decent house for his wife and family. And if he can't do that for them, what can he possibly do for me?' As a result, most Belgian politicians live in massive houses, which are intended to symbolise their political power and influence.

If you build a house in the Netherlands – in so far as such a thing is still possible – you will inevitably be confronted at some stage with the long arm of the dreaded Aesthetics Committee. It is the task of the members of this local government committee to decide whether or not your planned dream house 'fits in' with its intended surroundings. These professional busybodies are liable to comment on the colour of the walls, the shape of the windows, the layout of the garden, etc., etc., but without their blessing there will be no house.

A committee of this kind in Flanders would be regarded as the very worst kind of administrative fascism, an unacceptable intrusion by the state into what is seen in Belgium as essentially a 'private' matter. True, nowadays the Flemings have to make sure that they site their houses in the correct 'zone' and there are more regulations than there used to be, but building remains fundamentally a question of personal taste. To a Fleming, the right to 'build as he pleases' is every bit as important as the American's right to carry a gun.

I was looking forward to returning to Flanders to live, although I had enjoyed my time in my apartment on the stately Frankenslag in The Hague. This was a 'socially correct' part of town, with respectable people: civil, friendly and courteous. On Dynasty Day, the street was transformed into a sea of orange, interspersed with the national tricolour. On summer days, lined as it was with elegant trees, shrubs and lawns, the Frankenslag even reminded me of the Garden of Eden.

My landlady – an elderly widow in her seventies – was a model of decency, propriety and good manners. I visited her on the first Monday of every month to pay my rent. She prepared almost ritually for my arrival, dressed in her Sunday best for our 'pleasant little rendezvous'. I called her 'Madam', even though I had been living there for seven years. In all that time we had never progressed to a more informal style of address. 'How do you do, Mr.Eppink?' she enquired politely as she opened the door, stretching out her hand for me to shake.

As always, she had prepared tea and biscuits for our 'rendezvous', because she knew – and expected – that I would arrive on time. And if I was just a minute late, she was guaranteed to be standing at the open door, waiting for me. She seemed to enjoy the hour-long chat which accompanied the monthly paying of my rent. For the most part she had little company. True, she did let another room on the third floor, but this was to a certain 'Miss' Hansen, who had lived there for thirty years and had now reached the grand old age of 94. As a result, Miss Hansen could no longer manage the stairs, so that she hardly ever saw her. In fact, I had never seen her at all.

This ceremonial paying of the rent was a social ritual to which we both became attached and which led to a mutual bond of trust and respect. I listened in fascination to her stories about the district where she lived and its past. During the war the whole area had been cordoned off and belonged to the so-called 'Sperregebied'. Within this 'no-go' area the Germans destroyed all sanitary facilities, in an attempt to make the houses uninhabitable. As a result, the residents were forced to move elsewhere. The Germans wanted to remove all the local people from this strip of land along the coast, partly to prevent them from trying to sail across to England and partly because they needed to use this zone as part of their defences against a possible Allied invasion.

At the end of the 1930's Madam had worked as a secretary in the Ministry of War in The Hague. Yet in spite of the existence of this Ministry, the Netherlands was totally unprepared for war when it eventually came in 1940. 'There was total panic when we heard that the Germans were invading', she once told me. 'We thought it must be some kind of mistake. We were neutral! Surely all those German planes must be on their way to England. They couldn't possibly be here to attack us!'

Unfortunately, they were. German parachutists were dropped all around The Hague and quickly seized key positions in the city. 'The electricity was cut off and the officers began to ask: 'How can we work without power? It's an absolute disgrace.' Others complained about the 'unfairness' of being attacked without warning. One even moaned about the fact that he had been unable to shave properly that morning!'

Other sections of the local population reacted with similar indignation to this German lack of good manners. In those days there was a tramway between Leiden and The Hague, which was a popular means of transport for the civil servants travelling into the capital. 'The parachutists stopped the train and all the passengers were furious. 'You can't stop us here. We'll all be late for work!' We had no idea what a war would mean', added Madam. 'But the invasion quickly put an end to our naivety...'

After the war, the local residents returned to their shattered houses in the Frankenslag. Everything needed to be rebuilt and the general shortage of housing meant that homeowners were forced by the government to accept 'lodgers'. Madam had a whole series of these uninvited guests, the most exotic of whom were two 'sisters from the Dutch Indies'. Not only did they believe in evil spirits, they also dressed as evil spirits, in the hope of keeping their imaginary demons at bay! Madam knew how to tell a good story, bridging the gulfs of time and yet remaining true to the forms and customs with which she herself had grown up.

After drinking our two cups of tea, I paid her my rent. I put the money on the table and she quickly transferred it to a drawer, 'out of sight of the street'. Once this financial part of our ritual had been completed, she invariably asked: 'And now, Mr.Eppink, would you like something a little stronger?'

I answered with a polite nod and a bottle of sherry and a plate of cheese cubes were instantly produced from a nearby cupboard. As with the tea, our consumption of sherry was also strictly limited to two glasses – no more and no less. Traditionally, the period between the first and second glass was the moment when I tried to broach the thorny question of improvements to my apartment: minor repairs, new wallpaper, a new carpet. I knew that my requests had to be carefully worded and presented: Madam did not like spending money.

Her first reaction was always to be appalled at the potential expense: 'But Mr.Eppink, that will cost a small fortune!' Nevertheless, I continued to try and persuade her and when I agreed to pay a share of the costs, we usually managed to come to some agreement.

When I left The Hague, I left behind me a suburb of a kind that has almost ceased to exist. It was like a museum piece, a world such as Louis Couperus might have described: a never-never land inhabited by elderly widows and model citizens, all of whom are all loyal to King and Country and all of whom regard 'keeping up appearances' as a matter of the highest honour.

I knew that living in Belgium would be more fun, but also less formal and less ordered. Flanders does not have the same rituals, the same unwritten conventions, which govern the relations between 'people of a certain standing' in the Netherlands. Flanders prefers to leave such matters to chance. As a result, life in Flanders is full of unexpected surprises and mad situations. I had already had some experience of this when I arrived in Brussels as a young trainee.

Thanks to the help of some friends, I had managed to find a basement flat in the Stevinstraat. The landlady was Madam Bisqueret, a veteran of the 'Secret Army', with a heart as big as a house. She lived a few streets further away with her 'friend', a helpless soul who had turned to drink and whom she had taken under her wing. 'The poor dear', she said to me one day, with a protective note in her voice. 'I'm all he's got. He'd be lost without me.' Madam owned a whole block of houses in the Stevinstraat, all of which were let. The room above mine was rented to another old drunk, who had covered every inch of wall with pin-up photos from what were then called 'dirty magazines'. Madam remained tolerant and forgiving. 'He does like his young girls. But at his age, what can you expect?'

Paying rent to Madam Bisqueret was a very different experience to paying rent in The Hague. For one thing, her friend refused to lower the volume on the television, so that we could hardly hear ourselves speak. He just sat staring at the screen – he was a great fan of Westerns – with an open bottle of wine within easy reach. His standard answer to any question was 'What?'.

After a year, an apartment came free on the second floor of the same building. I decided to ask Madam if I could swap it for my basement flat. I was tired of my damp cellar, with its barred windows and its limited view of people's passing feet. There was too little light, too much fungus and my upstairs neighbour was too busy with his 'young ladies' to do much about the leak seeping through the ceiling.

To my delight and surprise, Madam Bisqueret agreed to my request and I dragged my few possessions up the stairs to my new home. The second floor apartment consisted of just three rooms and some old furniture, but for me it had an air of luxury that I had never experienced before. Until then I had always lived in single rooms, but now I had three whole rooms all to myself, with a view of the street and a bathroom to boot. At last, I began to feel at home in Belgium: I finally had a place of my own. Or so I thought.

The first thing I did was to turn one of the rooms – which already contained a beautiful wooden writing table – into an office. This gave my self-esteem a massive boost. Here was a place where I could write seriously; here was a place where I might even win the Pulitzer Prize! My first efforts were more modest. About that time the Japanese Embassy was organising an essay competition, with a two-week holiday in Japan for the winners. I decided to enter and wrote a witty piece about the arrogance of Europeans in describing Japan as a country in the 'Far East'. After all, the Japanese don't describe Germany as being in the 'Far West'! Why should we say that the Japanese live in the Far East, with all that this implies?

I sent my entry to the Embassy in the Netherlands. The essay had to be in English, French or German and I knew that there were lots of people living in Brussels who spoke these languages far better than I did. Back in Holland, I reasoned, there would be far less competition. And so it turned out. Two months later I was telephoned by an excited gentleman from the Japanese Embassy in The Hague. 'Mr.Eppink, you winner in Netherlands. You go Japan.'

I was thrilled and regarded my journey to Japan as a major triumph. My landlady was also impressed and celebrated my victory with a big, wet kiss. I had never travelled so far before, but now I was off to visit Tokyo, Kyoto, Yokohama, Hiroshima and all the other cities I had only ever read about in the history books.

Two weeks later, I returned to Brussels, tired but happy. I headed straight for my apartment, where I planned to sleep for a week. As soon as I entered the door, I realised that I was not alone. There was a woman in the bathroom polishing the taps and a child in the kitchen eating pap. I assumed that Madam had hired a cleaner to tidy up before I got back. 'That was kind of her', I thought and stumbled off to the bedroom, waving a hand at my unknown guests.

Next morning I was awakened by the crying of a baby. 'Bebe el thé', shouted a woman's voice. The child screamed louder. 'Bebe el thé', repeated the woman angrily. At this point, the screams of the child went off the Richter scale.

It took me some time to realise where I was. Was I still in Japan? Was I dreaming? The continuing noise from the kitchen brought me back to reality. I dressed and went to see what was happening. The woman and the child were still there. From the woman I soon learned that they came from Spain.

'Are you still cleaning?' I asked her in my best schoolboy Spanish.

'No, we live here.'

I couldn't believe what I was hearing.

'You live here?' I repeated incredulously. 'But I live here, too.'

She looked me straight in the eyes: 'Then now we live here together.'

I was stunned. I had hoped to have a few days rest after the exertions of my journey but now I found that my apartment had been taken over by strangers. Clearly Belgium was more full of surprises than anything I had seen in Japan!

At lunchtime, I went in search of Madam Bisqueret, to ask her what was going on. Had she thought that I would not be coming back?

'Ah, Mr.Eppink', she replied, 'I am sorry, I forgot to tell you. But you see, the Spanish want to become a part of Europe and a lot of them are already coming to Brussels. These people were looking for somewhere to live and I thought: "Mr.Eppink lives alone, he will take them." I found this all very difficult to grasp. The Spaniards were not yet a part of Europe, but they were already living in my rooms. The first Spanish invasion of the Low Countries since 1648 was beginning, and they had chosen to start with my apartment!

'But Madam, why did you say nothing?' I asked, trying hard to keep the indignation out of my voice.

'But Mr.Eppink, you were not here and I thought you would not mind. You are a kind man.'

Totally demoralised, I returned to my apartment. The only room I still had left to myself was the bedroom. My beautiful 'office' and the sitting room had been taken over by the Spaniards. The bathroom was now shared and I hardly ever got into the kitchen, since the Spanish lady was almost always cooking. Olive oil coated all the walls and the young child began crying each morning after the loud and imperious order: 'Bebe el thé!' The woman turned out to be slightly neurotic, smoked like a chimney and had a temper to match. As soon as I saw that she was also beginning to acquire a certain Belgian 'suppleness', I decided that this was no longer a place where a decent Dutch lad could live. After two months of being more or less confined to my bedroom, I decided to look for somewhere new: a place where there was no chance that Madam would saddle me with hordes of 'new Europeans'.

I had already seen an apartment near the Jourdan Square, a little further up in the European Quarter. It was in a new building, comfortable and modern. There was no Madam and the owners lived at a safe distance – in Spain, as coincidence would have it. Everything was arranged through the estate agent and there was also a caretaker to keep an eye on things.

I was delighted to be back on my own, free from all danger of enemy occupation. The caretaker, a small, thick-set man in an overall, seemed helpful, but complained continually about the neighbours. 'Do they make problems?' I asked him innocently. 'You see, Sir, it's like this. They're Congolese and they bring all kinds of things with them in their suitcases: vermin, insects, that kind of thing. If I was you, I would keep my windows and doors shut!'

But they were kind people from Congo, who never gave me a moment's trouble. Nor did I ever see a poisonous spider or snake in all my time there.

The caretaker also advised me to have a close look at the inside of my apartment. 'Because the bloke from the estate agent will be around in a minute, to draw up the inventory.' Inventory? This was the first I had heard of it. 'What's this 'bloke' going to do?', I asked. 'Note down everything that's in the apartment and what's wrong with it: every mark and every scratch.'

The 'bloke from the estate agent' turned out to be a large man with an even larger moustache. He was, he informed me, the official representative of the owner and showed me the long list on which he intended to note the inventory. As the caretaker had warned me, he went through the apartment with a fine toothcomb. He noted every blemish, counted every fork and spoon and went over the carpet more closely than a vacuum cleaner. He completed his forms in silence and asked me to sign.

'Now you must deposit a sum of money in a blocked bank account', he said. 'It is a guarantee payment against possible damage. You will get it all back when you leave, providing there is no serious damage, of course!' This sounded comforting and I thought that my involvement with this aspect of Belgian bureaucracy was over for good. How wrong I was.

A year later I wanted to leave the apartment, to take up a new job with the NRC. I assumed that the owners would not make any difficulties, but it soon became apparent that it was not going to be easy to recover my guarantee payment. In fact, it was going to be impossible. The owners refused point-blank to sign for its release and the 'bloke from the estate agent' returned with a new form, this time to note down all the terrible things I had done to their property.

'Rest assured, I will be taking a serious look, Mr.Eppink', he announced in the tone of a police inspector. His earlier friendliness was gone and had been replaced by suspicious hostility. Pen in hand, he poked his nose into every nook and cranny in the apartment. 'There's quite a lot to note, isn't there?' he said in a disapproving voice.

According to this self-appointed house controller, there were major cracks in the walls and the ceiling, excessive wear to the carpets and door frames, leaks in the bathroom and behind the cupboard. He made it sound as though the apartment had been occupied by a demolition expert for the past 12 months. The amount for the so-called 'damage' was surprisingly high: in fact, as high as the total amount of the guarantee payment.

I refused to sign this new inventory and a few days later I received a registered letter from the owner in Spain. It was written in a strange combination of French and Dutch, but the message was clear: the owner expected that I would release the guarantee and pay it all to him. 'I insist that you realise your obligations and transfer the money.'

I was genuinely shocked by the level of deception, the meanness of the owner and the duplicity of the 'bloke from the estate agent'. It was clearly time for a counter-attack.

On a Saturday morning, I removed my furniture from the flat, loaded it into a hired van and drove it to my new home in the Netherlands. Nobody – not even the caretaker – had suspected a thing. All my furniture was of the Ikea type and could easily be dismantled: it just looked as though I was shifting a load of wood. At least now my things were safe.

Next I tried to find out some more about the owners. It seemed that they were a retired couple from Brussels, who spent nearly all their time in Spain and who had placed their business affairs in the hands of my moustachioed friend from the estate agents.

I began to make some calculations. The bank account with my guarantee payment would remain blocked, unless both sides agreed to release it. My landlords were already well past pension age, so if I waited another ten years there was a good chance that they would both have snuffed it. At which point, the money would be mine, simply because there would no longer be anyone left to oppose my claim. In short, all I had to do was to let time do its grisly work.

The owners continued to send me angry letters, demanding that I should 'repair the ruin', but I no longer bothered to reply. After a while, the letters stopped.

10 years later (by which time I was back in Belgium) I judged that the moment had come to pursue the matter once again. I had heard nothing further from Spain and had no idea whether my landlords were alive or dead. I gambled, however, that the laws of demographics would be on my side. I thought it best not to act on my own behalf and decided to appoint a lawyer: this was certain to make a better impression with the bank. A friend of mine said he knew somebody: 'A smart girl from a good Flemish family. Give her a ring. She'll help you.'

My lady lawyer phoned the bank and enquired about the account. She learnt that it was still blocked. Via her personal contacts with the bank, she arranged what she called a 'supple solution' and what I called a 'Belgian compromise'. It was agreed that she should send a registered letter to the old address of the owners in Spain. If there was no answer within three months, the money would be mine.

'Have you heard anything from Spain?' I used to ask her every other day on the phone. She assured me patiently that she had not and nor was she likely to. She was confident the account would soon be made free. As the end of the three months approached, I began to grow increasingly pleased with myself. I had been too smart for the crook from the estate agents and my greedy landlords. For all their deviousness and trickery, I had beaten both of them.

One morning, my lawyer telephoned me: 'The daughter of the owners has called. They are still alive and they're still furious with you. The daughter called you 'the biggest bastard in all Brussels' and demands that you pay them the money at once.' In one sense, I could understand their anger: it was certainly a dirty trick that I was playing, even though I was doing no more than they had tried to do to me. To call me a 'bastard', however, was taking things too far. There are no bigger swindlers in Brussels than the landlords, who fill their pockets with over-priced rents for substandard properties. They are generally small, mean and nasty little materialists, who appear normal to the outside world but who would sell their own grandmother to get their hands on a guarantee payment. They lie, they cheat, they threaten and they exploit the ignorance of unsuspecting foreigners. To me, they are the lowest form of low life.

I sensed, however, that the daughter might make trouble and would probably try to blacken my name with the bank (where, by now, I had a mortgage). I couldn't risk this and so decided that it was time to try another 'Belgian compromise'. Over the years, interest on the guarantee payment had gradually been mounting up, so that the amount in the account was now almost exactly double what it had been ten years ago. I phoned the lawyer – who by now was as fed up with the whole business as I was – and said: 'Offer them a fifty-fifty split.' I reasoned that the owners couldn't risk waiting another ten years. Besides, their sort can never resist the temptation of easy money. I was right. The daughter agreed with hardly a moment's hesitation. 'But she still thinks you're the biggest bastard in all Brussels', my lawyer friend informed me politely. This didn't bother me in the slightest. I was just relieved that the matter had been settled. It might not have been the resounding victory I had been hoping for, but it was, at least, an honourable draw.

After all this trouble, I decided that the only way to avoid future problems with landlords was either to build a house myself or to buy a house and have it renovated to my own taste. This is what most Belgians do. Building and renovation are social phenomena in Flanders. During my time with the *De Standaard* newspaper, it used to occur regularly that colleagues would disappear for weeks on end. Their absence was normally justified by the fact that they were 'building a house' or 'putting in a new bathroom'. Their triumphs and disasters were openly shared in the editor's room, where most of their fellow-reporters had experienced similar successes and tragedies.

On many occasions 'doing it yourself' is a question of necessity, since contractors of all kinds – tilers, carpenters, painters, electricians, plumbers, plasterers, bricklayers – are notoriously unreliable in Belgium. This makes building or renovating a house a dangerous and unhealthy business and is liable to lead to a kind of depression known as 'builder's syndrome'.

To free myself from the grip of greedy landlords, I decided to buy an apartment in the Dijlemolens, not far from the House of the Lay Sisters in Leuven, one of the oldest parts of the city and included in the UNESCO world heritage list. Originally, the building was a mill which spanned the River Dijle, allowing easy delivery and shipment of both corn and flour. The giant mill stones were turned by an equally large water wheel, but in the course of the centuries the whole complex fell into disrepair. The property was bought by a developer in the 1980's and was transformed into a block of luxury apartments. This was intended to be an environmentally friendly project, with the water mill providing electricity, supplemented by a number of windmills on the roof. Sadly, all these praiseworthy plans came to nothing. When in action, the rotating water mill shook the building to its very foundations, whilst the windmills – which all had the shape of an Apollo capsule – threatened to tear the roof off and launch it into outer space.

An old couple in the Dijlemolens had decided to leave Leuven and move to Hasselt, in order to be nearer their children. I got to hear of their plans through a mutual friend and rang them up to see if they would be interested in selling. The couple were very charming and very traditional. The lady of the house made coffee, whilst I did business with her husband. Thirty minutes later everything was agreed: the purchase, the price and the date when I could move in. Never in my life had I made so many financially important decisions with such speed. 'Good', said the man pleasantly. 'That's that, then.'

Agreeing terms with the sellers was one thing; agreeing terms with the Belgian State was quite a different matter. In Belgium the sale of each house is taxed at almost 20%, a rate which most Belgians regard as little more than state-sponsored robbery. As a result, the ever-inventive Belgians have devised a system to overcome this, or at least to make the consequences less painful. This system involves 10% of the purchase price being paid to the seller 'under the table'. In this manner, the official selling price can be kept lower, thereby reducing the amount of tax to be paid. It is a typically Belgian solution to a typically Belgian problem. Everybody knows it is illegal, everybody does it and the tax office turns a blind eye, unless the under the table payment assumes unreasonable proportions. It all seemed very strange to me but in the circumstances it was difficult to avoid making use of this Belgian 'custom'. 'When in Rome, do as the Romans!'

For the signing of the deed of transfer, the couple chose a solicitor's office in the sleepy little Limburg village of Zussen-Zichen-Bolder, near Maastricht. I drove through the gently rolling countryside, the praises of which are so eloquently sung in the songs of old Limburg. Arriving in the village, it was not difficult to find the solicitor's house. Big, not far from the church and with a huge – one might even say regal – driveway. This was clearly one of those old fashioned communities, where the parish priest was still a figure of respect and where the notary also counted as one of the local notables. The notary himself was a precise, fast-talking man, who read the deed of transfer as though he had been doing it all his life. I understood very little of what he was saying and gradually began to pay less and less attention. Until, he stopped and asked us bluntly: 'I assume that you have not agreed a different sale price to the one mentioned in this deed.' By now he had my full attention and I was certain that I was about to be exposed as a fraud who had paid 10% 'under the table'. The old couple gave me a stern look and then turned to face the notary. 'No', they replied formally. 'No, of course not', said the notary – and gave us all a huge wink. The deed – and the deal – was done.

After the signing of the necessary papers, the notary invited us all for a meal in an old farm that had been converted into a pleasant rural restaurant. He seemed particularly interested in my views on the political situation in Belgium. 'If the Walloons don't get what they want at home, they will come and take it from us here', he said with his finger raised. 'Just look at Voeren.' I was having difficulty in pinning down his political sympathies. The reference to Voeren seemed to suggest that he leaned towards the Flemish nationalists. However, in the very next sentence he told us about his attendance at the Te Deum for the royal family in Tongeren. Was he then a monarchist, perhaps? I never did find out. Maybe that's just the way notaries have to be: blowing with the wind, to fit in with the opinions of their customers and contacts. After the meal, all three of them waved me off at the door of the restaurant. Possibly they thought that I was a 'nice Dutchman' – a title that is difficult to acquire in the Belgian Limburg. I never saw any of them again but their memory stayed with me: I had done a deal 'Belgian style'.

Living in the Dijlemolens is really something special. The view over the medieval House of the Lay Sisters makes you feel that you are sharing in a centuries' old drama, where time is relative and only man is transitory. The building had been completed a number of years ago and I had little desire to take part in the renovation craze. Not so my neighbours who were also good friends. They devised a scheme to enlarge their living room. The plans seemed sensible and easy to implement, and so I asked them if they would like to stay with me, while the work was being carried out.

'How long do you think the renovations will last?', I asked. 'We start in September and the contractors have promised that everything will be finished by Christmas. Three months maximum.' This didn't sound too bad. After my experience with the Spaniards, three months living with good friends should be easy.

Things, however, didn't quite turn out as planned. It quickly became apparent that building is not an exact science, particularly when it comes to setting completion dates. Three months became four months, four became six, and six eventually became ten.

Our building misery crept up on us unawares, like some kind of mysterious virus. The plans were ready and the major structural work was completed to schedule. It was then that the problems began. My friends took a day off work to meet the plasterer, to give him instructions and to lend him a helping hand, if it was necessary. It wasn't: he never turned up. On the telephone that evening he promised faithfully that he would be there the next morning. My friends took another day's leave but again it was all for nothing: the plasterer still failed to show. Day 3: same story, same result – no plasterer. After that, he didn't even bother to ring to say that he wasn't coming. It took six weeks of pleading, lying and bullying before he eventually arrived.

By this time, the building plans were in ruins. Because the plasterer had failed to do his work, the electrician had to be postponed. And because the electrician was postponed, the painter had to be put off. It was the domino effect gone wild. All the carefully-made appointments with a whole chain of contractors went up in smoke.

Weeks went by and the enthusiasm of the first days quickly turned to anger and despair. My friends spent hours on the phone, talking to contractors and subcontractors who continually promised improvement but never provided any. This is the key dilemma for anybody building or renovating a house in Belgium. Will the craftsmen come, or won't they? In the final analysis, we are all totally in their power.

Even when the plasterer had finished his work, the problems were still not at an end. By now, all the other contractors had already made new appointments with other customers for other projects. Getting them back to my friend's apartment was not going to be easy. Most of these tradesmen showed the same kind of reliability as the plasterer: plenty of promises but little action. And every time one of them failed to turn up, so the whole process of making new appointments had to be started all over again.

I shared in my friends' misery, in their daily hope that today a contractor would finally come and in their daily disappointment when he didn't. Before long, I, too, was suffering from 'builder's syndrome' – and I wasn't even building!

Ten months after they started, my friends were finally able to move back into their apartment. It was the realisation of a dream, but at times it had seemed more like a nightmare. With their departure, a certain calm returned to my life: no more phone calls, no more angry discussions, no more endless complaints about 'bloody contractors'. 'Builder's syndrome' quickly became a thing of the past and the restored peace and quiet almost put me into a holiday mood in my own flat!

As for myself, I have become very cautious with regard to all matters relating to building and renovation work in Belgium. You know where things are going to begin, but you are never quite certain where they are going to end. Not so long ago I drew up plans for the modernisation of my own bathroom. On reflection, I think I might wait for another couple of years....

BRUSSELS BY NIGHT – AND DAY

My first impressions of Brussels were not favourable. As my train pulled into the North Station, I thought that I had arrived in some kind of monster city – grey, cold and sad. The buildings were haphazardly arranged, as though thrown there by some careless giant, and the streets were dirty. It was a nightmare in iron and concrete – a city with a rich past but a grim present. Before our distant ancestors first came to settle in Brussels, the area was little more than marshland, dotted with trees and crisscrossed with streams. It was inaccessible, unpredictable and wet. In many ways, it has changed little during the intervening centuries: the streams have given way to concrete and tarmac and the trees have been replaced by brickwork, but Brussels still looks a recipe for instant depression.

Initially, I wanted nothing to do with the city, but I quickly realised that this was impractical. It is impossible to live in a place and yet be totally divorced from it mentally. However hard I tried, Brussels just kept bursting in on my consciousness. I may have begun as an accidental tourist, but after a while I was embarked on a journey of discovery through the largest city in the Low Countries. A city of paradox and contradiction. Brussels is the capital of Flanders, but few Flemings live there and you seldom hear Flemish spoken. Brussels is also the capital of Belgium – the faceless centre of a faceless country that scarcely exists.

Finally, Brussels is the capital of Europe – the heart of a community that has no soul.

It took me years to get used to the city and to accept it as a part of my life. At first, I used to just laugh at Brussels. I once described it to a friend as 'a mad city full of mad people and mad things.' To prove my point, I took him on a visit to the military museum in the Jubel Park – a sad collection of old uniforms and even older weapons, which are supposed to testify to Belgium's 'glorious' military past – a past which only exists in the crazed minds of one or two retired generals. From there we moved on to the famous but disappointingly 'small' statue of Manneke Pis. It somehow seemed to typify the city as a whole: long on expectation, short on substance...

As time passed, my attitude began to change. From being a disinterested tourist, I gradually became a supporter of my adopted city. I came to see a certain homeliness amidst the disorder and chaos. After each return visit to the Netherlands – where the box-like houses all stand in neat rows – I longed for the confusion of Brussels, a confusion in which everyone was free to make his own world. In the Netherlands, every citizen is under almost constant supervision, in a misguided attempt by the Dutch state to make sure that everything is done according to the letter of the law. Take parking, for example. If you are just five or ten minutes late back to your car in Amsterdam, there is a good chance that your wheels will be clamped. This kind of administrative fascism would be unthinkable in Brussels. In Brussels the police would just leave your car where it is, providing it is not blocking the road. And even if it was blocking the road, all they would do is write out a parking ticket for a small fine: a fine that will almost certainly never be collected, due to a shortage of staff in the appropriate Ministry!

As my knowledge and experience grew, I came to realise that Brussels is not really a city at all. It is more a metropolitan district, merged together with 18 outlying villages – villages which were once separate and independent but which have now been swallowed up by the expansion of 'Greater Brussels'. Each of these villages has its own special character.

Ukkel, for example, is a prosperous, French-speaking residential area, whilst Anderlecht is little more than an urban slum, where the old Flemish-speaking majority has now largely been replaced by North African immigrants. It is still possible to find some Flemings in Ganshoren, near the Basilica, but in Elsene (Ixelles) they have all but disappeared. For the convenience of its well-heeled inhabitants, the fashionable Louisalaan was also included in the Brussels administrative region (with postcode 1000) and it now acts as an exclusive corridor leading to the Terkameren Woods, the green heart of the city.

The Belgian constitution stipulates that Brussels, as the capital city of Belgium, must be bilingual in Dutch and French. There is, however, a huge difference between constitutional theory and local street practice. If you try and buy a newspaper from a kiosk in Dutch, it is almost certain that you will be answered in French. This applies equally in many of the shops and bars. True, many of the stallholders at the Sunday markets do speak Flemish, but most of them come from outlying Flemish towns. The situation is little better in local and central government. In almost every public building, a Dutch-speaker is likely to be met at best with ignorance, and at worst with indifference or outright hostility.

Yet it is precisely this bastardised quality – this gap between what Brussels is supposed to be and what it actually is – that gives the city its charm. In Brussels, there is a place for everybody. The Louisalaan is all fur coats and Armani suits, whereas less than a kilometre away the streetscape of the Madou Square is dominated by colourful costumes from all around the world. The area around the old Namur Gate has been 'colonised' by the broadly-smiling Congolese, while just a stone's throw away Schuman Square plays host to the officials of the European Union.

For obvious reasons, Brussels is the most European of all capital cities. However, I have often been struck by how little sympathy the employees of the great European institutions – the EU, NATO, embassies, etc. – have for their adopted home. For most of them, Brussels remains something of a mystery. They live in the city but are not part of it. They remain shut up in the European complex, complaining about the terrible chaos and the even more terrible traffic. Their attitude remains resolutely British or German or Dutch or French, and they prefer to stay in their own enclaves. For them Brussels represents a strange 'rite of passage', a stepping stone on the way to bigger and better things. It is a paradox that in this most European of cities, the majority of its European guests try to avoid all contact with local people and local customs. As a result Brussels remains largely unknown and unloved.

And if the Europeans make little effort to get to know Brussels, they make even less to get to know Flanders. They often master French and see Belgium, Brussels and Flanders through the eyes of *Le Soir*, *La Libre Belgique* and the RTBF, the French-language service of the Belgian television network. As the French-speaking press and media are notoriously partisan in their reporting of both domestic and foreign events, this gives the visiting Europeans a one-sided – one might even say distorted – picture of the country in which they live. That being said, the Flemish also do very little to try and make the Brussels Europeans feel at home. Most Flemings have the same suspicion of Brussels as the Europeans, whilst the concept of Europe seems a long way away. By contrast, for the Europeans it is Flanders which seems a long way away, while the abstract idea of Europe seems very real.

As a result of all this misunderstanding, the European community in Brussels lives alongside the local Belgian population, but not with them. This is a pity. The Belgians – be they from Flanders, Wallonia, Brussels or even from the German-speaking cantons – all have Europe in their blood. They have pro-European reflexes. Sadly, few Europeans have Brussels in their blood, let alone in their heart.

Fortunately, I had a different view of the city. For me Brussels was not the outsized centre of the great European family of nations. Instead, it was a patchwork collection of hidden corners and lost alleys. I knew only a fraction of the city but it was in this fraction that I lived. And it was this fraction that I came to love. As a Dutchman, I finally managed to feel at home in 'my Brussels'. Moreover, it was a Brussels that was continually changing, as I stumbled across new and exciting neighbourhoods: one day it might be the antiques quarter near the Zavel, the next evening the trendy night-life scene in the Dansaertstraat.

The discovery of each new square and each new restaurant was a constant source of joy. It had taken me some time to get used to the idea that you could eat well in a city as ugly as Brussels. Bad architecture and good cooking just somehow didn't seem to go together. True, in the beginning my needs were fairly modest. During the 1960's the Dutch very seldom went out to eat in restaurants. As a teenager, we had occasionally visited the local Chinese takeaway, but anything more exotic than this was either seen as showing off or a waste of money. We were brought up to eat whatever was put on our plate and most of it was simple fare. My favourite meal was kale (a kind of cabbage) and smoked sausage. I was less keen on sauerkraut and I didn't like sprouts at all. As for the rest, I would eat anything, providing it filled my belly and didn't give me the runs! During my student years, I gradually moved on from Chinese to Greek and Italian restaurants, but here my culinary experimentation came to an end. In those days, I had no interest in gastronomy: as far as I was concerned, *la Grande Cuisine* was a small amount of food on a large plate, followed by a large bill. It all looked very nice, with a sauce here and a sauce there, but it couldn't compare with a steaming plate of cabbage and sausage.

Once I moved to Belgium, it was almost impossible to escape *la Grande Cuisine*. Brussels is the culinary capital of Europe and eating out is an important part of both the social and political scene. In the Netherlands, culinary excellence is a fairly recent thing. It was not until 2002 that a Dutch restaurant – the Parkheuvel in Rotterdam – was finally given three Michelin stars. In the whole country there are only seven other restaurants with two stars and fifteen or so more with one star. By comparison, in Belgium there are two three star establishments, thirteen with two stars and more than seventy with one star. The Dutch might at last be outgrowing their preference for smoked sausage, but in Belgium 'eating out' out has a much longer tradition, at all levels of society.

From time to time, my work brought me into contact with some of Belgium's very finest chefs. On one occasion, they came to Brussels to lobby Parliament, which was planning to abolish tax deductibility for business lunches. This would have been a disaster for the restaurant industry, since it would have lost them most of their best customers: the businessmen and the politicians. As part of their protest, the chefs 'took over' the kitchens in the parliament building and cooked a series of meals for the assembled MP's and journalists.

This PR-stunt was arranged by the VLD senator, Leo Goovaerts. Goovaerts had already come to my attention by virtue of the fact that he was a member of no less than six separate parliaments: the National Senate, the Flemish Parliament, the Brussels Metropolitan Parliament, the Council of Europe, the Assembly of the West European Union and the Inter-Parliamentary Union. Even by Belgian standards, this was something of a record and perhaps not surprisingly many of Goovaerts most fervent supporters were in the catering business. It was these gentlemen who took over the parliamentary restaurant, which saw its longest lunchtime queue in recorded history. Needless to say, the politicians were 'persuaded' that cooking of such quality was a fine advertisement for Belgium as a whole and the favourable tax regime was maintained by a huge majority! With equal predictability, the press were 'in full agreement' with this 'wise' decision!

As a result of this unusual protest action, I came to know a lot more about the better places to eat out in Brussels. The undisputed jewel in the crown is Comme chez Soi. This restaurant dates back to 1926 and owes its name to one of its earliest customers, who told the owner: 'I enjoy eating here: it's *just like home*' (*comme chez soi* in French). The business passed by marriage into the hands of the Wynants family, who were originally butchers from the town of Tienen. Pierre Wynants, the present owner, has taken Comme chez Soi right to the very top of the culinary tree. Comme chez Soi has a pleasing, family atmosphere, but it is something of an exaggeration to say that it is 'just like home'.

The variety of the meals and the richness of the wine cellar are beyond most of the 'homes' that I have ever been to!

Homeliness is also an important element in the success of one of Brussels' other great restaurants: Bruneau's, near the Basilica. Jean-Pierre Bruneau opened his business in 1975 in a specially converted town house where he still lives on the top floor. A first Michelin star came in 1977, followed by a second in 1988 and a third at the beginning of the 1990's although with typical Michelin fickleness this was lost again in 2004.

Another of Brussels' gastronomic top-spots is the Villa Lorraine, which takes its name from a nearby avenue in the Zoniën Woods. The restaurant is housed in an elegant country mansion, and with just one Michelin star is probably, in my humble opinion, the most underrated eating house in the city. Equally good but somewhat heavier – both in terms of style and menu – is the Maison du Cygne on the main Market Square. This restaurant has some interesting historical associations. It was here that Karl Marx wrote much of his 'Communist Manifesto' and it was also here that the Belgian Socialist Party was founded. Strange that such a bourgeois-looking establishment should have such a proletarian past!

This is typical of Brussels – nothing is quite what it seems. It is a unique city, because it has no recognisable face. London is a showcase for the treasures of the once-mighty British Empire. Paris is the embodiment of national pride. Berlin – in spite of all its trials and tribulations in the 20th century – is still Europe's gateway to the East. By contrast, Brussels has no clear identity. It has always been a crossroads. Its present-day inhabitants include Flemings, Walloons and a whole host of European nationalities. In the past, it has been occupied by Spaniards, Austrians, the French, the Dutch and the Germans. All these foreign influences managed to leave something behind them. The Spanish left a cathedral, the Austrians left impressive government buildings and the Dutch left the 'Société Générale'! The French provided the city with a cultural veneer, whilst the Germans, true to national character, tried to absorb the surrounding villages into a Greater Brussels. This last undertaking was doomed to failure. Even the Führer and his henchmen should have realised that the citizens of Brussels will stomach just about anything – apart from uniformity. In this sense, Brussels is typically Belgian: it is not one city, but rather an amalgamation of different small cities. This is what gives it such a polyglot feel: more international than national.

In the course of the years Brussels has undergone many changes, both in terms of its structure, its economic activity and its social composition. After Belgium achieved its independence in 1830, the city suddenly found itself elevated to the status of a national capital. Before that it had been little more than a local centre for industry, trade and banking. Leopold II decided that this provincial town needed an imperial facelift. He constructed a large avenue running out to Tervuren and laid out the Jubel Park as a monument to his own and his nation's greatness. Belgium lay at the heart of Europe and Leopold wished to acquire for his country both an empire and superpower status. Sadly, once the fighting started in 1914, Belgium's true status became all too clear. For the second time in less than a century, the armies of France, Britain and Germany all converged on Brussels and the city passed once again into foreign hands.

Not all of Brussels' many transformations have been imposed from the outside. Some of the changes came from within. During the second half of the 19th century, as the city gradually became a true national centre, large numbers of industrial workers flooded in from Flanders. Throughout their history, the Flemish have shown themselves to be an adaptable race – and so it was now. French, the language of the metropolitan bourgeoisie, quickly replaced the local Flemish dialects of the newcomers and the city acquired the strong Gallic feel which it still has today.

The end of the Second World War saw the opening of a new chapter in the city's history. Brussels was chosen as the capital of Europe and it quickly became a centre for European integration and a home for the most important European institutions. The first to arrive were the officials of the EEC, followed shortly thereafter by the soldiers, sailors and airmen of NATO. Brussels was now expected to play the role of a world city. Its existing thoroughfares – such as the Koningstraat, a boulevard of elegant palaces and government buildings built by the Austrians, or Leopold II's broad avenue between the Jubel Park and Tervuren – were no longer deemed to be adequate. A whole new series of roadways, tunnels, and viaducts were driven through the heart of the old city, with an underground railway system thrown in for good measure. The development had a momentum all of its own and the planners seemed powerless to stop it. Almost without a second thought, historic sites were demolished to make way for new office blocks and hotels. The World Exhibition of 1958, coupled with the first post-war economic boom, focused people's attention on the future. Everything that was 'old' was 'outdated', and had to make way for the relentless march of progress. In less than a decade, Brussels lost many of its finest buildings. They were replaced by some of the ugliest architecture in Western Europe.

Ironically, the euphoria of the 1958 World Exhibition hid the fact that Belgian power had already passed its zenith and was actually in decline. Two years later the colony in the Congo was lost. Ten years later the federalisation of the country began. Under this process, Belgium was divided into various semi-autonomous regions and communities. Brussels was designated as the Metropolitan Region, with its own government and its own parliament, but still retaining its 19 separate local authorities. Brussels was also declared to be a province in its own right, equivalent to say West Flanders. As a result, the city now plays host to every administrative level of government in the Belgian political system: it is a municipality, a province, a region and also the seat of the national parliament!

As the city grew, so it fell into the hands of an unscrupulous political elite, corrupted by property speculation and by the bribery that went with it. The building companies were prepared to pay huge sums to the officials in the Public Works Department, in order to have their planning applications 'expedited'. As a result, close ties grew up between particular political parties and particular contractors.

In this respect, one name stands out in the history of post-war politics in Brussels: Paul Vanden Boeynants. Originally, he was the owner of an abattoir and meat factory, but this conflict of interest did not prevent him from becoming Minister for Small Businesses in 1958. From then on, he never looked back. In the course of his long career, he later held positions as Alderman of Public Works, Minister of Defence, Prime Minister and Chairman of the then powerful French-speaking Christian-Democrat party.

Vanden Boeynants – whose name was invariably shortened to VDB – was the ultimate 'Mr. Fix-it' and he had a finger in every Brussels' pie. During the golden age of property development, he was closely associated with Charly De Pauw (also known as

CDP). De Pauw was a major project manager and boss of a multi-storey car park empire. He was also awarded the lucrative contract for the 'modernising' of the Noordwijk. Between them, VDB and CDP demolished half of Brussels.

All these shady goings-on had taken place long before my arrival in the Wetstraat and I had never had the chance to meet VDB. In the meantime, he had been forced to retire from politics, but I was still fascinated by this larger-than-life figure, who had dominated the post-war political scene in Belgium for so long. Everything about him was exotic – not only his role as the spider in the web of Brussels' corruption, but also his famous kidnapping which many believed he had engineered himself, to avoid a number of pending legal prosecutions.

The courts eventually caught up with VDB and he was convicted of fraud. This prevented him from becoming Burgomaster of Brussels, a post he would dearly have loved to fill. Not dismayed, VDB tried to keep his hold over the city by securing the election of his figureheads to the Burgomaster's office. Unfortunately, these puppets were weak and unimpressive men. The first – Hervé Brouhon – was an alcoholic, who eventually drank himself to death. Next in line was the colourful but unstable Michel Demaret. Demaret was a figure from Brussels café life (he had once been a bouncer in a bar) and he was regularly to be seen in the Marollen, a popular city centre district. None of the city's 'waitresses' were safe from him and he was famed for slapping them on the bum and calling out: 'I'm glad to see they've got some new flesh in here at last!' Demaret also had a drink problem and it was only a matter of time before he brought embarrassment to the city he was supposed to represent. During a state visit to Brussels by the French president, he wandered around drunk and sweating in front of a bemused François Mitterand and King Boudewijn.

Not surprisingly, this was the last straw. The Court and the Government decided that VDB and his cronies must be removed from the political scene for good. As a result, during the 1994 election campaign not a single VDB supporter was selected as candidate for the French-speaking Christian-Democrats. His power was irrecoverably broken, but even then he refused to lie down and die. He continued to operate around the fringes of political life in Brussels, using his new position as director of the satirical magazine PAN to poke fun at the men who had forced him into retirement. For the rest, he withdrew to the seclusion of his exclusive villa in Knokke: '*Ons Hoekske*' (Our Little Corner).

I thought it might be interesting to interview this black sheep of Belgian politics, but he seldom gave interviews and was particularly careful to avoid foreign journalists. On a sheet of parliamentary notepaper, I sent him a short message, asking if he would be prepared to see me. I added that I was the first Netherlander since 1830 to take an interest in the workings of the Wetstraat. This must have intrigued him, since a few days later I received a handwritten invitation to visit VDB in '*Ons Hoekske*'.

His welcome was warm and he was especially pleased with the number plate of my car: PAN 477. 'Ah, I see you are already making publicity for me', he joked. He was smaller than he appeared on the television and his health had recently been giving him trouble, but it was clear that he still felt that he was a force to be reckoned with. From his villa next to the Royal Zoute Golf Club, he kept a close watch on the activities of the politicians in Brussels. He filled his pipe and began to lecture. 'Politics is a virus – and once you've caught it, there's no cure. As director of

PAN it's my turn now to dish out the criticism. And let me tell you, it's much easier than always being on the receiving end!' At the time of my interview VDB was 77 years old. His voice was strong and his handshake was firm, but he was obviously having trouble with his hearing. My Dutch accent hardly helped matters and so Vanden Boeynants' mistress sat next to him, screaming my questions into his ear. He had just returned from a health cure in Germany and was still dressed in his holiday clothes. 'I still play tennis and ride my bike', he informed me proudly in his incomprehensible mixture of Flemish, French and Brussels, one of Belgium's most difficult dialects. And if the conversation was moving in a direction he didn't like, then he would say so: 'trop is too much and too much is trop!' His use of language had a certain charm and his general attitude was friendly – one might even say genial. It was obvious that VDB was not one of those power politicians who enjoy biting everyone's head off. I soon found myself quite liking him.

During the 1980's one of Belgium's leading newspapers had written that 'VDB is not criminal – just sentimental.' Even so, he will go into Belgian history as the prime minister who raised political 'fixing' into an art form. Not that he saw it this way. His conviction for fraud in 1986 still irritated him, not least because of the public ticking off he had received from the trial judge. 'I was only doing what most people in the business world do', was VDB's reply. He accepted a plea bargain and escaped with a heavy fine. But the political damage was irreparable – he would never become Burgomaster of Brussels.

VDB felt at ease in *'Ons Hoekske'*, as if he had found peace. The floor of his sitting room was covered with a full-size lion skin. 'I shot that myself', he said. 'In the Kalahari.' To prove it, he pointed to a photograph taken just after the kill. In the photograph alongside, he was shaking hands with Charles De Gaulle. As I looked around the room, I could see dozens of other world leaders on similar display.

'This is the first time that I have ever given an interview to a member of the Dutch media', he announced suddenly, making an effort to keep his Brussels dialect under control. 'I have often been asked, but I thought it was better to keep Belgian politics out of the foreign press. I don't like Nosey Parkers.'

This didn't stop the foreign and domestic press from giving him a real roasting through the years. VDB is undoubtedly Belgium's most talked about and most controversial prime minister. Whatever the scandal was, you could be certain that someone would accuse VDB of having a part in it. He had sold VDB meat to the army. He had sold building permits to property speculators. He had been planning a right-wing coup d'état. He had been the brain behind the Pink Ballet, a high-class prostitution network for Brussels high-society.

'If anything happened in Belgium, I was always responsible. If I sneezed in public, the next day the papers would say I was causing a flu epidemic! I got the blame for everything. I was behind the Nijvel Bandits. I was working to – what is the word in Dutch? – "overthrow" the state. He made a throwing motion to emphasise his point. I was even shipping cocaine in my frozen meat! I remember one time....'

If he wandered from the point as he sometimes did, 'Madame' gave him a quick nudge to bring him back to the subject. 'Yes, and then there was that affair of the Pink Ballet, where I was supposed to be providing young men and women for the "amusement" of senior political figures. All lies, Mr.Eppink. All lies.'

If it was all lies, I asked, how come that his name kept on being mentioned? He continued as if I hadn't spoken.

'From the very beginning of my career, I was an anti-communist. Just after the war I worked for the *Vrai* magazine, a right of centre journal for young Christians. As a businessman, I was also against communism. My friends used to say: 'Paul, you are a born anti-communist.' Nowadays I am very proud of this fact. Communism was much worse than people ever realised. A member of the French Secret Service once told me: 'The Reds want you out of the way.' They never succeeded. I always did well at the elections. The voters were either for me or against me. There was no middle ground. "VDB – you love him or you hate him", they said.'

VDB might have been a born anti-communist, but this didn't stop him from doing a lucrative trade behind the Iron Curtain, even during the darkest years of the Cold War – a period when he was either Prime Minister or Minister of Defence. 'But what is wrong with that?' he demanded. 'Business is business and politics is politics. I did very well out of my dealings with the East, especially in Poland and Hungary. Do you know what the good thing was about trading with the East Bloc? You were always dealing with one organisation – not with many. And besides, their meat was very cheap. I made a lot of money without any complicated negotiations. I had the right partners. Voila.'

VDB saw no problem in the combination of businessman and politician. He simply couldn't understand my objections. 'The two things are really very easy to combine. Lots of people think I made a fortune, but that's not true. Politics cost me a lot of business. All those long meetings with ministers and cabinet staff took up an awful lot of time. And for a businessman, time is money. If I had to do it all again, I probably wouldn't go into politics. I would certainly be a lot richer, but perhaps not quite so satisfied. As I said before, politics is a virus.'

I continued to press him on this point. What about the rumours that he had sold meat to the Belgian Army? Without warning, VDB became very agitated: clearly I had touched a nerve. 'Sir, I swear on my word of honour that I never sold a single kilogram of meat to our armed forces or to any other government agency. Never, *jamais, nooit*. The Department of Justice investigated this matter, and what did they find? Nothing, *rien, niets.*'

At the end of the 1980's, VDB was kidnapped from his Brussels home. His abductors clearly believed that he was as rich as everybody said he was and hoped to make a fortune from the ransom money. A similar kidnapping of a member of the Heineken family had earned the kidnappers several millions. 'There is one important difference between Heineken and me. Heineken is a very rich man. The kidnappers thought that I was rich. Their leader, Patrick Haemers, had read in the newspaper that I had pots of money. But after 15 days of negotiation, they let me go for a paltry 63 million Belgian francs (1.5 million euros). The ransom was paid by a businessman, Jean Natan, who is now a good friend. I didn't have the money myself. Some people said that I had arranged the whole affair, in order to smuggle my fortune out of the country. What nonsense! If I had wanted to flee the country, I would have just got on an aeroplane, like everyone else.'

After his release, Heineken had surrounded himself with bodyguards and drove around in an armoured car. In *'Ons Hoekske'* there wasn't a security man in sight. VDB had a philosophical view of the matter. 'When I was abducted, I had good health and plenty of will-power. I was not tortured or starved. In fact, I was treated quite well. I wanted to survive and I did, without much difficulty. The affair has changed me very little. True, I am more careful now and I carry a gun – I practise regularly at a firing range. But if they want to capture you in a military style operation, then even an armoured car won't save you. I don't worry any more. I have just set the whole business behind me. Patrick Haemers committed suicide in prison and there is one other suspect awaiting trial. As far as I am concerned, it's all over.'

VBD had plenty of experience with the Belgian legal system and particularly with its failure to solve several major cases. 'But Sir, I ask you: is this so strange? In all countries there are always a number of cases which remain unsolved – even in the Netherlands. It's now far too late to track down the Nijvel Gang – the trail has gone cold. It might still be possible to clear up the Cools' murder, but it will not be easy. The hired killer came from abroad and was back across the border before the police had even begun with their enquiries. As for the men behind the killer, that is another question....' He paused and looked sad. 'André Cools was a very good friend of mine. Shortly after my own kidnapping, we dined together in Namur, where he was a Minister of the Walloon Community. He said to me: "Pol, men like you and I were not made to die in their beds." When I heard that he had been shot dead, I remembered these words.'

VDB became equally emotional when I began to ask him about his role in the 'redevelopment' of Brussels, which swept away so many historical buildings and replaced them with office blocks. 'But who says that Brussels is not beautiful? In 1914 it was just a provincial town. By 1940 it had become a national centre. Now it is a world city! This all had to happen very quickly. It was inevitable that there would be problems. Some projects were halted half way through, due to a change of management or lack of funds. By the time the buildings were eventually completed, they were already out of date. Nevertheless, they were all used. You say that there are too many office blocks in Brussels? But they are still building new ones, even today! And these, too, are all used. And if the European Union continues to expand, they will need even more. Many people want to see the EU leave Brussels. But I tell you, sir: this would be an irreversible disaster for our country!'

He regarded his close contacts with project manager Charly De Pauw – the famous VDB-CDP partnership – as the most natural thing in the country. 'In politics you have to have good contacts with lots of different people. Like myself, Charly De Pauw was criticised because he had vision, because he saw things on a grand scale. But look at the World Trade Centre! It is the tallest building in the country, but also one of the most beautiful. And do you know what stood there before? Slums. Long rows of derelict slums. And now it is one of the wonders of the modern world. That is what Brussels also needs as the capital of Europe – its own Manhattan. Charly saw it that way, too. People used to complain that Charly financed my election campaigns. So what? In those days it was allowed. But I never did any favours for him in return. Never! My hands are clean.'

The curtain finally fell over VDB's political career in 1994, when the Chairman of the Christian-Democrat Party, Johan Van Hecke, blocked his nomination. VDB talked with a degree of malicious enjoyment about the subsequent fate of his liquidator, who was himself forced to resign in 1996, following a very public extramarital affair. Van Hecke had even sneaked out of his party's offices via the fire escape and had flown off to Africa to be with his lover. VDB smiled as he recalled the scene. 'Yes, he ran off to Africa to be with his lady friend, abandoning all his responsibilities. Van Herck' (as he persisted in calling his ex-opponent) 'was the Robespierre of Belgian politics. He wanted to impose his will on everybody! And then he sets the worst possible example. *Allez*, how is it possible? People no longer wanted VDB because they were scared of VDB.'

Our conversation had lasted a long time and VDB's partner made it clear that it was almost time for his afternoon nap. I had just one last question: what kind of business had he done with the Netherlands throughout the years?

'Do you mean politics or VDB meat? In both cases, business was good. When I was Minister of Defence we agreed with the Netherlands to buy the F-16 jet fighter. This won us a whole string of compensation orders from the United States. I had very good relations with my Dutch counterpart, Henk Vredeling, but the negotiations were not easy. The Dutch government had its own ideas but I saw through them. They wanted to keep the fat and give us the bones! I wouldn't agree. The talks lasted months and a summit was held at the Egmont Palace to finally settle matters. The Prime Ministers, the Ministers of Defence and the Ministers of Economic Affairs from both countries were present. There was some tough talking. Den Uyl – a bandit but a clever man – said: "The Belgian Minister of Defence does not like Dutchmen." Prime Minister Tindemans looked out of the window in embarrassment. I replied that I liked Dutchmen very much. To prove it, I even sold my meat to them. But I added that my father had always taught me: "If you think a Hollander hasn't tried to rob you, check your pockets again."'

I stood up, shook VDB's hand and left *'Ons Hoekske'*. 'Enjoy our Belgian politics', he said at the gate. 'And remember to read PAN – then you will know what VDB is thinking.' I drove out through the green hedges and VDB went inside to have his nap. I never saw him or spoke to him again.

VDB died in 2001 and I couldn't help but feel sad. He was a politician from another era and another political culture. Throughout his career he was operating in a country where the straight and narrow path leads only to a dead end, whilst a twisty back alley will at least bring you temporarily to the right place. VDB was a man who knew these twisty back alleys better than anyone, but he was also in many respects a man of the people. And he was certainly not the crook that many people took him for.

VDB helped to build Brussels as we know it today: a city with nearly a million inhabitants and almost as many daytime workers. How many of these daily commuters – Flemings and Walloons – would have found work if Brussels had remained just a provincial backwater? If the European institutions had moved to the capital of one of the larger nations? As VDB said, this would have been a disaster for Brussels, but also a disaster for Europe. The European idea works because it has found its capital in an unpretentious city of an unpretentious country. In short, Brussels and Europe were made for each other.

1.

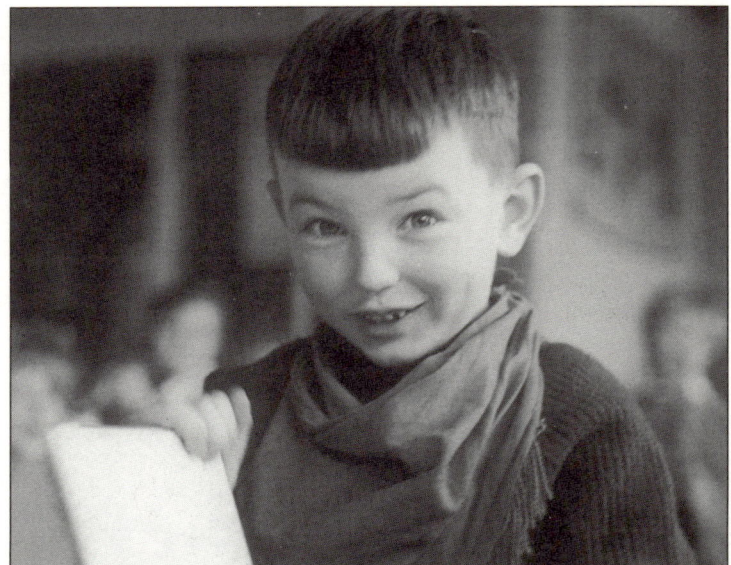

Derk-Jan Eppink – complete with cowboy scarf – as a toddler in Steenderen, his home village in the Achterhoek.

2.

Derk-Jan Eppink with his childhood friends at nursery school.

3.

In 1983 Derk-Jan Eppink undertakes a study trip to the Soviet Union. Here he is posing before the Ministry of State Planning in Moscow.

4.

Belgian newspapers: totally unintelligible for Dutchmen and Frenchmen.

5.

The Flemings are kings of their own castles.

6.

Brussels prefers architectural anarchy.

7.

Europe takes over the last small pieces of Belgium: the Luxembourg Station in the shadow of the European Parliament.

8.

Speaker of the House Herman De Croo prefers to inspect his 'estates' by horse.

9.

Paul Vanden Boeynants (VDB) lights his pipe. Note the sly look!

10.

3 June 1998: Herman De Croo becomes Minister of State. A pillar separates Derk-Jan Eppink from Guy Verhofstadt. 'Reconciliation' lunches will soon bring them together.

11.

In 1988 Guy Verhofstadt ousts Annemie Neyts as party chairman of the PVV. Guy laughs, while Annemie cries.

12.

23 April 1998. Premier Dehaene has just heard that Marc Dutroux has escaped. Belgium is in crisis.

13.

6 May 2002. Pim Fortuyn is murdered. A revolutionary mood grips the Binnenhof – for the first time since 1672.

14.

Flag-waving in Flanders: popular celebration during the Ronde van Vlaanderen.

15.

Catholic Flanders remains faithful to its traditions: the Holy Blood Procession in Bruges.

16. A crossroads in Belgium: who has right of way?

A state banquet for constituted bodies: King Albert and Queen Beatrix.

18.

19.

The best restaurant in Brussels: 'Comme chez Soi'. Cooking at home is cheaper but not quite so chic!

20.

21.

In Brussels you can drink until you drop. An example in the Jugendstil café 'A la Mort Subite'.

22.

The best chips in Brussels, on Jourdan Square.

23.

The founder of Opus Dei, Josémaría Escrivá, portrayed on postage stamps from various Catholic countries.

The compass-shaped layout of the Park in Brussels, between the Palace and Parliament. Only visible with a bird's-eye view!

25.

With a glass of Hoegaarden beer and a Belgian flag. 'Belgified' at last!

A BURGUNDIAN GENTLEMAN

Herman De Croo is a busy little man, who breezes and laughs his way through the corridors of power. I first met him at a VLD reception, shortly after he had been elected chairman. I didn't know him at the time, but I saw him making a bee-line for me across the room. He carried on making jokes and shaking hands left and right, but there was no mistake: he had me firmly in his sights. It was like watching some kind of whirlwind coming towards me: a gesticulating and talkative apparition, who made his way through the crowd with a skill that was almost artistic.

My colleagues at the paper had told me that De Croo was an 'out-of-date figure', one of the last dinosaurs of the old-style political culture. He was a great believer in the use of patronage and his philosophy was 'you scratch my back and I'll scratch yours.' I accepted the comments of my fellow-reporters at face value and after his election I described him as being 'yesterday's choice'.

At the Liberal Party headquarters in the Melsenstraat – known as the 'little blue factory' – the champagne was flowing in buckets. The liberals enjoy a good party and know how to celebrate with the best of them. They will always offer their guests champagne, while the Christian-Democrats make do with fizzy wine and the socialists stick to beer. And as always, there was plenty of booze to go around. De Croo had entrusted the organisation of the reception to the Sabena Party Service. As an ex-Minister of Transport, he had excellent contacts with the Belgian national airline. He was still an adviser to the company and, as new party chairman, was able to make sure that 'his people' were given seats on the board. Sabena also knew how to play the game of favour and counter-favour, and had no doubt provided the reception for a 'reasonable' price. And politicians got huge discounts when they flew Sabena. No wonder that the company went bankrupt some years later!

As the evening drew to an end, I finally found him standing at my side. 'Ah, so you are the Dutchman who has come to write about us all', he said, a little sarcastically. I answered that I was indeed the new boy and that, yes, I had come to write about Belgian politics. He looked at me askance and began to speak in his typically spluttering style. It was as if he was preparing for some kind of confrontation. I soon discovered that he was. 'And you say that I am an out-of-date figure?' He looked irritated and tried to drag some of the other bystanders into the conversation. They very wisely kept silent, since it was clear that he intended to give the press – in the unfortunate person of myself – a good hammering.

'If I am so out-of-date, how do you explain the fact that I always have the most preferential votes in Flanders?' he said in a voice that could be heard on the other side of the room. It was true, of course. In the East Flanders Zwalm district – his own personal political stronghold – he had long been the king of the preferential votes. But everyone knew why. I sipped my champagne and answered him. 'People say that you dispense favours. You bypass the normal channels to help your friends.' De Croo took a step back, as if he wished to distance himself from anyone who could say something so scandalous. 'Sir', he said, raising his voice and wagging his index finger under my nose. 'You know nothing about Flanders. You come and you see but you do not understand.'

A group of De Croo's political cronies had gathered around us and nodded earnestly in agreement with their leader. Even my journalistic colleagues, who were often much more critical of De Croo than I had been, held their tongues. In their eyes, I could read the unspoken message: 'don't get us into trouble with the new party chairman!' Strengthened by my obvious lack of support, De Croo continued haughtily: 'I do not dispense favours. I provide services. Services to people who ask my help.'

This was not the kind of evening I had had in mind and I tried to get away from De Croo and his gang as quickly as possible. Nevertheless, I had the impression that my remarks had hit the target, no matter how hard he tried to disguise the fact with extravagant gestures and flowery language.

A little later on, he took me to one side. 'Mr.Eppink, it is perfectly normal that you do not yet understand how Flanders works. I would like to invite you to my house in Michelbeke on a Sunday. If you like, we can go for a horse ride. Then you will see something of the real Flanders.' To show my good will – and perhaps also to mend some fences – I said 'yes'.

On my way back to the office, I started to doubt the wisdom of what I had done. I wasn't used to visiting politicians at home for a cosy, fireside chat. In the Netherlands, such a move would have been viewed with deep suspicion. It smelt of favouritism, some might even say of bribery and corruption. In The Hague I had never been to an MP's house, nor even had lunch with a politician. The most we ever risked was a cup of tea in the parliament bar! To have done otherwise would have been to commit professional suicide.

For all these reasons, I now felt slightly embarrassed at De Croo's invitation but I saw no way of getting out of it. Besides, like he said, it would be a good opportunity to see something of the 'real' Flanders.

If the truth be known, I was less worried about my professional reputation and more concerned by the fact that I would have to ride a horse. I had told De Croo that I had some experience of horse riding but this was a gross exaggeration. I had once taken a few lessons at a stable near Scheveningen, in the hope that one day I might be able to gallop across the sands of Holland's North Sea shore, like some kind of latter-day Errol Flynn. Sadly, my riding career was not a great success. My first lesson got off to a bad start, when another rider fell off his horse and broke his leg. The sight of the ambulance carting him away to hospital did my confidence no good at all, and matters didn't improve when I was actually asked to get on a horse. My instructress – a strapping girl with thighs like tree trunks – was able to control even the largest steeds, whereas I seemed to have trouble with even the smallest ponies. Nevertheless, I decided to stick it out, although I refused point-blank to sit on some of the bigger stallions.

After ten lessons there was a test for beginners. If you passed, you were allowed to ride on the seashore. The instructress stood in the middle of the training ring, whip in hand, and the other pupils gathered around to watch me perform. The plan was that I would do ten circuits of the ring at a canter and then another ten at a gallop. My horse, a moody-looking white beast, followed my instructions perfectly and we completed the canter section without mishap. As we started the gallop, I began to feel that I might actually get my riding diploma after all. Unfortunately, at this point the instructress unexpectedly cracked her whip. My startled horse raced off at an alarming speed and then suddenly hit the brakes. Before I knew it, I was flying gracefully through the air and landed with a bump in the manure-stained sand.

I was the only pupil in the group who failed the test and consequently I had to do a further series of lessons. By the time the next test came around, I was feeling more confident. I hadn't fallen off a horse in the meantime, but each new lesson had been a severe strain on my nerves and I was always glad to get home in one piece. The instructress had chosen a supposedly docile mount for me to ride and I had to perform the same exercises as last time. As far as I was concerned, it was a question of 'do or die', although I hoped not literally. Once again the cantering section passed off well. So much so, that as evidence of my improved riding skill, I decided to let go of my reins and wave at the instructress. 'Look how well it's going', I shouted smugly. I should have known better. Feeling the relaxed pressure on the reins, my horse sprang forward like a tiger. With a curious feeling of déja-vu, I was launched backwards out of my saddle, did a neat somersault and once again landed nose-first in the brown coloured sand.

Suffice it to say that I never did get a riding diploma and I never galloped romantically across the sands of Scheveningen.

In short, then, I had two very good reasons for delaying my visit to De Croo for as long as possible: fear of losing my professional credibility and fear of breaking my neck. However, the little man was not to be denied. Every time I saw him, he would end our conversation by asking: 'And when are you coming to Michelbeke?' Finally, I gave in. After all, I had given my word, and a promise is a promise. 'When would be convenient?' I said. 'How about Sunday? 12 o'clock?'

So it was that I found myself on a bright spring Sunday in March driving through the Flemish countryside on my way to

Michelbeke. I had seen from the map that it was little more than a small village in the administrative district of Brakel – hence De Croo's nickname: 'the Oracle of Brakel'. This was in the heart of the Zwalm district, which in turn formed part of the Flemish Ardennes – a beautiful area of lightly-wooded hills and dales, politically divided by the language frontier between the Dutch and French-speaking communities. I left the E40 motorway at Aalst and tried to keep as much as possible to secondary roads. My winding route took me through the villages of East Flanders, each with a church in the middle and each with a café next door. Most of them were quiet and deserted, save for a few early churchgoers and a handful of cyclists, profiting from the unexpectedly warm spring sun. The roads were made of huge paved blocks, lined with gently waving linden trees, and I drove slowly to enjoy the delights of a hidden Flanders I had never previously seen.

With the aid of my map, I finally arrived in Brakel, only to discover that the road to Michelbeke was blocked off. A board marked 'diversion' told me that I would have to find another way to reach the land of De Croo. I followed the diversion signs along a series of narrow cobbled roads, but after a few kilometres the signs simply petered out. I was now stuck in the middle of nowhere, with not the faintest idea of the right direction. All I could see were church towers in the distance, any one of which could have been Michelbeke. 'If I carry on like this', I said to myself, 'I'm going to be late and then I'll look a right fool. I'd better ask someone.' The only problem with this brilliant plan was that there was no one about to ask! For ten minutes I waited in vain for a passer-by, but none came. In near despair, I drove to the nearest farm and rang the bell. The lady who opened the door looked at me with the kind of suspicion usually reserved for Jehovah's Witnesses. Clearly, this was not a region where they were used to strangers just dropping in. 'I'm sorry to trouble you on a Sunday, madam, but could you possibly tell me the way to Michelbeke?' The woman brightened at the sound of a name she recognised. 'Oh yes, that's not very difficult. It's quite close by. Are you looking for anything in particular?' she asked inquisitively. 'Yes, I've been invited to spend the afternoon with Herman De Croo', I replied rather stiffly. Her face lit up. 'Oh, we all know Mr.De Croo. He's one of us, our man. I can tell you exactly where he lives.' Now it was my turn to look relieved – in the middle of this deserted landscape I had at last found a reliable point of reference. She explained in detail how I first had to drive to Michelbeke, then turn left at the church and then look for a big white house some 300 metres further on. 'That's where Mr.De Croo lives', she said proudly.

I followed her directions and arrived safely in Michelbeke. It was little more than a hamlet, with a church, a café, a school and a bank building. The sun sparkled on the roofs of the houses and the village square looked neat and orderly, but there was not a soul to be seen. I wondered where on earth De Croo's 40,000 preferential votes came from. As instructed, I turned left at the church and drove on for 300 metres. A white house, long and low to the ground, came into view and I assumed that I had finally arrived at the De Croo residence. I parked my car and rang the bell.

The door was opened by an elegant lady. 'Ah, you must be the man from the newspaper', said Mrs.De Croo, in an accent which suggested a French-speaking education. 'Please come in. My husband is not here yet. He is on the television.'

For a horrible moment, I thought that I had got the wrong Sunday. The television was on and there was De Croo in the middle of the screen. The programme was the 'Seventh Day', a political magazine, and De Croo was debating education with Johan Van Hecke, chairman of the Christian-Democrat CVP party. A white-suited Van Hecke was defending the merits of Catholic schools, whilst the VLD chairman championed the cause of the secular state system.

The discussion was a fierce one – although 'fierce' is a relative term in Belgian politics – and it was difficult to imagine that within a few years Van Hecke would leave the CVP and cross over to join De Croo and the liberals.

Mrs.De Croo followed the debate with extraordinary passion. 'That Van Hecke is an odd type. All those stories about priests and nuns. What a lot of nonsense. He should look at himself.'

I sat down and started to watch as well. Each time Van Hecke defended Catholic education, Mrs.De Croo had great difficulty in controlling her anger. It was obvious that this was a delicate subject for her, but I was afraid to ask her why, in case she thought I was impolite. However, as a good Protestant boy, I could fully understand her sentiments when she began muttering about 'those damned priests'.

I assumed that the liberal leader would come straight home after his television appearance, particularly as his wife had already made clear that I was expected. However, it seemed that De Croo had other ideas. 'My husband won't be here for a little while yet', the lady of the house informed me. 'He has to do a few halls first.'

'Halls?'

'Yes, halls. Function halls. There are a number of family celebrations in the area today – golden weddings, hundredth birthdays, that kind of thing. He's just going to pop in, to say hello.'

At this rate it would take De Croo hours to reach his White House and I was afraid that I would be kept hanging around for most of the afternoon. Mrs. De Croo must have seen the look on my face. 'Don't worry. It doesn't take very long for Herman to do a hall. And there are only three. Normally in an evening he can do thirteen.'

'Thirteen?' I repeated. She made it sound like the most natural thing in the world, to traipse around thirteen Flemish village halls on a dark Saturday night.

'Yes, thirteen. He goes in, shakes hands down the left hand side of the hall, then shakes hands down the right hand side of the hall, and then he leaves. Afterwards, everyone will say: 'Did you see? De Croo was here.' And, of course, he was – even if it was only for 3 minutes. He never stays longer than 3 minutes. His driver stands with a watch by the door, to make sure he gets away on time.'

I was amazed at such purposefulness and efficiency in a region better known for its relaxed and casual approach to life.

An hour later the front door opened and De Croo came in. 'Ah, my dear friend, you are here already. A thousand apologies for my lateness. I had to do the television interview and on the way back I dropped in at a few halls, as a favour to some people I know. It makes them happy and it is the kind of thing they remember at election time.'

De Croo took me by the arm and led me through his large house. Originally, it had been an ordinary sized villa, but a huge new wing had been added, which gave it its long and low appearance. The house had a splendid view across the Flemish Ardennes, a gently rolling mosaic of trees and fields, which formed the soft underbelly of Flanders, close to the border of the linguistic divide with Wallonia. This view was sacred to De Croo:

it was his window on the world. If anyone had ever had the idea of setting a building somewhere on this magnificent horizon, the liberal top man would have made sure that planning permission was never granted. All the local burgomasters were placemen of the king of the preferential votes.

'The language barrier doesn't exist here', said De Croo cheerfully. He wanted nothing to do with Flemish nationalism, flag-flying and language disputes. 'It's only the provinces far from the linguistic border that get excited about language issues. Here we hardly notice it. People just get on with enjoying life.'

He walked through to his study, which was full of rustic furniture and souvenirs, including spears and shields from Zaire. On the wall, there was a large photograph of De Croo standing next to the Zairian leader, Mobutu Sese Seko. 'I am proud of my association with the president', he said sadly. 'It is a pity that things turned out the way they did.' The two men had been friends and De Croo had regularly visited Mobutu in Kinshasa or at his summer palace on the French Riviera. He had even been invited to the dictator's 60th birthday party.

The shields and spears were a reminder of the close ties between the boss of the VLD and the boss of Africa's largest country. 'He called me recently. I was sitting in that very chair. I have his number and he has mine. I have the numbers of most of the top men in Zaire. If the Ministry of Foreign Affairs wants to get in touch with someone in Kinshasa, they usually ask me first. Premier Vanden Boeynants once told his secretary: "Get me Mobutu on the line." She answered: "But I don't have his number." "Then ask De Croo!" the premier replied.'

De Croo had seen 'the Congo' (as he still called it) become independent and had regarded Mobutu as the only guarantee of stability in a land that had always been internally divided. But he had been cruelly deceived. Instead of saving his country, the new president destroyed it, dividing its wealth amongst members of his own clan and leaving the rest of the population poor and destitute. During the final days of his regime, even his own supporters began to turn on him. Despised and rejected, he was forced to flee Zaire and to seek refuge abroad.

France refused to take him and Belgium also closed its doors. He spent his final years in Morocco, where he eventually died, unloved and unmourned. De Croo spoke of Mobutu in terms of a drama, a Greek tragedy on an African scale.

During his last days, the sick ex-president had phoned his old friend: 'My dear Herman, what have I done wrong? I am the President, the Chief. I did everything for my country. I did everything for Belgium. Why has everybody turned against me? How has this happened? For the rest of the world, I have become evil personified.'

De Croo had sympathised. He may not have agreed with Mobutu but he understood him. They were two politicians, whom the fates had treated differently. The Sun of Zaire and the Son of the Zwalm. When De Croo looked at Mobutu, he did not see a merciless tyrant but an unfortunate and misguided friend. And his office, with its melancholic air of nostalgia, was a memorial to that strange and ill-fated friendship.

The guided tour continued. When I thought that I had seen everything, I turned to him and said: 'You have a very impressive house, Mr. De Croo.' He looked surprised. 'But you haven't seen most of it yet. The best is still to come!' Now it was my turn to look surprised. The house was a bungalow, with no upstairs floor. What could he possibly mean? He quickly told me. 'Yes, the largest part of the house is underground. You have forgotten my cellars. That is where I keep my personal files – all 70,000 of them.'

I didn't know what to say, and so I simply followed him downstairs into a labyrinth of corridors and passages. It was like being in the catacombs of ancient Rome, although instead of bodies the walls were lined with row after row of files, all beautifully ordered and classified. De Croo explained. 'Look, I do things for people. I have a weekly session and people come to me with their problems. I listen, make notes and try to find a solution for their problem. And I don't care which party they vote for. I simply offer them my services.'

I could hardly believe what I was seeing and hearing. I had wandered into a chamber of horrors, which would not have been out of place in the police states of the old Communist Block – or even in Mobutu's Zaire. This was political patronage and favouritism run wild.

I wanted to try and find out more. 'But how do you do things for people, Mr. De Croo?'

He looked at me with an expression which said: 'This stupid Hollander still doesn't understand.' 'I have lots of contacts', he explained. 'Burgomasters, councillors, businessmen. I call them up or write them a letter and I ask them to help.' This was how he liked to see himself. Herman the Helpful. He even gave the local old age pensioners jobs, sorting out his files.

It slowly began to dawn on me that these catacombs were the real basis of De Croo's political power. He fixed things for people and at election time they repaid the favour. As a result, his number of preferential votes continued to grow in direct proportion to the number of files in his cellar. In his district, even the nuns voted liberal – the local Christian-Democrats never got a look in.

I suggested that this way of 'doing business' was morally questionable, to say the least, but De Croo thought it was the most normal thing in the world. 'I am a social person and I like to help people.' We had now reached the point of my visit. 'And if journalists like you call that old-style political culture, well, in that case I am an old style politician – and proud of it!'

After the cellar, I had hoped that our tour of the house would be at an end. Regrettably, it wasn't. With typical enthusiasm, he insisted that I should go and see his 'zoo'. He took me outside, where a garden the size of several football fields was divided up into a series of pens. From one of the pens an animal grunted. 'Look! That's my Vietnamese pig. And over there, between the geese and the ducks, you can see a kangaroo.' He talked of his animals with great pride, even though they couldn't provide him with a single preferential vote.

In the meantime, his children had arrived home: Alexander, a sporty twenty-year old who was a student at the Free University of Brussels, and his sister, Ariane, a girl of bewitching dark looks, who was studying law at the same university.

We dined with a spectacular view over the valley of the Zwalm and talked about nothing in particular. Suddenly, the doorbell rang and Mrs.De Croo went to answer it. She returned with an enormous bouquet of flowers. 'They're from the De Gerlache's', she announced.

'Splendid', said De Croo, 'I'm glad to see they haven't forgotten that little favour I did for them.' I knew that he wouldn't be able to resist providing an explanation. The De Gerlache's were relatives of the famous polar explorer Adrien De Gerlache, who at the end of the nineteenth century had made a series of heroic voyages around Antarctica in his ship, the 'Belgica'.

'When I was Minister of Transport, a decision was taken to add a new branch to the Brussels underground. We had to find names for all the new stations and I arranged for one of them to be called *Belgica*. The De Gerlache's were very grateful and every year we get a bouquet of flowers.' And every election a preferential vote, I said to myself silently.

De Croo continued to talk enthusiastically about himself and his region. 'No doubt you have heard of the village of Sint-Maria-Horebeke', he said. He made it sound as famous as London or Paris, but I had to confess that I had never heard of the place. 'What? And you call yourself a Protestant?' Inevitably, he went on to explain. Apparently, Sint-Maria-Horebeke is a Protestant enclave in an otherwise predominantly Catholic area, a throwback to the age of William I and the period of Dutch rule. 'During the redrawing of administrative boundaries in the 1970's, the CVP wanted to rob the village of its independent status and merge it with a larger Catholic commune. I was against the proposal and stood up for the rights of the Protestants against the CVP and the Bishop of Ghent. I won, of course. I don't know if the Protestants still vote for me, but I don't rule out the possibility.' Tongue in cheek, I thanked him for his brave defence of this last remnant of the Protestant past against an otherwise invincible tide of Papist domination. Yet for all my mocking, it was an act of tolerance which somehow seemed typical of this deep blue liberal.

We had hardly finished with Sint-Maria-Horebeke before we were moving on to another one of De Croo's pet subjects: stations. As Minister of Transport, he had initiated a project to have all the small local stations renovated and improved. 'People don't vote for me just because of my good looks', he joked. 'They expect me to do something for them. I am closer to the ordinary people than all the prophets of the new political culture put together.' I was beginning to see that he might have a point. The true spirit of Flanders is not to be found in the Wetstraat, but in villages like Michelbeke and Sint-Maria-Horebeke.

During dessert, the conversation finally turned in the direction I had been dreading. 'I hope you have brought your riding boots with you. I usually go riding at eight o'clock in the morning but today I have waited for you. Shall we go and fetch the horses?' A shiver of fear ran down my spine, but there was no way I could refuse. 'Alexander, will you come too? We can show Mr. Eppink our region.' Like a condemned man on his way to the gallows, I followed De Croo and his son to a nearby farm, where he kept his horses. In the stable yard stood three large stallions, impatient that their boss had kept them waiting since eight o'clock this morning. The swishing of their tails made it clear that they wanted to gallop off across the fields and I knew my fate was sealed.

With a nimble movement, De Croo swung himself into the saddle. His son did the same. My efforts were less successful. Eventually, I had to go and find a chair, so that I could scramble onto my mount that way. I had hardly got my feet in the stirrups, before De Croo ordered the horses to 'walk on'.

'We'll ride to the village first', he said. 'This is the best time of the day.'

We entered the square and for the first time since my arrival in the Flemish Ardennes I actually saw people on the street. They all stopped to greet the liberal leader on his horseback.

'Good afternoon, Mr.De Croo. How are you today? Well, I hope?'

De Croo returned the greeting by putting two fingers to his riding helmet, in a kind of aristocratic salute. He seemed to know all the villagers by name and he always asked them to pass on his regards to the other members of their families. The whole of Michelbeke was bathed in the warmth of his social beneficence.

Suddenly, we turned off to the left and entered an orchard. We had come to inspect his fruit trees and he looked at his fruit buds critically. 'It's going to be a good year', he commented.

I had the feeling that I had drifted back in time. It was as if I was riding with some 19th century nobleman around his estates, checking on the fields and controlling the local peasantry. And wherever we turned, there were signs of his good works for 'his' people. 'I had that little dam built', he announced, pointing to a barrage in the River Zwalm. 'It was necessary for the drainage and to prevent flooding.'

However, not everything in the De Croo garden was lovely. We suddenly found our way blocked by a barbed-wire fence, much to the obvious irritation of my host. 'Hasn't this so-and-so moved that wire yet? He only does it to annoy me. I'll have to speak to the Burgomaster again.' Clearly there were still some of the local peasants who were in a rebellious mood.

We moved off in another direction, past streams and woods and meadows. I still hadn't fallen off my horse and was actually able to follow quite well, as I was bringing up the rear, behind De Croo and his son. After half an hour, however, we came to a large meadow. 'This is where we usually gallop. The horses love it. Hold on tight to your reins and off we go!'

Between my legs, I could feel my horse getting restless, building itself up for a mad charge across this wide-open country. 'Mr. De Croo, please don't gallop. If you do, I'm going to fall off!' I hardly had time to finish my sentence before my horse bolted. We left a surprised De Croo and his son standing and raced off across the field. I pulled on the reins as if my life depended on it which it probably did. But try as I might I couldn't get the stupid animal to stop. Its natural urge to run free was greater than the pain of the bit.

In the meantime De Croo and Alexander had set off in pursuit. 'Sit tight', he called, 'and I'll try and head him off.' By this time I was sitting anything but tight. I had already slipped half way off my saddle and was holding onto the bridle with just one hand. I felt my strength ebbing and I was certain that I was about to fall, when De Croo finally came alongside and pulled my runaway steed to a halt. He jumped from his own horse and pushed me back into the saddle, probably remembering that I would otherwise need a chair to get back on.

'You have to hold on to the reins tightly', De Croo warned me. I nodded, breathed in huge gulps of air and hoped that this hellish journey would be over as quickly as possible. For the rest of the ride they kept a close eye on me. 'Alexander, you go in front of Mr. Eppink and I will stay behind him. Just in case the horse makes another run for it.' As the best guarded rider in the Zwalm district, I made my way at a snail's pace back through the orchard and into the farmyard. I let out a huge sigh of relief, but found that I couldn't get off the horse. During my adventures, I had clenched the muscles of my legs so tightly to the saddle that I was now unable to relax them. De Croo had to fetch a ladder to release me from this embarrassing position. My humiliation was complete.

When I had finally been separated from my steed, De Croo suggested that we go back to the house for a drink. 'It will give you a chance to get your wind back.' In his living room, I half collapsed into a chair and Mrs. De Croo brought me a glass of water. She seemed most concerned with my lack of horse skill.

'Mr. Eppink, you must be careful. You could have an accident riding like that.'

As always, De Croo himself saw the bright side of things. 'But everything is fine. He rode very well. It's just that the horses were a bit frisky, because we were much later than normal.'

He disappeared out of the room and returned five minutes later dressed in a suit and tie, with a small badge, a family heirloom, fixed to his belt. 'Mr. Eppink, I am afraid I must leave you. I have a few more halls to do. It was nice having you here. Please come again.' And with that, he was gone.

I never found the courage to go riding with De Croo again. I kept thinking of the 'Superman' actor, Christopher Reeve, who had fallen from a horse and been paralysed for life. If that could happen to Superman, what chance did a political hack from the Wetstraat have?

Even so, I kept in regular contact with De Croo although always without horse. I gradually amended my original opinion of him and came to see him as an affable man, social and warm-hearted. And this is the way he stayed, no matter where he was and no matter what he was doing. In the late nineties he was finally appointed as a Minister of State and after the elections of 1999 he became Speaker of the Lower House. De Croo was not only king of the preferential votes, he was now also 'first citizen of the country'. He enjoyed the prestige of his new position which he saw as the highest possible reward for his many 'services' but didn't shrink from making things difficult for his own government, if he thought it was justified. He also had the Parliament Building restored to its former glory, just like he had done with the railway stations in the Zwalm valley.

Time and time again, I asked myself what motivated a man to spend all his free time 'doing' halls and making people 'happy'.

Was he perhaps aiming for a permanent place in the history of his country? Were all his renovated stations, dams and buildings just his way of trying to leave something behind for posterity? De Croo has been an MP since 31 March 1968 and it is one of his ambitions to break the record of Camille Huysmans, who sat in the Lower House for half a century by which time he was well over ninety years of age. And providing the nuns and the Protestants of East Flanders all keep voting liberal, he will probably achieve his goal. After all, he only has another 14 years to go!

But he, too, will have to start being more careful with horses. One Thursday evening I turned on the television to watch the news and saw De Croo sitting in the Speaker's Chair. I noticed that he was wearing a big collar around his neck and that he seemed to be in some pain. I knew at once what had happened: he had fallen off his horse!

The next day I sent him a note, in which I alluded to the dangers of riding. As an MP, De Croo always replied to letters and the answer which I received the following week confirmed that my suspicions had been correct.

He wrote:

As far as the collar is concerned, it is part of my battle against the big-headedness to which all politicians are sometimes susceptible. More prosaically, a case of horse whiplash is causing me considerable embarrassment. A nerve was trapped between two of my neck vertebrae and I had to be operated upon, otherwise there was a risk that I would lose the use of my right arm. It is the first time that anyone has got me to lie still for three hours in more than 45 years.

Instead of the three months that civil servants take after such an operation and instead of the three weeks that was recommended in my case, I resumed work after just three days. A little too soon perhaps? But let us look on the bright side: now that my neck has been strengthened with coral and titanium, I can afford to stick it out more often!

I look forward to seeing you soon.

With kind regards.

Herman De Croo
Minister of State

RECONCILIATION LUNCHES

Before my return to Belgium, I only knew of Guy Verhofstadt from the television. He cut an unusual figure for a politician, with a lock of hair falling constantly in front of his eyes and a set of teeth you could park a bike between. His conversation was always animated – passionate, even – and he was often regarded as being a little too excessive in a country where good-natured moderation is one of the key virtues. He clearly stood for an ideal, but it was less clear whether or not the Flemish people shared this ideal with him. In short, he was a visionary prophet in a land of village politicians.

My first face-to-face meeting with Verhofstadt went well – very well. Our paper used to interview him regularly and shortly after my arrival I was allowed to tag along to a planned meeting at his offices in the Melsenstraat, the headquarters of the VLD (the Flemish Liberal Democrats). I immediately found him to be open, friendly and likeable.

'Ah, you must be the new Dutchman I've heard so much about', he said. 'We'll do the interview and then we'll go and have a bite to eat. I know a good, little restaurant just around the corner.'

His boyish good-humour instantly set everyone at their ease, as he shook hands, clapped shoulders and flashed his famous toothy smile. His office was on the third floor, to which access was gained by a ramshackle old lift, which looked as if it had probably been installed before the turn of the century – the 19th century. 'The lift has already jammed a couple of times, but we should make it, with a bit of luck.' Ignoring the warning bell, which told us that the combined weight of three journalists and one party chairman was too much for our ancient elevator, he pressed the 'up' button. It would have been quicker and safer to walk, but after much creaking and groaning we arrived at our third-floor destination. His office was a shambles, with loose papers and open files strewn everywhere. 'Don't worry', he said cheerfully, as he followed my eyes. 'I know exactly where everything is.'

Verhofstadt and his Liberals had now been in opposition for more than 10 years and he knew that he had to make a breakthrough soon. At the beginning of the 1990's he had remodelled the old PVV and turned it into the progressive VLD, which he broadened to include defectors from several other parties. He was convinced that this radical new alternative would bring electoral success and would help him to smash the political mould, which had been dominated for the best part of a decade by a Christian-Democrat/socialist alliance. Unfortunately, the expected electoral triumph had so far failed to materialise and the party faithful were beginning to get restless. Alone with his ideals, Verhofstadt was starting to discover that the political top is a cold and lonely place, when things begin to go wrong.

When he started to talk about politics, he almost became a different person. He was like a great cycling champion, who moves up a gear when he gets into the difficult mountain sections of a race – the sections where the race is won and lost. You could see his mind working at a higher rate and his speech became quicker and more excitable. Waving his arms and thumping his desk, as if he was delivering an address to a VLD party conference, he gave an impassioned vision of a bright liberal future to our limited audience of three.

'Come on, lads! Can't you see? The existing administration is intellectually and politically bankrupt. The Dehaene-Tobback regime has got to go!' And if the voters decided otherwise, he would resign. 'If we do not break the existing majority with a significant VLD victory, then I will be forced to draw my own conclusions.' This time, it was all or nothing. Death or glory.

I noticed how often he referred to foreign politicians during our conversation, which gave the impression that he was both broad-minded and well-informed. 'I agree with Wim Kok, the leader of the PvdA in the Netherlands, and also with Tony Blair, leader of the Labour Party in Britain. But I do not agree with Louis Tobback and his SP.' This looking outwards was unusual for a Belgian politician, most of whom look no further than their own back yard. At the same time, this was also part of Verhofstadt's problem – because most Flemings also look no further than their own back yard. Verhofstadt was a reformer in a land where change is always viewed with suspicion. As a result, he often appeared to be out of step with his own people and his own electorate. He was aware of this himself and he frequently quoted Marcel van Dam, ex-Director-General of the Dutch VARA broadcasting company, who once said: 'People will always choose for the quiet familiarity of the status-quo in preference to the uncertainty of change.' But it didn't stop him trying to convince them to the contrary.

As I listened to his monologue, I began to think that Verhofstadt was talking a good deal of sense. His enthusiasm was infectious and much of what he said sounded right, but I had the impression that the voters probably wouldn't see it that way. I saw before me an ambitious – if slightly chaotic – man who wanted to do so much but who, I feared, might never get the chance. It was as if I had met a latter-day John the Baptist: 'a voice crying in the wilderness...'

After the interview he relaxed and was once again the jovial young man we had met an hour before.

'Now, what about something to eat?' he said to me, as though it was a brilliant idea that only he could have thought of. He had chosen an Italian restaurant and had reserved a table through his talkative Brussels-born spokesman, Guy Vanhengel. 30 minutes later, we were seated at a table with the 'Two Guys', as they were commonly known.

'I've been here a few times already and it's not bad. In particular, the wine is very good. I usually choose Tuscan wines', said Verhofstadt, with a faraway look in his eyes. Tuscany is almost like his second home and he soon began talking about his holiday villa.

'I go there as often as I can. It gives me the chance to catch up with my reading and to relax. It's the best place I know to totally unwind.' I thought that he seemed fairly relaxed here in Belgium, but before I could pursue this line of enquiry any further, he switched the conversation to my own job and my Dutch background.

'You've arrived at just the right time. You are going to see things in the Wetstraat that you would never have dreamed possible. And you're not the only one that's going to be surprised, believe me!' I found this encouraging, but noticed at the same time that he was talking to me as though I was a member of his staff. It was clear that he was expecting me to confirm the truth of what he had just said, so that he could be absolutely certain in his own mind that he was right.

The meal was long and extensive, and after the wine I began to feel sleepy. 'But we're not finished yet', said Verhofstadt in a cheerful voice. 'Don't tell me you're not going to drink a *pousse café*? After an Italian meal I usually drink an Amaro Averna. It's a herb drink. Why don't you try one? It's more a sort of medicine, really.' I drank the dark, bitter-sweet liquid and I had to confess that it tasted very good. However, at three o'clock in the afternoon, with half a bottle of wine already inside me and a full evening's work ahead of me back at the office, it was all a bit too much. I made my excuses and went off to sleep in the car. Yet my first impression of Verhofstadt – like those of many journalists – remained a positive one. I had the feeling that this really was a 'good Guy'.

Not every Belgian politician was so approachable. Jean-Luc Dehaene came across as being curt and short-tempered although later on I realised that this was just his manner and was not intended to offend. His speciality was practical common sense, limited ideals and shrewd political management. This enabled him to build a broad political network, which led to stable coalitions, with practical policies and tangible results. In short, Dehaene was a doer.

In contrast to Dehaene, Louis Tobback was a verbal waterfall. He had a reputation within the Socialist Party of being dictatorial, but this was little more than a caricature which he himself had created and which he sometimes liked to play. He was an eloquent but sometimes brutal speaker, a power politician of the old school, who mellowed towards the end of his career and who finally found his ultimate political calling as burgomaster of his home city, Leuven.

In comparison, Verhofstadt was more open and therefore more vulnerable. He lacked the skill of Dehaene and the hardness of Tobback. He reminded me of Karel Appel, the abstract painter. Appel's technique involved throwing layer after layer of paint onto the canvas, which he then reworked with broad, sweeping strokes, to create something that he – and many others – thought was beautiful. Verhofstadt did much the same thing with political ideas, although whether or not the voters thought that the result was 'beautiful' is an open question. His language was full of '-isms'. He was driven by 'voluntarism', the strong desire to do something, and by 'verbalism', a form of rhetoric in which words sometimes seemed more important than deeds. The result of this pseudo-intellectual approach was political improvisation some would say 'chaos', disguised by a clever combination of deceit and bluff. If Dehaene was a doer, then Verhofstadt was a talker.

Not everyone was fooled and in particular many of his fellow politicians developed a strong dislike for Verhofstadt. Chief amongst these was the former Chairman of the Christian-Democrat Party, Johan Van Hecke. In 1993 he said: 'The so-called reform of the VLD is the result of the personal frustrations and, above all, the personal ambition of just one man. This man is a fervent exponent of liberalism in its most extreme form and his main concern is for the rights of one man: in other words, himself.' Van Hecke did not fail to join the VLD, once it came in power. In fact Verhofstadt convinced him to cross the floor and assured his former opponent a parliamentary seat in return. In Belgian politics controversies never last for long.

During the 1995 elections Verhofstadt failed to make the political breakthrough he had been hoping for and the press reacted critically. Strongest of all in its condemnation was *Het Laatste Nieuws*, which at that time still had close ties with the Flemish Liberals. Most of the other papers had long since broken their political affiliations. *De Standaard* – with its AVV/VVK logo – had once been the mouthpiece of the Christian-Democrats, whilst *De Morgen* was firmly tied to the socialists. However, both newspapers were now independent, leaving *Het Laatste Nieuws* as the only 'political' daily, with its foot firmly in the blue, liberal camp. Even so, Luc Van der Kelen, political commentator for *Het Laatste Nieuws*, was harsh in his criticism: 'Someone should tell Guy Verhofstadt that politics is more than setting agendas, making proposals and attacking your opponents. Politics is practised by people and people have their sensitivities. Whoever fails to take account of this fact is destined to remain in the political desert.'

This was not the first time that Van der Kelen had crossed swords with Verhofstadt. A year earlier, he had written a piece in *De Morgen* (of all papers!) entitled 'An Open Letter to the Liberals'. According to Van der Kelen: 'Verhofstadt wants to declare war on the entire social fabric of Flanders and seeks to replace this fabric with independent-minded citizens, who will decide everything for themselves, free from all outside interference. He should realise, however, that a war against the social fabric of Flanders is a war he can never win.'

Verhofstadt was furious at this attack and retaliated with a Citizen's Manifesto. 'The reaction of the editor (Van der Kelen) – the editor of a paper which still claims to be liberal – is unacceptable. He is a typical example of someone who calls himself a liberal but who is, in fact, nothing more than a reactionary.' This was internecine strife at its worst – blue fighting blue. It did the VLD no good at all.

After the election defeat, Verhofstadt kept his word and resigned from his position as VLD chairman. He gave a farewell interview to *De Standaard* and left by plane for Tuscany the morning it was published. The policeman at customs control in Zaventem was reading a copy as he passed through and wished him 'good luck'. Surprised passengers in the aircraft also offered him their condolences.

Nobody was more surprised than the editors of *Het Laatste Nieuws*. They had been tipped off that Verhofstadt would stay and had announced this in their paper. In the meantime, the bird had flown – to Tuscany. The staff at *Het Laatste Nieuws* were fuming and felt – not without cause – that they had been deceived. They instantly got on the phone to VLD headquarters, but all they got was Guy Vanhengel's answering machine. They vented their frustration by leaving a series of angry messages, in which the words 'lying' and 'bastard' were frequently used and the least insulting.

Van der Kelen was savage in his criticism: 'Guy Verhofstadt is the kind of man who kicks at half-open doors, with a juvenile bravado that you would scarcely expect from a grown man. In reality, the ex-VLD chairman was born ten years too late. His mentality is more suited to the year 1968, when a bunch of young hooligans lashed out wildly at the established order. This is precisely the problem of the late – and not so lamented – Liberal leader.'

I was only able to follow these goings-on at a distance: the angry comments, the slammed doors, the theatrical performances – the Wetstraat at play. At that time, I was more involved with the trials and tribulations of the socialists, who had become enmeshed in the so-called Agusta Affair. This scandal had a devastating effect on the whole party. Top figures such as Minister of Foreign Affairs Frank Vandenbroucke and NATO Secretary-General Willy Claes were forced to resign. Louis

Tobback reacted in characteristic fashion: 'Any journalist that follows me around is going to get his head beaten in.'

If anything, the mood of the French-speaking socialists was even worse. Half of the party executive was being held in Lantin Prison in Liège, while the remaining non-arrested members held crisis meetings in the party offices in the Keizerslaan. Party Chairman Philippe Busquin gave regular press conferences in the nearby Red House, where the foundations of Belgian socialism had once been laid. I went along every Monday morning to hear what he had to say.

Busquin was a reasonable man, whose French I sometimes found difficult to follow. After most of my interviews with him I had to more or less guess what he had actually said. With a little creativity and a lot of good luck I usually managed to get it more or less right. Busquin was also friendly and likeable, which is not something you could always say of his predecessors. Guy Spitaels was an almost unapproachable figure, who modelled himself on the French president, François Mitterrand – an 'imperial' socialist, if ever there was one. Spitaels was destined to be yet another victim of the Agusta Affair – he was convicted of bribery and, as a consequence, lost a number of his civil rights. Procurator-General Eliane Liekendael described him as 'a mean, despicable, power-crazed, Machiavellian devil.' It was the first time that a Minister of State had ever been treated in this way.

Before Spitaels, the party had been run by André Cools. Cools was an out and out bully, who made enemies wherever he went. Few people were surprised when he was gunned down in front of his mistress's flat in July 1991. The Tunisian hitmen were arrested several years later, but it was not until 2004 that the men behind the killing – a number of Belgian-Sicilian officials working in the cabinet of ex-Minister Alain Van der Biest – were finally given long prison sentences. In comparison with these men, Philippe Busquin was a sweetie.

But writing about the SP and the PS was not a lot of fun: both parties were in mourning and there wasn't a laugh or a free meal to be had anywhere. Champagne socialism was very clearly a thing of the past. I found it all a bit depressing and made my feelings known during our weekly editorial meeting.

'The socialists are such a miserable bunch', I said. 'They're angry, they don't say anything, they don't do anything. It's all so boring.'

My colleagues nodded in sympathy, but nobody seemed keen to take over the socialists. They were even less keen to take over the rightist Vlaams Blok. The last journalist to be allocated the Flemish Block had resigned and moved to the Netherlands. The senior editor was still looking for a suitable victim to replace him. He looked at me:

'You're a white, heterosexual foreigner. Why don't you do the Flemish Block if you're so fed up with the socialists?'

My colleagues all turned in my direction and I could see that they were all praying that I would say 'yes', so that the threat of them being given the Flemisch Block would be temporarily removed. The Nationalist Party was a difficult and politically dangerous assignment. Difficult, because the party congresses were little more than mass rallies, where Filip De Winter worked the party faithful into a frenzy. Difficult also because the Block closed ranks quicker than a crack Roman legion whenever a journalist started to ask probing questions about some of their more contradictory and divisive policies. This was one of the inevitable effects of the so-called *cordon sanitaire*, by which the more traditional parties hoped to isolate the Block from the political mainstream. Quite dangerous, because this party aroused such fierce emotions on all sides. Whatever I wrote, it was certain to provoke a strong reaction, and the risk was that this reaction would be directed against me personally. As for the culinary aspects, the Block was the worst party of the lot: it remained confined to the beer tap. No champagne around! Let alone caviar.

Even so, I didn't really see how I could turn down the editor's proposal and so I tried to make the best of it by putting forward a counterproposal of my own.

'O.K.', I said. 'I'll do the Flemish Nationalists and I'll even keep the socialists – but only if I get the VLD as well. That way at least I can have a bit of fun.'

It was an offer he couldn't refuse. He nodded his agreement and everyone in the office breathed a sigh of relief.

At that time, the VLD was in total chaos. Herman De Croo now stood at the head of the party, while Verhofstadt enjoyed a sunny semi-retirement in Tuscany. Even so, as vice-chairman of the Liberal group in the Senate he was still regularly to be found in the Wetstraat, holding court in his elegant red-carpeted office, decorated with historic statues and medieval tapestries. A mere shadow of his former self, he moved silently and unheard through the corridors of power. However, I always had the feeling that he was planning a comeback. He may have lost a battle, but, self-confident as he was, he didn't think that he had lost the war. Like a latter-day Moses, he still believed in his destiny to lead his people out of the desert and into the promised land.

As part of my new assignment, I began to look more closely at Verhofstadt and his background. He first came to prominence during the PVV ideological conference in Kortrijk at the end of 1979, when he put himself forward as the new leader of the Young Liberals. He was a strange mixture of political maturity and impatience. With his Radical Manifesto he wanted to drag

Flemish liberalism into the 21st century, by forcing it to declare war on what he called the 'techno-bureaucratic society'. He was an almost totally new phenomenon on the usually placid Belgian political scene and tore through the political landscape like some kind of youthful whirlwind. He quickly gathered a group of like-minded young liberals around him, of whom Patrick Dewael would become his most constant supporter and ally. His brother Dirk also played an important if somewhat shadowy role, particularly in terms of policy development. Several others came and went, eagerly accepted if they could contribute something to the Verhofstadt cause, quickly dumped if they could not.

His future political mentor, Frans Verleyen – editor-in-chief of the weekly magazine *Knack* and the intellectual father of Verhofstadt's Citizen's Manifestos – said of him in 1993: 'After the Kortrijk Conference, he barraged journalists with all kinds of self-written texts. He would drive around Flanders in the middle of the night, dropping them into people's letterboxes. I didn't even bother looking at them, until after the fifth or sixth time he telephoned me. When I did eventually read them, I was pleasantly surprised to find them well-written, well-structured and closely argued.' It was the start of a long collaboration between the two men. Verleyen became a political guru, with Verhofstadt as his pupil whose meteoric rise he later described in his book 'The Verhofstadt Factor'.

In 1982 Verhofstadt was elected chairman of the PVV in the Magdalena Hall in Brussels. He comfortably defeated the only other rival candidate – the ageing Brabant politician, Gust De Winter – and in typical fashion began bombarding newspapers with a whole series of articles, in which he announced the dawn of a new 'liberal arrogance'. At 28 years of age, he was in stark contrast to Belgium's other party chairmen, most of whom conducted their business in smoke-filled back rooms over a good cigar and a glass of whisky. By comparison, Verhofstadt was more open and more ambitious: he wanted nothing less than to change the world. Rather uncommon for a Belgian politician.

Preaching a new and aggressive type of liberalism, he promised his supporters 'a long march to victory', which would ultimately see the PVV as the strongest political party in the land. His confidence was almost unlimited. In the French-speaking newspaper *Le Soir* he wrote pieces with titles such as 'The Future is Ours'. He seemed to be in permanent revolt, as though institutionalised rebellion was his main aim.

As the leading figure in the PVV, in 1985 he was given the post of Budget Minister in Wilfred Martens' administration. CVP politicians still look back in horror to this time, when their young liberal 'partner' terrorised ministerial meetings, talking for as long as was necessary to get his own way. On occasions his manner was hostile, even offensive. Largely as a result of his influence, politics became more combative, with Verhofstadt always ready to fight in the front line. In budgetary terms, his arguments were generally sound, but his style of presentation made him several political enemies for life. Leading Christian-Democrats, Martens included, were determined to be rid of him: the 'boy' was too brutal, too demanding and too asocial. This was a reputation which would follow him for many years and his opponents made good use of it, first to isolate and then to marginalise the man they now saw as public enemy No.1. Before too long, he was known universally as 'Verafstoot' – a play on his name, which in Dutch means 'repulsive'.

In 1988 the Christian-Democrats ditched the liberals and entered into a new alliance with the socialists. Verhofstadt felt betrayed and demanded the resignation of the government, however to no avail. It seemed that the 'long march to victory' was going to take slightly longer than he had planned and certainly longer than Chairman Mao's original 'long march' to Peking in the 1930's. In fact, the liberals were destined to remain a full 12 years in the political wilderness. 12 years in which Verhofstadt was tantalisingly in sight of the oasis of power, only to discover that it was just another fata morgana. 12 years in which the liberals argued and bickered amongst themselves, deprived of the one thing they wanted most: the chance to rule.

In 1989 Verhofstadt was elected to the position of party chairman for a second time, with a resounding 85% of the votes. Typically, he moved immediately onto the offensive. 'Martens has got to go and the liberals have got to resume their rightful place in the administration', he roared to the PVV conference. His new catch phrase was 'Don't wait – smash Martens Eight,' a reference to the fact that Martens was already busy with his eighth administration. Sometimes these aggressive methods were also applied to his own side. Particularly harsh was the manner in which he pushed aside the previous party chairman, Annemie Neyts. There is a famous photograph of the two of them after the leadership election, Neyts with tears in her eyes and Verhofstadt with a broad grin. His body language spoke volumes and showed a darker side to the man's character. Here was naked ambition, pure and simple. Only one thing counted: to become prime minister.

He thought his chance had come after the elections on 24 November 1991, which became known as Black Sunday. The CVP lost heavily and Wilfried Martens effectively disappeared from the political scene. The King appointed Melchior Wathelet to assess which party might best be able to form the next administration and after exhaustive investigations – he even consulted the Mufti, an Islamic religious leader – he finally recommended Verhofstadt. Verhofstadt immediately began negotiations with the socialists for a 'purple' coalition, so named from the merging of the respective party colours of blue and red. He was prepared to make a number of major concessions but there remained one important problem to be solved: who would be prime minister? The socialists put forward Willy Claes, but Verhofstadt wanted the job for himself. Neither side was prepared to budge and the coalition talks broke down. This opened the door for the CVP and at the beginning of 1992 Jean-Luc Dehaene took office at the head of a new 'Rome-Red' (Christian-Democrat/socialist) administration.

Disappointed but undaunted, Verhofstadt continued his one-man quest for power by other means. He issued his series of Citizen's Manifestos – actually written by guru Verleyen – in which he attacked the 'kleptocracy' of pressure groups, such as unions and medical insurance funds, which in his opinion 'lived off the state'. He also tried to add an international dimension to his image. Flanders was too parochial and Belgium too small. Unlike Herman De Croo he was not content to be 'king in his own back yard'. Instead he enlisted the support of men such as Karl Popper, Friedrich Von Hayek and Mario Vargas Llosa in his campaign to 'give the state back to the people'.

To achieve this goal, Verhofstadt felt that he needed a new social and political movement. As a result, in 1992 at the Sofitel Hotel in Antwerp the old PVV party was laid to rest and the new VLD was born, christened by some cynics as Verhofstadt's Last Dance. This was the party which would force the breakthrough, the party which would finally carry the liberals into power soon. Sadly, it was not to be. The first real test came with the European elections of 1994. The opinion polls had been favourable, but the results were disastrous. Flanders was still not ready for revolution and Verhofstadt and a tearful Dewael were left to drown their sorrows with the champagne that had been prematurely ordered for the victory celebrations. The party did better in the general election of 21 May 1995, but the 'Rome-Red' coalition just managed to hold onto power. Once again Verhofstadt flew off to Tuscany to read his books and to ponder his future. But everyone knew that sooner or later he would be back. At just 45 years of age, he was not yet ready to begin a new career as an Italian winegrower. His will to power was just too strong. The Wetstraat had not yet seen the last of him.

One day I bumped into him in the long corridor between the Lower House and the Senate, surrounded by statues of the Provisional Government of 1830 and other famous figures from Belgium's parliamentary past. We went to his office, a small but elegant affair. The Louis XIV writing table was covered with books on political theory, literature and poetry. Even so, I was surprised when he began to talk about philosophy instead of politics.

I soon began to realise that he had undergone a complete change of style, not only in his clothes but also in his general appearance. The expensive collar and tie which he used to wear had now been replaced by a trendy polo sweater and casual trousers. He seemed more relaxed, as if he had made a conscious decision to break with the aggressive image which had kept him in opposition all those years. He was equally keen to lose his reputation as a baby Thatcher, which had seen him move too far to the political right and had made him a hostile figure for the socialist movement. Suddenly, he was to be found at overtly 'leftist' events, such as anti-nuclear demonstrations, rubbing shoulders with the workers and the activists while carrying his son Louis on his shoulders. Verhofstadt the political prophet of doom had been transformed into Verhofstadt the family man. He had reinvented himself – again.

As my paper's 'VLD expert', I was required to watch all these developments closely. As a result, I saw quite a lot of him and occasionally called in at his office. His desk was invariably covered with files and papers, but he laughed off the heavy workload. 'It will pass', was all he said. This, too, was part of the new image. 'You shouldn't take it all too seriously. Tomorrow is another day. Recently I have become fascinated by literature. I think that I learn more out of a good novel than out of half a dozen non-fiction books. I try to read at least one book a week.'

This was the new Verhofstadt; a Verhofstadt of broader horizons and more balanced views. But I still wasn't sure whether this change of heart was genuine or just a facade. Had he truly seen the light? Or did he just want a new image for a new political start? He certainly seemed more relaxed in the public spotlight, but was he planning a new coup d'état behind the scenes? Perhaps the works of Francis Fukuyama and Jean-Marie Guéhenno, in which he now took such an interest, were merely used to cover up his real ambitions.

Gradually, he began to re-enter the political arena. One of his key speeches was entitled 'The Leap into the 21st Century', in which he exposed what he called 'the Belgian sickness'. As the new Verhofstadt began to take shape, so things became more and more difficult for party chairman Herman De Croo. It was clear that Verhofstadt was ready for yet another comeback and I felt that it was time for another in-depth interview.

In spite of his recent transformation, he had not lost his preference for Italian food. Not far from the Wetstraat, he had discovered Il Perugino, a stylish Italian restaurant run with an iron hand by 'the lady of the house'. While the liberal leader tucked in to his fresh pasta, grilled fish and Tuscan wine, I decided to try and see whether or not the new Verhofstadt packaging also held new contents. 'Have you really changed?' I asked him bluntly. It went quiet in the restaurant, as the other diners – many of them politicians – tried to overhear his reply. 'My commitment and my beliefs have not changed, but I now realise that you can't beat the world all by yourself.' This was quite a confession, coming from a politician who had been convinced for years that he was right and who, as a result, had never listened to others. 'Does this mean that the new Verhofstadt can accept criticism?' I pressed. He replied with a laugh. 'I wasn't always aware of just how self-righteous I was. We were sitting on a cloud, totally convinced of the justice of our cause. There was too little modesty, too little self-criticism. The past few years have finally shown me that the ultimate truth does not exist, is not the property of any one man.' It seemed to me as if he believed what he was saying. Certainly he was less inclined to preach than in the past and I found myself enjoying our talk. I also enjoyed the Amaro Averna – another habit he had not lost.

A few weeks later he was re-elected chairman of the party, but with just 52% of the votes. By the narrowest of margins, the VLD were prepared to give the new Verhofstadt another chance.

Little by little, I began to realise that the new Verhofstadt was not so 'new' after all. Just like the old Verhofstadt, he began to make all kinds of radical plans for the social, economic, fiscal and communal reform of Belgium – plans which were enshrined in the Declaration of Kortrijk, a kind of VLD version of the Ten Commandments. Moreover, the prophetic tone also began to creep back into his speeches. Perhaps this was not surprising. He was under great pressure from the liberal supporters to finally get the party into power, and so he had to come up with something new. At the same time, he was still keen to maintain his 'cool' image. This led to tensions, which sometimes erupted into old-style Verhofstadt outbursts.

On the day of the liberal's annual New Year reception, I wrote an article entitled 'Verhofstadt's Last Chance'. I argued that time was running out for the VLD's blue-eyed boy and wondered how long he could keep pulling political rabbits out of the hat. The 'new' Verhofstadt hardly batted an eyelid and gave his speech to the liberal faithful as planned. Inside, however, he was furious. 'If I ever get my hands on that bastard from *De Standaard*', he told journalists in private, 'I'll break his bloody neck.' However, when I bumped into him fifteen minutes later – closely shadowed by film teams from the main Belgian television stations – he simply put out his hand and shook mine. 'Thank you for the article', he said. 'It is a major contribution to the debate.' I was unsure how to react. Was this the new Verhofstadt or the old one? The genuine leader or just a cheap imitation?

If Verhofstadt was angry with an article, in the old days he used to ring up the editor-in-chief to complain. If he was really angry, he would insist that the offending journalist should be given the sack. I half-expected that he would break this habit, since it was hardly in keeping with his new image. I was wrong. The next morning my boss called me into his office.

'Guy phoned and he's not very happy. Go and have dinner with him. Get it sorted out.'

A little later Bart Somers, Verhofstadt's personal spokesman, called. He was a smart young man, full of talent and ambition, and he instantly tried to limit the damage. 'I'm sure it's all a misunderstanding. Guy would be pleased if you could come to lunch. Perhaps with some other members of our party. Then we can explain things better.' The first reconcilian lunch was bound to take place!

I was invited to Restaurant De Arenberg, a well-known eating house in Brussels and a favourite of Verhofstadt's political soul mate, Patrick Dewael who was then leader of the liberal group in the Lower House. When I arrived, I was shown to a set of private rooms upstairs. Here I was surprised to find almost the entire VLD leadership waiting to greet me: Verhofstadt, Somers, Dewael, party treasurer Jaak Gabriels and Geert Versnick, Verhofstadt's personal Mr.Fix-it. This was what my colleague Van der Kelen of *Het Laatste Nieuws* had once described to me as 'the blue blood cabinet'. Clearly, Verhofstadt had called out all his big guns to try and knock me into line. I was almost flattered.

'I hope you're not going to be difficult', he said in a cheerful voice. 'Besides, we've got you outnumbered!' This was undoubtedly the Verhofstadt of old: friendly and good-humoured. 'Let's have something to eat and then we can explain our plans to you in more detail. After that, I'm sure that everything will be fine.' I nodded in agreement. We ate, drank and were merry, rather too merry, if I recall, and we parted in mid-afternoon as the best of friends. By the time I got back to the office, Verhofstadt had already telephoned to my editor, suggesting a more formal interview later the same week, so that he could put his side of the story. The interview duly took place and my critical article was never mentioned again. As he had predicted, everything was 'fine'.

After that, our paths regularly crossed in the parliament building. He was usually in a good mood and it was clear that he bore me no hard feelings. He was one of those people who could shout and scream when he got angry but who didn't bear a grudge, once the anger had passed. This made him popular with many journalists, myself included, and I found that I had to make a conscious effort not to be overcome by his charm. However, this period of calm did not last long. Political crisis was just around the corner and, when it came, Verhofstadt quickly returned to his bad old habits.

It all began on a Thursday afternoon in April 1998. Everything seemed normal. Question time in the Lower House started promptly at two o'clock. The chamber was almost empty and ministers chatted with journalists in the corridors outside. Yet two hours later this same chamber was in uproar and it looked as though the end of the Dehaene government was in sight. What had happened to bring about such a change? Foreign invasion? An outbreak of the plague? Even worse – Marc Dutroux, Belgium's very own *state enemy nr.1*, had escaped from prison.

In all my time in politics, I had never seen a crisis blow up so quickly. I was sitting in the press box, following the usual ritual of question time. Prime Minister Dehaene was slumped on the government bench, with a bored expression on his face. Rik Daems of the VLD asked him a question about Belgium's poor showing in a recent international study. Dehaene quickly put him in his place. 'The study has nothing to do with the real facts and has been negatively influenced by false rumours and the Dutroux case.' As always, Dehaene was at his laconic best during question time. On one occasion, an MP had taken a full five minutes to ask the Premier a question. When he had eventually finished, Dehaene got to his feet, walked to the speaker's tribune, replied 'the answer is "no"' and then sat down again. After Dehaene, it was the turn of the Minister of Home Affairs, Johan Vande Lanotte, to answer a question on the legal regulation of prostitution. He was followed by Minister of Justice, Stefaan De

Clerck, who dealt with a query from Geert Bourgeois about the 'de-federalisation of justice'.

It was all very routine and, as question time moved towards its conclusion, the atmosphere in the chamber was relaxed. Outside the sun was shining and everyone expected that the sitting would be a short one. Some MP's were even phoning their wives to tell them that they would be home early. And then the bomb burst.

A colleague rushed up to me. 'There are some very nervous French-speaking journalists from RTL over there. They are saying that Dutroux has escaped.' He looked at me inquisitively but I didn't believe him. 'It must be a joke. Dutroux escaped? Impossible!' I tried to work further on my report about the 'de-federalisation of justice', but doubts began to creep into my mind. Dutroux escaped? It sounded fantastic – but in Belgian politics, you never know. I went out into the corridor to see if I could find out any more news. The RTL camera team were still there and rushed over towards Minister De Clerck as he left the chamber.

'Has Dutroux escaped?' they asked.

To my amazement, De Clerck refused to answer and simply pushed his way past them. He met Dehaene in the Lower House Reading Room and together they went into the Green Room, a small antechamber behind the Senate. When they emerged, the look on their faces spoke of disaster. 'There are problems with Dutroux', whispered De Clerck in my ear, but before he could say any more he had rushed off with Minister Vande Lanotte to a crisis meeting in Dehaene's official residence at Wetstraat 16. What had started as an ordinary day, was ending with a savage political sting in its tail.

The rumour spread like wildfire throughout the parliament building, but the MP's in the main chamber of the Lower House still knew nothing. They were talking, laughing and voting, as if everything was normal. A few of them began to receive calls on the telephones which stood in front of them. They couldn't believe what they were hearing. Dutroux escaped! Like me, they thought it was a joke. 'A bad Belgian joke', someone called out. They looked up to the press gallery for confirmation, but when they saw the serious faces of the journalists, they knew the worst had happened. The leaders of the opposition parties immediately demanded the floor and insisted that the sitting should be suspended. The House could not meet properly while 'public enemy No.1 was on the loose'.

The majority of MP's looked dazed, as they left the chamber. 'The bird has flown', commented Marc Eyskens in typical fashion. Others were more serious. 'What kind of a country are we living in?' asked one CVP member. 'It's a revolution', said VU Senator Bert Anciaux, his lip trembling.

Outside in the streets, the sirens of dozens of police cars could be heard. The whole police force had been mobilised but nobody knew what the coming hours would bring. Most MP's stayed in the parliament building and those who had left early rushed back. They were followed by hordes of pressmen, gathering like vultures for the kill. The government looked likely to fall and they didn't want to miss it.

Rumour followed rumour. 'He's been caught', somebody shouted. 'It's not been confirmed', said someone else. Dutroux had the entire country under his spell.

In the meantime, Guy Verhofstadt had gathered together the entire opposition and had marched to the entrance of the Lower House. Flanked by all the VLD's leading figures, he demanded the resignation of the government, which was still meeting in crisis session at Dehaene's residence. 'The two ministers responsible have got to go and the members of the government must ask themselves whether they are not collectively responsible.' The chaos was complete. Not only was the country on a semi-war footing, but the opposition was now attacking the government in the middle of the worst crisis in Belgian politics for almost fifty years!

Four hours after Dutroux's escape Dehaene called the party leaders together. 'We've got him', he told them. The country breathed a sigh of relief, since Dutroux's adventures threatened to tear apart the whole fabric of Belgian society. Ministers De Clerck and Vande Lanotte were sacrificed to public outrage, but Dehaene was able to hold on to office and called back his old political ally, the socialist Louis Tobback, as Minister of Home Affairs. The opposition had cried victory too soon.

This was a great blow to Verhofstadt. He had genuinely believed that the government would fall and that he would be the next prime minister. Instead, Dehaene had survived and now began to implement much needed measures for the reform of the police and justice systems. To make matters worse, the French-speaking liberals were prepared to support the Dehaene government in these measures, which in turn forced Verhofstadt and his Flemish liberals to do likewise. I wrote an article on these political manoeuvrings entitled 'Verhofstadt Changes Course' and once again I struck a painful nerve.

When I next saw him at a VLD congress in Ghent, he almost bit my head off. 'It's all lies. We're not changing course. How dare you write such a thing?'

The congress itself was very long and very boring. It covered almost every aspect of Belgian society that you could think of –

and a few that you probably couldn't. The VLD made more plans than East European bureaucrats at their Stalinist worst. The Liberal Party faithful wilted under this barrage of largely useless information. They left the conference hall in large numbers and there were soon more people in the bar than in the hall. Verhofstadt was not pleased and ordered that the bar should be closed. The delegates were furious. The VLD had already had five study days and five regional meetings that year, and now they had to sit through a three-day conference with no booze! This was too much for the rank-and-file. 'We come to a congress to meet each other', said one senator. 'Not to scrutinize dots and commas in dozens of different policy documents.' One of the liberal MP's put it differently: 'A congress is like foreplay – it shouldn't last too long.'

I knew how they felt. By the end of the congress, I too was tired and irritable. As a result, my report of the proceedings was perhaps a little more peppery than usual: 'Verhofstadt, the spiritual father of the citizen's democracy, subjected his loyal troops to a level of zeal that would frighten even a Jehovah's Witness.'

Early next morning, the phone rang in my editor's office. One of my colleagues heard that it was Verhofstadt. 'Guy is on the line and he wants you to be given the push.' Not for the first time in my career, my fellow reporters turned to look at me with sympathy, expecting that news of my dismissal would follow within minutes. I decided not to wait. I walked into my boss's office and asked him bluntly: 'Did Verhofstadt call?' 'You know he bloody well did. And guess what? He's not very happy. He thinks that your article is far too "personal" and he didn't like that Jehovah's Witness comment one little bit.' I agreed that the reference to the Jehovahs was probably a bit over the top, but pointed out in my defence that it was made in a moment of weakness after three days of mind-numbing boredom. My editor gave me the by now familiar advice. 'Ring him up, go and have a meal with him and get it sorted out!'

Twenty minutes later I was on the line to his spokesman. 'Yes, Guy is very upset. But if you have lunch with him at an Italian restaurant, I'm sure it will all be fine.' By now he had discovered yet another 'favourite' restaurant and this time we met at a nice establishment on the Louisalaan in Brussels. 'Let's see what pastas and wines they've got', said Verhofstadt, apparently more concerned about culinary problems than political ones. We talked about politics, Belgium, Europe, the world – just about everything other than the offending article which had brought us together in the first place. It was clear that his anger had subsided and by the end of the meal we were once again the best of friends. Afterwards, his chauffeur drove us back to the Wetstraat. As I stepped out of the car, he turned to me and said: 'You see? I knew it would be fine.'

For several months thereafter, things remained calm on the political front. I did a number of interviews and articles and Verhofstadt went off to Tuscany to put some of his latest thoughts down on paper. When he returned, he was keen to share these thoughts with the press. I wandered along to VLD headquarters and found him sitting behind the chairman's desk in his office. It was our most painful interview ever – at least for Verhofstadt. 'I was working in the olive grove and fell off my tractor', he told me with a wince. I later discovered that he had four badly bruised ribs but he insisted that we should carry on with our conversation – it was that important to him to get his new holiday ideas into the newspapers.

The period of calm soon came to an end and the new source of discord was Marc Verwilghen.

Verwilghen was chairman of the parliamentary committee charged with investigating the Dutroux Affair. He was a rising star in the political firmament and he was as popular as Verhofstadt – perhaps even more popular. The two of them were boyhood friends but rivalry had grown between them. Verhofstadt wanted Verwilghen to stand as a candidate on the VLD list in Antwerp or Brussels during the forthcoming elections. Verwilghen – who lived in Dendermonde – refused. Verhofstadt decided to try and hide the tension between the two of them by suggesting a double interview in *De Standaard*. He had already tried something similar a few months before, when journalist Hugo Camps had been called in to write a 'reconciliation book' with the two liberal top men. Unfortunately, they were unable to agree on a final text. Verhofstadt wanted to make the book ideological, while Verwilghen wanted it to be more biographical. A disappointed Camps – who had spent two days in Tuscany and two days in Dendermonde – withdrew from the project. He was later to write: 'The root of the problem is that Verwilghen wants to present himself as a man of conscience, who stands up for the rights of victims, while Verhofstadt is more a man of power, who wants to run the country.'

The double interview took place in Verhofstadt's work room. The atmosphere was good-natured but the comments were predictable and pre-rehearsed. Verhofstadt had wanted to paper over the cracks between them, but he wasn't sure that his plan had worked. Before I left, he asked me: 'Could I read the text before it is published?' I was surprised, as this is most unusual in Belgium, but in a moment of uncharacteristic flexibility I said 'yes'. I sent him a draft version of the article, but when I got it back it was almost unrecognisable. Entire sentences had been re-written by Verhofstadt, whilst others had been deleted altogether. As a result, the whole tone of the piece was altered.

I immediately phoned spokesman Bart Somers. 'This is unacceptable', I told him. 'He's turned the interview into a personal pamphlet!' Somers hardly knew what to say. 'Yes, I know. It's very delicate, but Guy is very insistent.' We went through the article line by line, using the tape recording I had made during the interview. I agreed to accept some of the changes, but only if the deleted questions and answers were re-instated. Somers still wasn't very happy. 'Talk to Guy about it', he suggested. 'Why not take him for a meal?'

I did and we managed to reach a compromise but it was getting more and more difficult to interview Verhofstadt. The 1999 elections were approaching and election fever was growing fast. As I expected, the VLD tried to increase its pressure on the press corps and media adviser Noël Slangen watched over his leader's public image like a hawk. Slangen was a spin doctor and he played much the same kind of role as Verleyen had played in the past: that of guru. At bottom, Verhofstadt is an uncertain and insecure man, the kind of person who has constant need of a guru figure, someone who can act as a mental anchor and a psychological crutch in difficult moments. Verleyen was the guru for Verhofstadt's political message. Slangen was the guru for Verhofstadt's political marketing.

In the months leading up to the elections, I had no fewer than six 'reconciliation' lunches with Verhofstadt, each of them in an Italian restaurant; my personal favourite was the Crèche des Artistes. Whilst these were generally pleasant occasions, their frequency was becoming something of an embarrassment. 'Off for another reconciliation with the chairman?' my colleagues would ask me sarcastically, as I left the office at lunchtime. It was the same story in the parliamentary press box. 'A good meal with Guy, was it?' I tried to reply with as much dignity as I could: 'A politician, like a soldier, marches on his stomach…'

The touchiness of Verhofstadt was in marked contrast to the studied indifference of Jean-Luc Dehaene. Dehaene had the skin of an elephant and seemed impervious to media criticism. Unlike so many of his other Wetstraat colleagues he never phoned the press, never complained about them, never even seemed to notice that they were there. I once did an interview with the liberal politician, Jaak Gabriels. We were sitting in a fish restaurant on the Fish Market, where else?, just a stone's throw from the VLD Central Office. I got on well with Jaak and had visited him several times in Bree, where he was Burgomaster. As we were sipping our champagne this was a VLD lunch, remember, he suddenly said: 'Dehaene is just like Benito Mussolini!' I suggested that this might be a slight exaggeration, but he continued to insist in an ever-louder voice which enabled all guests to hear his view on the Belgian parliament. 'I'm telling you! Just like Mussolini. Put it in your paper!' This was hot stuff and I did indeed work it into my next day's article. However, I felt honour bound to give Gabriels one last chance to retract. I called him on the phone: 'Look, Jaak. Are you really sure about this Mussolini comment?' I had assumed that once the effects of our lunchtime alcohol had worn off, reason – or at least political common sense – might prevail. Not a bit of it. 'I stick by every word. You just print it.' So I did.

All the next morning I waited for an angry reaction from Dehaene, or at least from his charming but not always communicative spokeswoman, Monique Delvou. Thinking of my run-ins with Verhofstadt, I began to select possible venues for my 'reconciliation' lunch with the Premier. My colleagues assured me that I was wasting my time. 'That's not his style. Besides, he eats so fast that you'd be back outside in half an hour.' Even so, I continued to wait into the afternoon for a call from the Wetstraat 16, but it never came. I was at a loss to understand what was going on. If a Dutch journalist compared the Dutch prime minister to Mussolini, there would have been a veritable storm of protest. 'Maybe Dehaene doesn't read the papers', I said to myself.

Later the same afternoon, I bumped into Herman De Croo in the corridors of the parliament building. 'My dear friend, I have just had the Premier on the phone complaining about Jaak. Did he really say that about Mussolini?' I assured him that he did. De Croo could scarcely hide his distaste. Gabriels had crossed over to the VLD from another party some years before and had never really been fully accepted. 'I have often said to Guy that these turncoats are travellers without luggage.' Even so, the comment did Jaak Gabriels little political harm. He became a minister in the 1999 federal government and in 2004 was appointed Minister of State by King Albert.

Even though I had been denied my 'reconciliation' lunch with Dehaene, the stomach continued to play an increasingly important part in Belgian politics as a whole. The 1999 dioxin crisis meant that for weeks on end it was impossible to eat chicken in Belgium. This was too much for the Flemish voters. They are flexible in most things, but not when it comes to food and eating. The Sunday chicken – fresh from the market and covered in fatty sauce – is almost like a religious ritual in Flanders, a centuries old social and cultural tradition, in which the whole family is involved. The dioxin crisis emptied the shops of poultry and filled the television screens with images of hundreds of thousands of chickens being massacred. Understandably, the voters blamed the ruling Christian-Democrat and socialist coalition. Both parties lost heavily at the election, whilst the ecological 'green' movement made huge gains. In spite of more modest gains, the liberals became the largest single block in the land and Verhofstadt finally got his wish: at last, he was prime minister. And all thanks to the rumbling stomachs of his fellow countrymen!

Two days after his victory, I visited him in his office. He was calm and relaxed. The heat and fury of political battle had subsided and in a nearby restaurant, Italian, of course, we made an analysis of the results. It was a pleasant talk and he offered a thorough and shrewd assessment of sociological and political developments in Flanders. I got the impression that a huge weight had been lifted from his shoulders.

However, the process of forming the new government quickly turned the pressure back up. Verhofstadt had to work with six different parties to reach a majority: the liberals, the socialists, the greens and their French-speaking equivalents. After each consultation meeting with one of these partners, he held a press conference in Hall D of the Senate. He clearly had great plans for Belgium, which he aimed to transform into a 'model' state. After he had finished speaking, none of my colleagues seemed anxious to upset him by asking difficult questions. I was less intimidated and asked the question that most of us wanted to hear. 'Mr.Verhofstadt, what's the price ticket for these great plans of yours? What's it all going to cost?' A reporter from the Walloon paper *La Dernière Heure* turned on me: 'Why are you deliberately trying to annoy our future prime minister?' Verhofstadt himself was even angrier. 'I've been a budget minister', he shouted. 'I know how to pay for all this, don't you worry.' I was shocked by the aggressive nature of his reply. It seemed to me a logical question: whoever makes a plan has to say how he is going to pay for it. Instead, Verhofstadt had reacted like the spoilt schoolboy of years gone by. He stormed out of Hall D and went to an adjoining room to release his pent-up emotions. I later heard that it took the combined efforts of Marc Verwilghen and Johan Vande Lanotte to calm him down. For my part, I was also shaking as I left the Senate: I hadn't expected to see this darker side of Verhofstadt's nature ever again.

I tried to put the incident out of my mind and carried on with my other assignments. Two days later, while I was shopping in the supermarket, my mobile phone rang. It was Verhofstadt's secretary. 'The Prime Minister-Designate would like to see you.' 'No problem', I replied, 'As long as my senior editor can come along too.' I was getting tired of the usual reconciliation routine. Besides, it was starting to increase my weight and my suits didn't fit me anymore.

'I'm sorry, that won't be possible', she said. 'Mr. Verhofstadt wishes to see you in private.'

I was intrigued and worried. In private. What on earth did he want? We agreed to meet in the la Rotonde Restaurant, near the parliament building. It was our first meeting in a restaurant that wasn't Italian. It seemed like an omen.

When he arrived, Verhofstadt was friendliness itself. 'That question about the financing? Don't worry. It will all be fine.' In a few short minutes, he explained his country's financial future on the back of a serviette. When he had finished, he quickly switched to another subject – the subject that was the real purpose of our meeting.

'How would you feel about working on the other side of the political fence, as a member of my personal staff?'

I had half been expecting this question and had already prepared my answer. First, however, I had to listen to all Verhofstadt's arguments in favour of his proposal: 'You could leave the paper and work for me. It would give you a chance to be a player in the game, instead of just a spectator.'

'Thanks for the offer, Guy', I replied, 'but no thanks. I am a full-time journalist and that's the way I want to stay.' I failed to add that I didn't fancy the idea of working with someone who could fly off into a rage without a moment's warning. I also failed to add that a few days earlier I had had a similar offer to work in the European ambit. This seemed more my cup of tea. After my adventures in Holland and Belgium, I felt that maybe the time was right to move on to Europe.

He accepted my decision with good grace and we left the restaurant. At the entrance to the parliament building, I shook him by the hand. 'Good luck, Guy', I said. He gave me a pat on the shoulder and walked off to run the country. As he climbed the steps, I thought to myself: 'An interesting but difficult Guy.'

I saw little of Verhofstadt after he became prime minister. However, I did bump into him one Sunday, during 'grape-picking' at his new Minister of Telecommunications, Rik Daems, who was owner of a vineyard near Leuven. Verhofstadt had brought his children, Louis and Charlotte, along. They drove the tractor which took the harvested grapes from Daems' farm to the collecting point in the nearby village of Rillaar, where there was a wine press. The adult guests were all given a basket and a pair of secateurs and were sent out into the fields to do the picking. Rik's mother, a fine old lady, provided soup and coffee and at the end of our labours we were able to indulge in every Belgian's favourite hobby: wine-tasting.

Centuries ago, this region produced a fine white wine, but Napoleon had all the vines destroyed at the beginning of the 19th century, in order to protect the French wine monopoly. Father Daems replanted the vineyard during the 1970's and his 'Hagelanden' label became quite well-known and respected in the region. His flamboyant son treated us to tastings of several vintages, but Verhofstadt – who sees himself as something of an expert – was not convinced of their quality. Some of them were 'OK', whilst others were condemned as 'too watery'. Daems was not impressed. 'There's nothing wrong with my wine', he kept repeating, and proceeded to drink large quantities of the stuff to prove it. As one of the other guests commented in a pointed aside: 'Gentlemen, it's all a question of taste.'

It was at about this time that Verhofstadt announced his intention to introduce an 'open debate culture' in the Wetstraat. This seemed to me a good idea. His predecessor, Jean-Luc Dehaene, had been anything but 'open'. Dehaene moved through the corridors of the parliament building at such a pace that it was quite difficult to actually ask him a question. Even if a breathless journalist did manage to catch up with him, his only reply was 'no comment'. It was with this style of politics that Verhofstadt wished to break. According to the Premier everyone was free to engage in this new culture of debate, since 'it is only within the context of a free and frank exchange of views that the power of argument can make itself felt.' It sounded like the start of a new golden age. But how long would it last, I wondered?

De Standaard asked me to make a series of regular reports on this new phenomenon. Open debate – genuine open debate – was something that had never really existed in Belgium up to that time. For most party chairmen, 'open debate' meant toeing the party line and putting the boot in on the opposition at every available opportunity. This same discipline was also exercised on and by journalists, which often led to a form of self-censoring that I had always found disturbing. Now this would all be at an end.

Full of enthusiasm, I began to think about how I should approach this new culture. I decided that humour and criticism would not be out of place and wrote a number of articles laced with sarcasm and biting comment. These articles were directed against some of the country's leading politicians, but it could hardly be otherwise. With whom else could you be expected to engage in political debate? The reactions from readers were positive, but as time passed I was surprised by the lack of response from the politicians themselves. No letters, no phone calls, no heated denials in parliament or the press. This was hardly my idea of a debate. Where were my sparring partners?

Out of the blue, I was given a friendly warning by a minister with whom I was on good terms. 'You'd better be careful. Guy is not happy. He's already complained in cabinet about you.' Initially, I was pleased: at least it showed that my articles were being read! I now expected that the government's counterarguments would begin to appear in rival newspapers. I was mistaken. On the contrary, instead of open debate, I received more veiled threats. I had been scheduled to take part in a discussion about Pim Fortuyn and his impact on politics in Belgium, held by the Union of Flemish Liberals (LVV) in the stylish Metropool Hotel. There were about 200 people in the auditorium and the atmosphere was animated. Before I mounted the rostrum, the Chairman of the LVV pulled me to one side and whispered in my ear. 'I just want to warn you that the party Chairman has sent two spies to check up on you.' He referred to Karel De Gucht's private secretary and also to the party's official spokesperson.

Both sat poised with pen and paper, ready to note down every uncomplimentary word I would say.

I sensed that things were coming to the boil: had my cutting remarks been perhaps a little too cutting? Certainly, the government seemed to think so. De Gucht had already telephoned *De Standaard* to demand that my series of articles should be scrapped. The paper had refused, but I doubted whether Verhofstadt would let the matter rest there. I decided that maybe it was time for another 'reconciliation' lunch. I chose an Italian restaurant in Elsene, Tutto Pepe, where I had once been on Valentine's Day with my fiancee. It wasn't cheap, but I realised that a major gesture was needed on my part to get me back in the PM's good books. I was even prepared to pay the bill myself: and for a Dutchman, there is no bigger gesture than that!

But this time I had miscalculated. Turning his back on the culinary habits of a lifetime, Verhofstadt refused my offer of a free lunch. He felt that he had been 'insulted in my position as Prime Minister' and complained to powers beyond my grasp. My series of articles was to be quietly dropped and I was told to calm down and enjoy life, rather than to anger the Belgian Premier. Instead of applying knife and fork to a delicious *osso buco* in Tutto Pepe's, as I had planned, the knife was being applied to my throat! It was not a pleasant feeling.

The end of my articles also marked the end of the 'open debate' culture. I asked myself how such a thing was possible. I just didn't understand. First Verhofstadt proclaims that open debate will be 'the icing on the cake of this government's policy'. A few months later he uses all the considerable power of the prime minister's office to ensure that the first tentative efforts at such debate are strangled at birth. Perhaps it was all the result of a cultural misunderstanding? Belgians and Netherlanders both use the word 'openness', but clearly they mean something different. For a Netherlander 'openness' is saying what you think, irrespective of the consequences. For Belgians, 'openness' is saying what you think somebody wants you to say, with a very clear eye on the possible consequences. In Holland 'openness' is as clear as crystal. In Belgium, it is as clear as a look through a steamed up window. In Holland, those in authority are always the targets of 'openness'. In Belgium, it is those in authority who decide what 'openness' is. As a result, a Dutchman practising his kind of 'openness' in Belgium is likely to cause a crisis, without him even knowing it. Which is precisely what I did.

After this sorry affair, I found myself temporarily in the political wilderness, due to the man who spent there 12 years himself! During my time in the Wetstraat, I had seen many other politicians in this same wilderness. Every party has its share of mavericks and loose cannons, men who are avoided by their colleagues and who are marginalised to the point of intellectual extinction. I had always found it interesting to watch these men and their struggle to cope with their isolation. It was less interesting, however, to actually experience the same thing myself! After the initial shock of this realisation, I decided to try and make the best of it. Many had passed through this desert before me and many had found their way out of it. Besides, a desert, even a political one, can sometimes be a fascinating place to be. It has a unique fauna and flora all of its own – and there are oases everywhere!

I went to discuss my situation with Herman De Croo, the Chairman of the Lower House and the 'first citizen of the country'. De Croo is so proud of this honorary title that he seldom takes a holiday, so that even in the middle of summer I knew that I would find him in his offices at Wetstraat 10, just a stone's throw from the prime minister's residence at Wetstraat 16.

He greeted me with open arms and in his typically flamboyant, exaggerated style. 'My dear friend, what brings you to my humble door, here in the House of the People?' I replied that I wished to speak to him about 'a not-unimportant incident'. He asked me to wait a few minutes in his waiting room, whilst he first dealt with another 'client'. This 'client' turned out to be Princess Esmeralda, the daughter of King Leopold III and Liliane Baels, both of whom had also spent some time in the political wilderness. Baels lived in the castle of Argenteuil near Waterloo, but was not on speaking terms with the rest of the royal family. Her breech with King Boudewijn – and above all with Queen Fabiola – had occurred when they had more or less forced her to leave the royal palace at Laken. As a matter of courtesy and discretion, the King and Queen went away on holiday while Baels moved out, but returned to find that she had taken all the furniture with her! In the circumstances, it seemed likely that Princess Esmeralda was consulting the 'first citizen' on a family matter.

De Croo suddenly called me into his office. 'My dear chap, I'm afraid that I will have to keep it short: the Princess is still waiting. What's the matter? Tell me all about it.' I related how my articles had been spiked and how, as a result, I would also be forced to postpone publication of this book which had originally been planned for the autumn of that year. 'This is unbelievable', he muttered. 'Things have really gone too far this time.' It was clear that he knew nothing of what had happened. 'I am amazed', he said. 'Me, too', I replied. 'But I thought that as "first citizen of the country" you should be made aware of what is going on.' De Croo sighed. 'I have told Guy dozens of times: leave the writers and the journalists alone. But he just gets angry whenever I suggest this. He finds it so difficult to accept criticism.' I thanked him for his concern and allowed him to return to the Princess, who was probably not used to being kept waiting. 'If you ever feel the need to apply for political asylum, you know where to find me', he joked as I left. It was a kind offer, but I thought that the Prime Minister might view the matter differently.

News of my 'muzzling' also began to filter into the Wetstraat. The secretary of Verhofstadt's private office told Willy De Clercq, prominent liberal politician and minister of State, that they had 'silenced that bloody Dutchman once and for all'. De Clercq – a true blue liberal in heart and soul – was genuinely shocked and began to spread the story. Soon everyone was talking about it, so that *De Standaard* felt obliged to issue a statement which at first glance seemed to be a masterpiece of vagueness, but left nobody in any doubt that my series had been terminated because of the intervention of the 'big boys'.

The opposition parties were quick to support me. Ex-Prime Minister and Minister of Foreign Affairs Mark Eyskens sent me a note in which he suggested that the unvarnished truth of the affair should be 'leaked secretly'. I was flattered but felt it was better to keep a certain distance from the CVP, since I knew that in their time the Christian-Democrats had also done their best to have critics silenced. The prominent television reporter Walter Zinzen once told me how he had been forbidden for 17 years from making a documentary about Zaire. By the end of the 1970's, Zinzen had come to the conclusion that President Mobutu Sese Seko was a ruthless dictator, which is now common knowledge, but was not so evident then. Zinzen wanted to expose Mobutu for what he was, but failed to reckon with the power of the royal court and the Wetstraat. Mobutu was a friend of King Boudewijn and also a central pillar in Belgian foreign policy in Central Africa. Neither of these vested interests was prepared to see their placeman embarrassed and so the Belgian government – then led by the CVP – put pressure on the state broadcasting company to torpedo Zinzen's plans. 'I knew everything about that country', Zinzen told me. He had lived and worked there for many years. 'And for 17 years I was allowed to say nothing. And let me tell you, friend: 17 years is a very long time.'

The reaction of ordinary men and women in the street also gave me encouragement. The sympathy of the public is like water in the desert: it quenches your thirst and makes everything blossom. Your average Fleming is not really a political creature, but he has always had a strong feeling for the underdog. Throughout their history the Flemish people have been oppressed by foreign invaders and by their own French-speaking elite, so that they know exactly how it feels to be bullied and ignored. People often stopped me on the street to express their support: one genteel lady told me that it was 'a disgrace', whereas her husband was somewhat more expressive: 'Don't let the bastards grind you down.' My own favourite was a comment from an elderly gentleman, who sat next to me in a restaurant. 'Sir, you must remember that this is Belgium. Small country, small minds.'

I still carried on giving my regular talks, and the halls where I spoke seemed fuller than ever. Everyone was curious. 'Is it true that Verhofstadt had you silenced?' When I confirmed that it was, their indignation knew no limits. During my period in the political wilderness, I began to learn something of a different kind of Flanders. Not the Flanders of three-star restaurants, champagne and fast cars, but a deeper and more compassionate

Flanders, a Flanders of ordinary men and women, earning little and living in terraced housing, but with a strong sense of right and wrong. Without my sojourn in the desert, I might never have experienced the warmth of these people and somehow their fellowship seemed to make my period in exile worthwhile. It was certainly a feeling that I had never experienced in the Wetstraat.

Not that all my political contacts deserted me. Jef Valkeniers, a Liberal MP, remained a true friend. We shared a common passion for South Africa and I visited him regularly at his villa in Dilbeek, built in the Dutch Cape style. Jef eventually married a South African lady and I was invited to attend the reception in Groot Bijgaarden. Not surprisingly, most of the VLD hierarchy was present. 'Are you still allowed to write?' asked Hugo Coveliers with an amused grin. 'Or is the VLD Stasi still giving you problems?' Coveliers was soon to have his own problems with the party leadership and he told me all about a 'sensational book', his words he was going to publish.

We were still chatting when the door opened and in walked the three VLD top men: Verhofstadt, Dewael and De Gucht. 'Look out, here comes the Holy Trinity', I heard someone whisper. I made no effort to turn around and just carried on talking as though nothing had happened. I knew, however, that the threesome would make a tour of the room, shaking hands and dispensing the meaningless pleasantries which are second nature to all politicians. I knew equally that this meant that they would eventually work their way around to me. Verhofstadt hadn't recognised me, but when he tapped me on the shoulder I turned to face him. Things in our part of the room went quiet and all eyes focussed on the two of us. Some people were clearly anticipating a slanging match, perhaps even fisticuffs. However,

I decided that this was a moment to rise above petty personal feelings, to avoid the confrontation that everyone seemed to be expecting. Or, to put it another way, I decided to behave like a true Belgian.

'Ah Guy, my good friend', I said in a jovial voice. 'Long time, no see. How's things?'

'Well, well, well', he replied, 'If it isn't my most recent victim. Everybody seems to think that I had you muzzled.'

'Yes, I read that in the papers as well, so it must be true,' I said. 'Who would have thought that a nice man like you would do a thing like that?'

'Verhofstadt had a deep sigh. Maybe we should talk about it over lunch. I know this really good Italian…'

THE COBBLE EATERS

Cycling has always exercised a strong hold on my imagination, possibly because it is the hardest and most physically demanding of all sports. The long hours on the bike, the punishing changes of pace, the strength-sapping climbs – all combine to put the body under the very greatest pressure. Cycling is struggle; cycling is sweat; cycling is suffering.

And the poor old cyclist must do it all by himself: there is nobody who can help him.

Lonely are the brave.

My fascination with the sport began at an early age. I used to keep an exercise book, in which I religiously copied down the daily results of the *Tour de France* from the newspaper. And each year I used to pester my parents to let me go and watch one of the post-*Tour* criterium races – I wanted to see all these great sportsmen in the flesh. Finally, my nagging paid off and one summer's morning, under the watchful eye of my mother, we set out by bike for Dieren – where the Gazelle factory is – to watch the local criterium. Mother dropped me off at a suitable point on the course and then disappeared into town to do some shopping. She returned two hours later to find me rooted to the same spot. I had sat transfixed, as such famous figures as Jan Jansen, Rini Wagtmans and Rik Van Looy had all passed by. For the most part, they had ridden at a gentle pace – only in the final lap of the race did the speed increase, to try and give the impression that it had actually been a serious competition.

By 1980 I was old enough to travel to Paris by bus, to see the triumphant arrival of Joop Zoetemelk, only the second Dutchman ever to win the *Tour*. It was an unforgettable sight. The Champs Elysées was bathed in sun, Zoetemelk was embraced by the then Prime Minister of the Netherlands, Dries van Agt, a colourful figure with a penchant for the dramatic and also by the Burgomaster of Paris, a certain Monsieur Jacques Chirac.

My own modest ambitions in the world of cycling came to nothing. I once entered a local competition but after just one lap I was already tailed off at the back of the pack. Cycling was clearly more difficult than I had thought. The good riders accelerated out of the bends, whilst I just freewheeled around them like a Sunday afternoon tourist. However hard I tried, I simply could not follow the pace and soon I was far behind. With much puffing and panting, I eventually struggled across the finishing line – in last position.

My own cycling career was very definitely at an end but I still cherished the hope that one day I might get the chance to go behind the scenes of one of the great classic races which pass through Belgium. There was the famous *Waalse Pijl*, which ended on a steep hill in the town of Huy and there was also the much tougher *Luik-Bastenaken-Luik* (Liège-Bastogne-Liège). However, both these races were held in Wallonia, where I knew none of the organisers.

I had more contacts – and therefore a far better chance – in Flanders. Here the cycling season opens each year with the *Omloop Het Volk*, which, as the name suggests, is sponsored by the newspaper *Het Volk*; or, as it is unflatteringly known in East Flanders, 'the little liar'. Naturally, I had even better prospects with the king of the Belgian cycling classics, the *Ronde van Vlaanderen*, sponsored by my own newspapers, *Het Nieuwsblad* and *De Standaard*. After a brief word with the editor of *De Standaard*, I was promised that I would be able to follow the race, which sends Flanders into a frenzy of sporting passion each Easter. This is the best opportunity of the year for the famous *Flandriens* – the Flemish hard riders – to show what they are made of and also offers a foretaste of the great tour events which follow in Italy, France and Spain.

Then, the race began on the market square in Sint-Niklaas, a sleepy little town near Antwerp, from where the racers pass through the hilly landscape of East Flanders, before arriving at the finish in the village of Meerbeke. I had expected to be able to get a place in the motorcade without much difficulty, but it turned out not to be quite that simple. A few weeks before the race I went to see the formidable lady who was responsible for promotion and publicity. In an unnervingly forthright manner she asked: 'What do you want to come along for? You're not a sponsor, you're not a politician, you're not a sports journalist. Why on earth should a political writer be interested in a bike race?'

I explained patiently that I wanted to go along out of love for the sport. I understood fully that the sponsors had absolute priority: after all, it was their money that made the whole event possible. Similarly, I accepted that a place had to be found for the politicians, for whom this was an ideal chance to meet and greet the local voters, not to mention keeping well in with the papers. However, if there was just one place left... 'O.K. – I'll see what I can do', replied my interrogator, clearly softened by my sympathetic approach. A few days later she rang back. 'It's all arranged. You're in a car with two Spanish journalists from Barcelona.

Your driver is Fernand. It's his thirtieth year, so he should know what he's doing.'

Relief flooded over me. I was going to follow the *Ronde van Vlaanderen*: a childhood dream would finally become reality.

I made sure that I arrived in good time at the rendezvous point, a cafe on the market square in Sint-Niklaas. The cycling entourage shared the available space with a funfair, giving the whole square a feel of popular celebration. The air was already thick with the smell of chips and the main attraction seemed to be a giant ferris wheel. Inside the cafe, there were a number of sport journalists and other fringe figures, drinking coffee and speculating over the day's events. Who was in good form? Who would have the 'best legs'? Out of the corner of my eye, I saw Bernard Thévenet pass by, dressed in jeans and carrying a plastic bag stuffed with folders. Back in the seventies Thévenet had won the *Tour de France*, but now he seemed to be just another cycling groupie. I had no idea what he was supposed to be doing, but he looked sad and slightly pathetic: a once great racer reduced to the cycling equivalent of an errand boy. He lacked the leadership qualities of a Bernard Hinault, who worked his way up to become director of the *Tour de France*: a small man, but with an iron will.

Suddenly, my name was called out. 'Will Mr.Eppink please come to the bar?' I worked my way obediently through the crowd and arrived at the bar, where I was greeted by a young man in a t-shirt. 'This is Fernand. He will be your driver. The two Spaniards are there. Take them with you and make sure you get away on time, otherwise you won't see a thing.'

Fernand was a pensioner from Sint-Niklaas. At first glance, he seemed a bit aloof, an introvert who mumbled when he spoke.

He had been driving visitors around the *Ronde van Vlaanderen* for decades and he gave the impression of being a man in a hurry.

Outside the cyclists were already riding up onto the starting platform, where they had to sign off their names on some kind of competitor's list. Within seconds the race would be under way. All over the market cars were driving off, horns blowing, jostling to take up their place in the motorcade.

Fernand was getting nervous. 'We can't wait too much longer, otherwise the race will start and we'll be left behind. Where are the two Spaniards?' Prompted by Fernand's obvious unease, I went in search of our Spanish guests.

'*Señores, tenemos que partir*', I suggested, in the hope of finally getting them on the move. Without a word, they rose and walked in the direction of the car, dragging their huge suitcases behind them. After the finish of the race in Meerbeke, they were travelling straight back to Brussels for the evening flight to Barcelona. Fernand was already behind the wheel of his Mercedes and I jumped in beside him. The Spaniards made ready to get in the back.

Suddenly and without warning, Fernand hit the gas pedal and the car shot forward. Behind me I heard a cry of pain and turned to see one of the Spaniards lying at the side of the road. 'Jésus Maria', he screamed, to which blasphemy he added a stream of unintelligible Spanish curses. The reason for this outburst soon became apparent. Fernand had driven over his foot, while he was still trying to get inside the car! Happily, the offending foot was still attached to the leg, but the unfortunate Spaniard seemed to be in some considerable pain. Fernand was unimpressed. 'Should have bloody well watched where he was going. Come on, we've got to go.'

I jumped out and raced back into the cafe, where the owner quickly provided me with a bag of ice cubes. These I offered to the Spanish reporter, in the hope that they might reduce the swelling and ease some of the pain. For the rest, we would simply have to trust to luck.

Fernand showed little remorse for what he had done and without a word of apology we sped off after the race. Fernand turned on the radio to find out where the main pack of riders was and, using a series of back roads, managed to bring us close up behind them. He was obviously pleased with himself. 'Now, at last we'll see something', he said to me in Dutch. To the groaning Spaniard and his colleague he said very little, other than an occasional *'allez, ça va?'* Gradually, I, too, began listening to the radio, since on the road ahead I could see next to nothing, other than the rear lights of the other cars in the motorcade. We did occasionally manage to catch sight of a cyclist who had had a flat tyre or who had stopped for a pee, but for the time being this was the limit of our sporting excitement. Far more exciting was the competition between the various cars to try and get prime position behind the pack – a competition which showed scant respect for the rules of the road.

'I'm used to this', said Fernand confidently. 'I know all these roads like the back of my hand.'

Suddenly, he saw his son, who was driving one of the other courtesy vehicles. Fernand wound down his window and began an informal chat about last night's football, still keeping one ear on the radio and looking everywhere except at the chaos on the road ahead of us. All around cars were accelerating, braking or trying to push past each other. It was like a Wild West show on four wheels.

'Isn't it difficult driving in these conditions?' I asked Fernand, in the hope that this might bring his eyes back to the road.

No such luck. Ignoring me completely, he simply carried on his conversation with his son. Up ahead, one of the leading cars slowed down and some of the others also began to brake. Lost in a world of his own, Fernand saw nothing and I watched in horror as the rear bumper of the car in front began to approach us at great speed.

'Look out!' I yelled. Fernand gave a start and instantly hit the brakes. The Spaniards – who had lapsed into a moody silence on the back seat – shot forward and began a new stream of obscenities. Fernand somehow managed to avoid the car in front but we skidded off the road and came to rest against a grassy bank. My heart had leapt into my mouth, where it was operating at twice its normal speed, but otherwise I was unharmed. Nobody said a word, although the looks of the Spaniards spoke volumes.

Totally unruffled by this near disaster, Fernand reversed out onto the road and edged his way back into the motorcade. After a few minutes of silence he muttered: 'Shame about that. We've gone and lost our good place.'

In the meantime, the main pack was moving ahead over the highways and byways of Flanders. The first part of the route was relatively uninteresting. It was too flat to make an attack of any kind worthwhile, so the riders just idled along at a pace that even most amateurs would have found slow. All along the course the streets were decorated with yellow Flemish flags and in every village the Flemish Lion was waiting to greet the riders. The pavements and roadsides were thick with people, who began spontaneously to applaud as the race and its caravan of cars passed by. Even the roads were painted with the names of famous Flemish racers, the so-called *Flandriens*.

The race only came to life when the hills of East Flanders came into view. The tempo increased and the racers began to speed through picturesque little villages, where the sun-drenched cafes and terraces were packed with cycling fans. Clearly, the *Ronde van Vlaanderen* was more than just a bike race: it was a popular celebration of Flanders and the Flemish way of life.

After our near accident, Fernand was keen to get us back to the front of the motorcade and so once again we took to the back roads. 'I know this region like my own back garden', he reassured us for the twentieth time. 'I drive here almost every day.' The roads became narrower and narrower, until eventually they were little more than paths. All the time, Fernand continued listening to the radio (which he had now switched to a French channel, for the benefit of our Spanish companions), in an attempt to track down the location of the race leaders. 'Got them!' he shouted. 'If we can just get by here, we'll see everything.'

I was not so sure. Stretching away in the distance, I could see a thin but colourful ribbon of flag-waving supporters, all of whom still seemed to be waiting to cheer their heroes. 'Fernand', I suggested cautiously, 'I don't think we're behind the pack – I think we're ahead of it.' Fernand wouldn't hear of it. 'Impossible', he mumbled under his breath.

Impossible or not, a large group of riders began to close in on us from behind, winding across the countryside like a snake through the dust. Gradually, even Fernand began to realise that I was right and he was wrong. 'But they shouldn't be there', he protested. 'They should have passed here ages ago. They're riding too slow!'

Suddenly, we were surrounded by the lead vehicles of the race. Horns began to sound and drivers began to gesture, casting clear doubt on both Fernand's parentage and his sanity. Policemen on motorbikes pulled alongside our car and made it plain that we had better get out of the way – and fast. Fernand the hunter now became Fernand the hunted. There seemed no way of avoiding the pack – the roads were too narrow and the cyclists were approaching too fast.

Fernand ground his teeth and tried to increase speed. Unfortunately, under the pressure of the moment, his driving skills were no longer up to the task. On more than one occasion he almost drove off the twisting roads and gradually his panic began to increase. 'We've got to get out of here', he shrieked, 'otherwise they'll overtake us.' After a brief pause he added plaintively: 'This has never happened to me before.'

To make matters worse, the police motorcycles now turned on their sirens. The Spaniards, finally realising that the pack was close behind, turned to look through the back window of the car, in the hope that they might finally see something of the race. But it was not to be. At this moment we entered a village and Fernand, by now at his wit's end, turned sharply into the first available side street. As we came to a screeching halt, we heard the hissing sound of bike tyres pass behind us. By the time we turned around, the race was gone.

Not only was the race gone, but five minutes later the motorcade was gone as well. The Spaniards were at a loss for words. They had travelled all the way from Barcelona to make an exciting report on the *Ronde van Vlaanderen*, but all they had seen was 150 kilometres of Flanders' less interesting minor roads. I understood their disappointment. At the start of the day it had also been my great wish to follow the *Ronde*. By now, I had modified this wish into a simple desire to get home in one piece.

A little later, Fernand managed to pull himself together. 'Let's go and have a beer', he said. 'I know a nice spot.'

He drove us to a cafe near a mill, in the middle of the Zwalm district. This is the political stronghold of Herman De Croo. Apparently, De Croo was in one of the other cars that had been ahead of us in the motorcade. Little wonder. The race always passes his very own front door in the village of Michelbeke – a public relations opportunity that was just too good to miss. As soon as the riders had sped by, on their way to climb the steep slopes of the Berendries, De Croo simply stepped out of his courtesy car and went home. To complete the publicity exercise, the VRT helicopter following the race circled over De Croo's house, allowing an excited commentator to announce to the watching public: 'And this, ladies and gentlemen, is where Herman De Croo lives.'

The cafe by the mill was a popular place, full of reporters and ex-riders, all bent on enjoying a glass of good Flemish beer before the final denouement of the race. Whilst the racers sweated their way across the Flanders countryside, their accompanying circus of sponsors, politicians and journalists all seemed more concerned with taking a refreshment break.

We, too, needed a break, particularly the wounded Spaniard. His foot was still giving him trouble and our recent adventures on the road had left him cold with fear. The two of them sat there, silent and visibly disappointed – one might even say disgruntled. The bag of ice blocks had long since melted, forming a large pool in the back of Fernand's car. I went to the bar to get some more.

By now Fernand had recovered his old élan. 'Don't be too long', he warned me. 'We have to get back on the trail of the pack.' The Spaniards and I just had time to knock back our pints, before leaping into the Mercedes and roaring off in a new and even more desperate attempt to catch up with the race.

Fernand was in a jovial mood. 'I know things went wrong back there, but I'll make it up to you. This time we're going all the way to the "Wall" in Geraardsbergen, right behind the leaders.' This sounded promising.

Even the Spaniards began to brighten up, cheered at the prospect of at last seeing something of the race. Fernand said he knew a couple of back roads in a village close to Geraardsbergen. These would bring us onto the route of the *Ronde* and would allow us to squeeze into the motorcade. We raced through the valley of the Zwalm at breakneck speed, finally turning off at a church in the centre of a small village. This was Fernand's 'secret road', the road that would lead us back to the race. Or so we thought. A few hundred yards further on, we found that the secret road was firmly blocked. A barrier manned by a large policeman barred the way, not only for us, but also for several other drivers who had thought to try the same shortcut. We were stuck.

Fernand was furious. 'This isn't possible. I've been coming along here for thirty years. It's a disgrace, an absolute bloody disgrace.' His anger soon turned to self-pity. 'Why did this have to happen to me, today of all days?'

I got out of the car and walked towards the barrier. I had seen a driver talking to the police and I thought I recognised him. It was André Denys, a Liberal member of the Flemish Regional Parliament and a fervent cycling fan. He was sharing a car with Herman Van Springel, a well-known ex-professional, who had lost the 1968 *Tour de France* to Jan Jansen by the smallest of margins. 'Ah, Mr. Eppink', cried Denys. 'We have to get through here as quickly as possible; otherwise we will miss the pack!' Denys and Van Springel nagged away in turn at the policeman and eventually he let them through. Denys turned and waved, as Van Springel put his foot down and the car sped away.

We tried the same trick, but the policeman was not to be fooled twice. 'You're not getting through here', he said to Fernand in a stern voice. 'It's too dangerous. Turn around and drive straight to Meerbeke.'

This was the end. We would never catch up with the pack now and we wouldn't even make it to Meerbeke in time for the finish. Fernand sat slumped behind the wheel, while the Spaniards hissed their disapproval. Via the Bosberg and a number of villages, we drove in the direction of the finishing line, almost within touching distance of the riders, but unable to see them. In silence we listened to the final sprint on the radio. The race was won by somebody called Sörensen.

By the time we arrived in Meerbeke everything was over, even the presentation of the winner. Tired and demoralised, I got out of the car and thanked Fernand, more out of politeness than gratitude, and made my way to the hospitality tent, where journalists and politicians were discussing how the race had gone. I, of course, had little to tell and decided to go home early. At least that way I could catch up with the reply of the race on television.

I took my leave of the two Spaniards, who did not bother to thank Fernand. They seemed pleased to have survived their drive through the 'Flemish hell', but disappointed that they had missed just about everything they had come to see. They climbed into a taxi and headed off towards Zaventem and the Spanish sun.

I, too, reflected upon my day in the *Ronde van Vlaanderen*. I had seen nothing of the race but felt that I had learnt a little more about Flanders!

THE POWERS THAT BE

When I came to Flanders, I never imagined that I would get to meet the Belgian royal family. For an ordinary citizen, the idea of meeting a king is almost beyond comprehension. For by definition, a king is unapproachable. He is the personification of the State; he embodies an ancient, almost mythical concept; in some cases, he might even be a living legend – in short, the kind of person we ordinary mortals never get to meet. Kings and presidents are meant to be viewed at a distance – usually on television. This is what makes their institution so remote. Almost as if they come from a different planet.

Even in my own country, the closest I had ever got to Queen Beatrix was to see her golden State Coach speed past at the opening of Parliament. As a journalist, I had been given a special press pass to get me inside the Binnenhof. In reality, however, I was little more than a tourist. My only useful journalistic contribution that day was to hold a white cloth for our photographer who assured me that this was something to do with correct lighting and exposure. For the rest, I just gazed at the spectacle like everyone else.

As a Dutchman in Flanders, the royal palace seemed further away than ever. I assumed that if any journalist was ever going to make it past the gates of the Royal Palace, it wouldn't be one with a Netherlands passport.

Even so, there was one royal event which intrigued me: the annual reception of the constituted bodies. The mere mention of the name was enough to bring a rueful smile to the lips of my other colleagues in the political section. At first, I had no idea why. Constituted bodies? What could this possibly mean? It sounded like something which might conceivably be discussed at a convention of undertakers. Or perhaps it was more in the medical line?

On a cold day in January the chief political editor breezed into the office and announced: 'Point one on today's agenda is the constipated bodies.' This was clearly intended as a play on words, but it confirmed my earlier impression that the whole subject was something for a medical man. 'Shouldn't we get our public health correspondent to cover this one?', I suggested. The room exploded into laughter.

'Eppink', explained my boss, as though he was talking to a not very bright child, 'when we talk about "the constipated bodies", we actually mean "the constituted bodies."' The look on my face must have made it clear that I still didn't have the faintest idea what he was talking about. 'The constituted bodies are the official institutions of the State. In French, they are known as *"corps posés"*, but in Flemish we say *"de gestelde lichamen"* – the constituted bodies. Every year, their representatives are all invited to a fancy New Year's reception at the royal palace.'

Now that I understood, I quite liked the sound of this. 'Could I go along and have a look?', I asked. 'I somehow don't think they'll be inviting you', came the reply. 'The only constituted body around here is the Editor-in-Chief!'

Still curious, I found an excuse later in the day to drop in at the Chief Editor's glass-walled office. I found him flicking through today's paper, a bored look on his face. I asked him directly:

'How was it, then, at the reception for the constituted bodies?' He looked at me blankly. 'I didn't go. I never go. The whole thing is a waste of bloody time.' Clearly the paper's constituted body had little desire to meet his political equivalents. This was useful information: it meant that the paper's annual invitation to the reception went unused. All I had to do was bide my time.

The following January I was back in the Chief Editor's office. His secretary informed me that he was away on holiday. 'Has he received his invitation for the reception of the constituted bodies?' I asked innocently. 'Yes, it's here somewhere', she said, searching through a large pile of correspondence. 'He never goes, of course. Do you want to keep it? As a kind of souvenir?'

Back at my own desk – and careful that nobody should see – I took the invitation out of my jacket pocket and started to read. It was written in a grandiose style befitting an important royal occasion and informed me that 'full court dress must be worn' and that I should 'RSVP' as soon as possible. I weighed the answer card in my hand, trying to decide what to do. 'Why not?' I thought. 'The Chief Editor is away, so he won't mind. The political editor won't mind either – it will save him from going.' I filled in the card and popped it in the evening's post. I was on my way to the royal palace in Brussels as a constituted body.

On the day of the reception, I arrived at the palace amidst a stream of fast moving limousines. It was struck by the fact that I was one of the few people driving my own car – most of the guests were simply being driven up to the door, where they got out and went straight in. Guided by a burly policeman, I drove off to the parking area – happily we had all been given a special badge for a reserved space – and returned on foot to the entrance, clutching my invitation in my hand. If I was going to have problems, now would be the time. A quick examination of my identity card would show that I was not the person whose name was on my invitation. In short, I might become the first and only Dutchman ever to be thrown out of a Belgian royal reception. I could already see the headlines.

I quickly flashed my invitation card at the palace guard, holding it upside down, so that it would be more difficult to read. I backed this up with a friendly wave, which I hoped would give the impression that I had been coming here for years. The guards nodded politely in reply and ushered me through the doors. I was in! And nobody had even asked to see my card! The first hurdle had been cleared.

The entrance hall was full of court officials, all of whom wore traditional 19th century dress. One of them appeared silently at my side. 'Would you like to give me your coat, Sir?' I did as I was asked and wandered through into a marble corridor lined with large mirrors and even larger chandeliers. I followed the red carpet up the stairs to the first floor. On each step stood a member of the gendarmerie, dressed in ceremonial uniform and holding a sword. It was as though I had stumbled into a fairy story, with fantastic visions wherever you looked. I buttoned my jacket, checked my flies and stepped resolutely into the next room.

Here I at last saw a familiar face – or at least a face I recognised. Van Ypersele de Strihou was the King's principal private secretary. He was sometimes known as the 'Deputy King', because of his powerful influence over the Belgian royal family, and he was famed for the half-smile which never seemed to leave his lips, as though he was always laughing at some secret joke. He wore that same smile now, as he greeted me. I had seen him a number of times in Parliament, following the debates from the special Royal Box. Happily, he did not know me and so he failed to realise that I was an impostor or 're-constituted body', as I now thought of myself. We shook hands and he led me through into the next chamber.

This turned out to be a kind of auditorium. The reception of the constituted bodies is always preceded by short speeches from the King and the Prime Minister. I had arrived in good time and so I began to look for my place. Another of the silent palace lackeys materialised at my side and whispered in my ear: 'Would you like to follow me, Sir?' He made it sound like an offer I couldn't refuse. I had expected that he would lead me to one of the blocks at the back of the room. At any public function, the press are always shoved in at the back. Why should a royal reception be any different, I thought? To my surprise he showed me to a row of chairs near the front, immediately behind a block reserved for 'the representatives of the Government and Parliament'. This was a large block, cordoned off with thick rope. With six parliaments and six governments, Belgium has a lot of constituted bodies.

I took my place amongst the magistrates and high-ranking army officers and began to look around. As the minutes ticked by, I was treated to a fascinating social and political spectacle, which seemed to have its own internal momentum. The very elite of Belgian public life passed before my eyes and moved to their appointed places with the natural precision of a ballroom dancing team: the speakers of the various parliaments and government ministers at the front, then the court officials, the judiciary, the military and the civil powers. The only thing – or things – that seemed slightly out of place were the chairmen of the various political parties. These are amongst the most powerful political figures in the land, but they were all seated several rows behind myself. Some of them were not impressed.

'Hey, Eppink, what are you doing here? My, my, we have come up in the world, haven't we? I didn't realise they let foreigners in to the reception of the constituted bodies!'

Before I could reply, a bell rang. A group of ministers moved forward and lined up on either side of a door at the front of the room. Clearly, they were intended to act as some kind of welcoming committee for the royal family: it rather reminded me of the ballboys at Wimbledon on Finals Day. A court official instructed everyone to stand and in his country's three official languages announced the arrival of *'De Koning, Le Roi, Der König'*. The King was on his way.

The door at the front of the room opened and in filed King Albert and Queen Paola, followed by Prince Filip, Princess Astrid and Prince Laurent who was known in our office as Prince Woof-Woof – a non-too-subtle reference to his position as patron of the Belgian Dog Association. There was a hushed silence, as everyone in the room seemed captured by the spirit of the moment.

The first to speak was the Prime Minister. He was a plain man known for his plain speaking, particularly in his more unguarded moments, but he too realised that the occasion required something different. 'Sire, Belgium is facing many great challenges. You can count upon the faithful support of the constituted bodies to give guidance and service to both yourself and your loyal subjects....'

The King replied in like fashion. 'I thank the constituted bodies for their tireless dedication in the service of our country.' In other circumstances, this speech might have sounded a bit over-the-top, but in the stately surroundings of the royal palace it had an almost inspirational quality. His Majesty seemed anxious to instil order and discipline into the work of his *'corps posés'*.

'Belgium is at the crossroads of Europe, a land with a unique experience of social co-operation. It is good that we concentrate on the things which bind us.' The King warned against tears in the fabric of society, such as are regularly threatened by the constant bickering between the Flemish and French-speaking communities. 'It would be strange indeed if Belgium should become divided, just at the moment when Europe is uniting.' The King spoke in French, Dutch and German. His knowledge of these languages followed roughly the same order.

After this somewhat formal ceremony, the reception proper began. The King and Queen were first to enter the reception room, each accompanied by a personal aide-de-camp. The constituted bodies followed at a discreet distance. As I was leaving my seat, a politician I knew grabbed me by the sleeve. 'Eppink, fancy you turning up here! Do you think you are going to be introduced? The aide normally selects the guests to meet the King, takes them over to him and lets them know when the conversation is over. And remember – it's only the King that is allowed to ask the questions; you just answer.'

Having been given this crash course in 'how to deal with a ruling monarch', I waited patiently, in the hope that I might receive the royal summons. All the eyes in the room were fixed on the King and who he was talking to. The aide never left his side and you could almost feel the tension each time the pair of them moved towards another group of guests. Was someone going to be asked? Was I going to be asked? Sadly, it was not to be. Next time, maybe.

The tables were full of delicious-looking hors d'oeuvres and the palace attendants served the very finest champagne. Receptions in Belgium, particularly parliamentary receptions are normally lively occasions, which frequently run on for hours and hours. Not this evening. After 45 minutes the King and Queen returned to the royal apartments and shortly thereafter most of the other guests also made ready to depart. I left with them, feeling nonetheless that I had taken part in something special.

At the main entrance, the police were calling up the drivers of the generals, ministers and magistrates with a loudspeaker. One by one, the limousines rolled forward and carried off their distinguished owners, back to their offices and homes. 'Can I call your driver, Sir?' enquired a policeman politely. 'That won't be necessary', I said. 'I'm driving myself!'

Back in our editorial office, the mood was playful. 'And how does it feel to be a constituted body?' my colleagues asked. I ignored their jibes and sat down to write a nondescript article about the King's speech. But deep down, I still thought that for a few brief hours I had been privileged to take part in a modern-day fairy story.

Following the reception of the constituted bodies, I assumed that my chance of a face to face meeting with a member of the royal family was gone for good. What prospect had an itinerant Dutch journalist of an audience with the King of the Belgians? None at all. Or so I thought.

A year or so later my telephone rang. A businesslike female voice asked if I was Derk-Jan Eppink. I replied in the affirmative and waited to see what would happen next. 'This is the Ministry of Foreign Affairs in The Hague. Your name has been included in the list of guests for the state banquet on the occasion of the visit by King Albert and Queen Paola to the Netherlands. Do you intend to come?'

I was dumbfounded by the question. A state banquet? I had seen them on television, of course, and also heard stories from political friends who had attended. But I had no real idea what one would actually be like. While I dithered in silence, the disembodied voice from The Hague continued: 'You will be required to wear a dress suit and for your overnight stay we can book you into the Krasnapolski Hotel in Amsterdam.' It was clear that she was working her way through a pre-arranged check-list of things she had to say. It was equally clear that she expected an immediate answer.

'Yes, of course I'll come', I replied.

'Good. I'll arrange a personal invitation for you as soon as possible. And remember – don't be late!'

I let this unexpected news sink in. I had never imagined that I would ever be invited to a state banquet. State banquets were reserved for people of power and importance – and I didn't come into either category! 'What on earth am I going to do amongst all those big shots?' I asked myself. 'How am I supposed to behave? What am I supposed to say? And what, in the name of all that is holy, is a dress suit?'

I decided to investigate this last point first. I assumed that a dress suit was another name for a dinner jacket, but I wasn't sure. I called some of my political contacts, who were more familiar with the niceties of protocol than I was, and asked their advice. I was quickly informed that a dress suit is very definitely *not* the same thing as a dinner jacket. 'No – a dinner jacket and black tie are what you would normally wear at an official dinner. A dress suit is hardly ever worn – only for state banquets, really. That's why most of us hire them.' I tried hard to control my growing panic – attending a state banquet was clearly a complicated affair. What if I turned up at the palace in Amsterdam wearing the wrong suit? I had only just managed to avoid being thrown out of the reception of the constituted bodies. And now it was looking as though it was all going to happen again!

Whatever else I got wrong, I was determined that I was at least going to get this clothing business right. I reached for a copy of the Yellow Pages and turned to the section marked 'Costumes, festive clothing and curiosities'. I quickly found a shop in the centre of Leuven, which claimed to rent out 'special clothing'. I rang and made an appointment.

The shop was near to Ladeuze Square. Seen from a distance, it looked ordinary enough. My first impression was that it seemed more likely to specialise in novelty bow ties than in dress suits for state banquets. However, as I got closer my hopes began to rise. The elegant front window contained a wedding dress and several top hats – a good sign. The moment I went inside I knew that I had come to the right place: as far as the eye could see, there were row upon row of suits, costumes and dresses.

And elderly lady came up to me. 'Are you looking for something special?' she enquired. I tried to make my reply sound as modest as possible. 'Yes, I've been invited to a state banquet and I need a dress suit.' I hoped that she would know exactly what I meant.

'A dress suit? But of course. Let me give you one to try on.' She disappeared through a door and returned thirty seconds later with a heavily laden coat hanger. 'Here, try this one.'

In the changing room, I carefully removed everything from the hanger. There was a lot of it. I recognised the shirt and trousers, but there was a strange waistcoat and a bow tie, which I had no idea how to put on. I slipped into the shirt and trousers which were far too long and stepped back into the shop.

'Excuse me, but I'm afraid I don't know how to put the rest on. There's just so much!'

The lady of the shop was already busy with another customer. She turned to me with a polite smile of amusement and said: 'You just pop back inside the changing room. I'll be with you in a minute.' After a brief delay, she pulled open the curtain. 'Now then, let's see what we can do with this suit.' It was a complicated business. Everything had to be done in a particular order. First the bow tie, held in place with a band. Next a kind of hardboard waistcoat, bolted into position with a number of buttons in the shape of little screws. Finally the heavy morning coat, complete with tails.

'The screws are the difficult bit', she warned. 'A lot of people seem to have trouble with them. If you are not careful, you will get your fingers tied up in knots.' I think she meant this last remark as a joke, but I wasn't laughing. She showed me what to do and I tried to copy her. It was a disaster. 'I will do it for you now but you will have to practise a bit at home', she said. 'Otherwise you will be going to the state banquet half-dressed!'

At long last, I was finally strapped into my dress suit. I felt like a medieval knight, locked inside a suit of armour. I looked, however, like a penguin. 'Do you need a top hat and white gloves?' I declined – I thought I looked stupid enough already. She packed everything into what looked like a mini-cabin trunk and handed it over with a smile. 'Good luck at the banquet', she said. 'Let me know how it goes....'

Several days later, I drove up to Amsterdam and booked in to the Krasnapolski Hotel. This was a hotel with style, a famous place in its own right, just a five minutes' walk from the royal palace. I had stayed there once before, and so I knew the little side street where the entrance to the hotel's garage is hidden away. Just as well: one wrong turning and I would have ended up in Amsterdam's famous red-light district! By now, I was no longer looking forward to the banquet. After my initial enthusiasm, I now realised that it was pompous, formal and elitist. The affair with the dress suit had made me see that the whole thing was little more than a glorified puppet show. Besides, I had a practical problem: how was I ever going to get the dreaded dress suit on?

I made a first effort in the privacy of my hotel room. I managed the trousers and the shirt, but the problems began with the bow tie and the stiff waistcoat with the screw buttons. I remembered the warning of the lady in the shop in Leuven, a warning which I had failed to heed. I had not practised at home and now I was about to pay the penalty. No matter how I tried, I couldn't fasten either the tie or the waistcoat in the required manner. The tie hung at a crooked angle under my chin and the buttons of the waistcoat kept springing open, just when I thought I had them under control. On more than one occasion, I had to retrieve the buttons from under my bed. Without them, I would never get the waistcoat closed. And without the waistcoat, there was no dress suit. And without the dress suit, I would never be let in to the royal palace.

After half an hour of stumbling around my room like a circus clown, I finally decided there was no other option: I rang down to the hotel receptionist.

'Excuse me, Miss. Could you send someone up to my room to help me? I'm having trouble getting dressed.'

There followed a brief silence, while the receptionist tried to assess whether or not I was a pervert, trying to lure some poor, unsuspecting chambermaid up to his room. In view of the proximity of the red-light district, it was a trick she was probably familiar with. Finally, she answered: 'Of course, Sir. I'll send someone straight away.'

Two minutes later there was a ring at the bell. I opened the door, only to find it blocked by a giant of a man.

'Is there some kind of problem here, Sir?' he asked, in a non-too-friendly voice.

Out of self-defence, I pretended to be a bit stupid, not that it required much pretence: 'Yes, I have to go to the state banquet and I can't get into my dress suit.'

He looked behind me into the room, trying to assess the situation. Was I a sexual deviant or was I genuinely a man in need? Fortunately, he decided that I was the latter and the look of suspicion disappeared from his face. He picked up the suit. 'It looks a bit complicated', he said. I explained about the bow tie and the screw buttons, whilst he studied them from every conceivable angle. 'Don't you worry, Sir. I'll get you inside this suit.'

And he did. But there was just one tiny drawback: I could hardly breathe. By the time he had finished, I wasn't so much wearing the suit: I was strapped and bolted into it. My bow tie was tightened to almost strangulation level and the big fingers of my newly acquired 'dresser' had simply forced the screw buttons into place, breaking the metal threads in the process. 'There', he said proudly. 'They won't move.' He was right. They didn't. The problem was, neither could I – at least not normally.

I thanked my helper and made my way down to the hotel lobby in a series of robot-like movements. A number of other guests for the banquet were already assembled. There was a special bus to take us the hundred or so metres to the palace and the Dam had been specially cordoned off with barriers.

Amongst the crowd I spotted the Belgian Minister of Justice, Marc Verwilghen. He, too, was wearing a dress suit. 'How did you manage to get into that thing?' I asked him. 'I have one with ordinary buttons', he replied. 'I can never get those screw things fastened.' Clearly, he was a man with experience of state banquets.

The private secretary of Queen Paola was waiting to lead us onto the bus and drove with us to the palace. Apart from Verwilghen, there was nobody else I recognised and so I stayed next to him: a friendly face in hostile territory. Upon arrival, we were led off to be introduced to the two royal families. Everyone was wearing a dress suit, but Verwilghen and myself seemed to be the only people who were not wearing medals and decorations. Most of the guests had just one or two medals, but a few, such as Viscount Etienne Davignon, seemed almost to be covered in sashes and crosses. They looked like overdone peacocks and I wondered how they managed to keep their balance without falling over. Everywhere I turned, I saw ministers and senior civil servants, top bankers and major names from the industrial world. It crossed my mind that if someone put a bomb under the palace that evening, the Low Countries would be robbed of their political and economic elite.

Gradually, we all joined the long queue, which was forming outside the hall where the formal introductions to the royal families would take place. I was standing behind ex-minister Van Mierlo and his partner, the writer Connie Palmen. To judge by their appearance, it looked as though they had both been to the same slightly eccentric hairdresser. Although I knew Van Mierlo, I didn't speak to him. He had once demanded that I should be sacked from the NRC, after I had written an article in which I suggested that he was the person most responsible for creating a Chinese-style mandarin culture in the D66 Party. He was a man who liked to talk, but he got upset if anyone dared to talk back.

The queue crept slowly forward, until I could finally see into the room where the royal families stood lined up, like two football teams before a match. At the entrance to the room, a palace official read out the names of the guests, before they went forward to be introduced. All eyes were on the royals, who looked like so many lavishly dressed waxworks. The lighting in the room served only to heighten this Madame Tussaud's effect. If they hadn't kept moving from time to time, you wouldn't have thought they were real! Ahead of me, Van Mierlo disappeared into the royal presence and the official at the door took my invitation.

'Mr. Derk-Jan Eppink', he bawled into the room.

I tried to look confident as I crossed the floor to meet the collective pride of the Houses of Orange and Saxe-Coburg. Queen Beatrix gave me a limp hand and clearly didn't have the faintest idea who I was. This applied equally to Prince Willem-Alexander and Princess Margriet. I had more success with the Belgian royals. King Albert gave a friendly nod, as if he knew me or had at least heard of me, and Queen Paola flashed a knowing smile. Nobody had told me what you are supposed to say on an occasion such as this, and so I confined myself to a polite 'good evening'.

After the formal presentation, we were led through into an elegant reception room, floored in marble and lined from wall to wall with massive guilt-framed mirrors. Here the social ritual began. We were handed an aperitif and I went in search of familiar faces. Luckily, I bumped into the Dutch correspondent of my own paper, *De Standaard*. As we chatted, I started to notice a lot more people I knew – mainly Belgians, some Dutchmen. At least, I wouldn't have to spend the evening alone. I attached myself to a group of Flemish-speaking guests and began to feel more at ease. Unfortunately, as I began to relax, so too did my clothing. A lady leant across and whispered in my ear: 'Your bow tie is undone'. Her words sent a shiver of horror down my spine. This was the nightmare scenario I had feared. The fixing band had torn and the tie was hanging limply down across my waistcoat. A childhood memory of Hans Christian Andersen's story of the 'Emperor's New Clothes' flashed into my brain – I felt naked in the middle of the royal court.

The wife of my colleague from *De Standaard* had seen my predicament and had tried to fix the tie in place with a temporary knot. It seemed to work, but even so, I hardly dared to move. I was certain that the damned thing was going to fall off at any moment, exposing me to instant ridicule and shame. I tried to shuffle my way forward into the banquet room with the other guests, hoping that no one would see.

I was still fingering my tie when a loud voice called out: 'Is Mr.Eppink here?' I almost fainted with shock, convinced that I had somehow committed some terrible blunder. Had my flies been open when I was introduced to the Queen? I checked quickly to make sure they weren't. Or had she found my simple 'good evening' insufficiently courteous?

Two men emerged from the crowd of guests, still calling my name. People who knew me pointed them in the right direction. 'He's over there.' I prepared myself for the worst. I recognised one of the two men as Queen Paola's private secretary and guessed that the other one must be the Chamberlain of the Dutch Court: he certainly strode around as though he owned the place. At last, they spotted me and came across the room. 'Ah, there you are, Mr.Eppink', said the private secretary. 'Would you come with us, please. The Queen would like to talk to you.' I had little choice and followed them toward the reception room, where the royal party was still standing. My heart was pounding. Why did the Queen want to see me? And which queen was it? I hoped that it wasn't Beatrix – she had a well-deserved reputation for severity. We entered and I was led forward by one of my escorts in the direction of the royal group....

It must have been my lucky day – not only did my bow tie stay in place, but it was Queen Paola who wanted to see me! The private secretary introduced us. 'Your Majesty, this is Mr.Eppink.' For the second time, I bade her 'good evening'.

'Mr.Eppink, I have read your book', she said in Dutch. I breathed a sigh of relief: I hadn't done anything wrong, after all. 'I thought it was a very good book, which said a lot about the differences between Belgium and the Netherlands. My husband and my son have also read it. They liked it as well. It is so strange that our two countries are so close, yet so different.'

I was pleasantly surprised by her compliment and explained why I had written the book *Vreemde Buren* (Strange Neighbours): 'If we understand our differences, it will help us to get on better with each other.'

It was not an easy conversation. The Queen spoke in a soft voice and there was a lot of noise from the reception in the background. I only understood about half of what she said and I gave answers which I hoped were appropriate. All of a sudden, she wished me 'Good Luck' and the private secretary indicated that our talk was at an end. I thanked her again for her compliment and turned to leave the room.

It was then that disaster struck: my bow tie sprang loose! It shot forward and dangled down to somewhere near my trouser belt. The only reason it didn't fall to floor was that one small piece of strap was still caught in the collar of my shirt.

Ex-European Commissioner Karel Van Miert was the first to notice this affront to the laws of protocol. 'Ah, your tie is loose', he commented in a loud voice. This caused everyone in the immediate vicinity to turn and look in my direction. I could see them thinking: 'Thank God it's him, and not me.' I wished the ground would open and swallow me up, but it didn't. I felt like Mr.Bean in that sketch where he head-butts the Queen.

Suddenly, a lady detached herself from the crowd of spectators and moved towards me.

'Sir, do not worry', she said. 'This is the most interesting thing that has happened here all evening. Enzo, come and help.' Enzo was her husband and turned out to be the retired politician, Enzo Toxopeus. He was from long before my time, but one of my first jobs for the NRC had been to write his obituary. All newspapers have obituaries for the rich and famous prepared well in advance. I had assumed that he was long since dead, but was pleased to discover that he was not.

'I am always ready for this kind of mishap', Mrs.Toxopeus continued. She rummaged in her handbag and pulled out a large safety pin. In the meantime, two other ladies had come forward to help me in my plight. Together, they took the torn fixing straps of my bow tie and pinned them to the back of my collar. 'That should hold', said Mrs.Toxopeus. 'At least until the end of the banquet. But don't make any sudden moves with your neck. Otherwise it might come loose again.' The crowd of onlookers smiled in amusement. I felt like a two-year-old and turned bright pink with embarrassment.

The bell for the start of the banquet sounded and I once again shuffled forward with the crowd. I was shown to a place next to the private secretary of Queen Beatrix. He was a clean-cut, pleasant man, who kept the conversation going throughout the meal. I had little interest in what he was saying. I was too busy trying to prevent any further problems with my clothing – like my bow tie falling into the soup. Every two minutes I kept fingering my neck, just to make sure that everything was still in place. The pin seemed to be holding, but to my horror the braces of my waistcoat now began to work loose. They had stretched out of place as I was bending forward to eat my soup!

I sat as still as I could, ate as little as possible and just hoped that I would be able to survive the meal. The banquet had a rhythm and an order all of its own. The food was served by a team of palace servants, who moved behind the guests with the natural flow of a river. Moreover, it was a river that swept away everything in its path. There was no chance of a second helping and the plates and dishes were removed in accordance with a precise timetable. The guests who ate slowly were likely to find their unfinished meal whisked away from under their noses!

After the royal families had left, the guests moved through into another room, where brandy was being served. By this time I badly needed a stiff drink, and so I stayed a few minutes, chatting to people I knew. However, when I saw the first people beginning to leave, I also headed for the door. I crossed the Dam, still looking like a lost penguin from the local zoo, and made my way as quickly as possible back to the hotel.

I closed the door of my room with a sigh of relief. The banquet was finally behind me: I was safe. I unpinned my pin, unscrewed my screw buttons and threw the dress suit onto a chair, glad to be free of it at last. I went to lie down on my bed, with cramps in my stomach. My adventures with hanging ties and sagging braces had done little to improve my digestion and I was quickly 'relieved' of my royal meal. My banquet with the constituted bodies had left me feeling like a constipated body!

In the morning I stuffed the dress suit back into its trunk. I never wore one again.

THE HOLY CROSS

When I first arrived in Flanders, I felt that I had come to a land of mysticism. Flanders has something that you simply do not find in Holland: symbols and symbolism. In Holland I had never seen a military parade or a religious procession. The world of secret societies was equally unknown to me. The only symbolic event I can remember was the annual aubade on 30 April: Dynasty Day. Each year as a child, I went with my class to the town hall, where we politely sang the national anthem. The Burgomaster gave a speech from the balcony, praising the Queen and thanking her for the beneficence of her rule. Then we all went home. Other than this brief affair, I have no recollection of any other ceremony or parade. Nor did I feel the lack of them. In this respect, the Netherlands is a bit like a Protestant church: cold, empty and bare.

In Flanders, however, there is a long history of statues, ornaments and saints. Everything is decorated, everything is coloured and – if at all possible – everything is shrouded in an aura of mystery. The Flemish people delight in attributing all their problems to the actions of small groups of agent provocateurs operating out of back rooms, or to the evil influence of black masses or to the unseen hand of corruption. In short, they are masters of the conspiracy theory.

When I joined the editorial team of the *De Standaard* newspaper, I had little intention of becoming involved in this shadowy world. Mysticism was totally alien to me and I didn't really feel comfortable with it. As for Flemish symbolism, I considered that this was purely a matter for the Flemings, knowing that a Dutch 'interloper' would not be tolerated lightly.

Sadly, I was unable to maintain this position of lofty detachment for long. During my very first summer the chief editor came into my office. 'I suppose even a Dutchman has heard of the IJzer Pilgrimage in Diksmuide', he commented scornfully from behind the coffee machine. He moved warily to the farthest corner of the room, seeking to gauge my reaction. To his obvious relief, I replied positively. Yes, I had heard of it, but I had never been there.

'Well, now is your chance', he said hastily. 'I'd like you to take a run down there and have a look at the ceremony from an outsider's point of view.' The speed with which he made this suggestion led me to suspect that I had just walked into a trap. The IJzer Pilgrimage commemorates the terrible horrors of the First World War, the endless battles in the mud which cost hundreds of thousands of young men their lives. At the same time, the war in general and the pilgrimage in particular have also come to assume important symbolic roles in the development of the Flemish national identity. In the trenches, most of the officers were French-speaking, whereas most of the ordinary soldiers were Flemings. As a result, both had difficulty in understanding the other, a communication problem which led to tragedy and needless loss of life on more than one occasion. These events highlighted a deep social division within the country. Belgium was a French-speaking land run by French-speaking politicians and a small French-speaking Flemish elite. This meant that the ordinary Fleming in the street was subject to the rule of a regime whose language he did not understand. The first steps to change this intolerable situation were taken along the muddy and bloody banks of the River IJzer between 1914 and 1918. Consequently, the IJzer Tower at Diksmuide does not simply remember those who died: it also commemorates the Flemish struggle for autonomy. It is not just another war memorial: it is also a monument to social emancipation.

These were dangerous waters, particularly for an 'outsider'. To make matters worse, the IJzer Tower – with its famous slogan 'All for Flanders, Flanders for Christ' – had also acquired a political dimension in the course of its troubled history.

A radical element within the Flemish Movement did not merely wish to achieve greater Flemish autonomy within Belgium, but actually sought to break away from the Belgian State and set up an independent Flemish nation. During the Second World War, these radical nationalists collaborated with the Germans, in the hope that this might buy them their freedom from the dominance of the French-speaking ruling class. In turn, the Germans used the Tower as a propaganda weapon to promote their idea of a Greater German Empire and to coax the Flemish Movement into still closer ties with the Nazi regime for example, by recruiting volunteers for service on the Eastern Front.

After the war, the Belgian State took its revenge. Almost the entire wing of the Flemish Movement was imprisoned. No distinction was made between moderates and hard-liners. All were tarred with the same brush and all were heavily punished – many by having their pension rights withdrawn, a source of grievance which still rankles with many of their descendants, even today. This was the so-called 'period of repression' and tension was running high. On two separate occasions the IJzer Tower was damaged by explosions. Although the perpetrators were never caught, many suspected the Belgian Government of being behind the plot.

The IJzer Tower had become a bitterly disputed symbol. Its praiseworthy message of 'No More War' had been stained through its association with Hitler's tyranny. To the less nationally-minded Flemings, such as the liberals and the socialists, the Tower was a symbol of the 'black shirts', a monument to 'collaboration'. For the more moderate nationalists, it remained a fitting symbol for the Flemish struggle. The radicals wanted to transform it into a symbol of Flemish independence. In other words, the Tower began to divide the Flemish people, instead of uniting them.

I asked my editor for some thinking time. 'This could be tricky', I argued. 'The whole IJzer business is a hornet's nest. And you're asking me, a Dutchmen, to write a piece for a Flemish public on the most famous and most divisive Flemish symbol of all!' He looked me straight in the eye and I knew my fate was sealed: 'But that's exactly why you're just the right person – we need a sober and unprejudiced point of view. And who better to give it than a Hollander!'

In the months before the Pilgrimage, the political struggle surrounding the Tower had once again become intense. The Pilgrimage was normally organised by the official IJzer Pilgrimage Committee, but this year there was a rival. The radical nationalists had set up the IJzer Pilgrimage Forum, which was said to have sympathies with the right-wing Flemish Block Party. Civil war seemed to be brewing among Flemish activists and it looked as if I was going to be right in the middle of it.

On a Sunday towards the end of August, I rode to Diksmuide to do my report. It was a long drive and so I left early – I wanted to get to the Tower in good time. Diksmuide has been beautifully rebuilt and now sits sleepily at the heart of the Flanders coastal plain. The town square is lined with cafes and restaurants, and the day of the pilgrimage is undoubtedly their busiest day of the year. The road to the memorial is a cross between a market and a fun fair. There are stalls everywhere, selling all kinds of Flemish memorabilia: pamphlets, t-shirts, sweaters, stickers, flags. The Flemish Lion is much in evidence and a beer tap is always somewhere close at hand. This is the Flemish nationalists' great day out and they mean to enjoy it. On the packed cafe terraces, activists swap stories of their contributions to the cause. The government gets its usual hammering for 'its failure to stop the Frenchifying of the Flemish zone around Brussels.' But it all seems a bit passé. The large-scale marches in Brussels took place during the 1960's and even the famous 'battle' for Voeren dates back to the 1980's. The 'glory days' are gone – all that now remains is symbolism and nostalgia.

In the old days, tens of thousands of nationalists made their way to Diksmuide for the annual pilgrimage. In recent times numbers have dwindled to between 5,000 and 10,000, depending on whether you listen to the police or the organisers. I followed the line of stalls down to the memorial enclosure and was shown to my place in the press box. Next to me was a tall, thin and very silent journalist from *La Libre Belgique*. I said 'bonjour' and he smiled briefly in return, but otherwise made no sound. It was clear from the expression on his face that he did not find the afternoon to his liking. An assignment to the IJzer Pilgrimage is a kind of punishment for the members of the French-speaking press – the very worst job of the year. I wondered what he had done to deserve it and left him to suffer in silence.

The ceremony itself was pompous and full of exaggerated symbolism. It was also much too elaborate, considering the limited numbers in attendance. I suggested to my French-speaking colleague that the whole event seemed a little out of date, as we approached the close of the twentieth century. *'Ah oui,* that is the very least that one can say.' It was his longest sentence of the day. Towards the end of the proceedings, the pilgrims sang three national hymns: the 'Flemish Lion', the anthem of Flanders; the 'Wilhelmus', the national anthem of the Netherlands; and also 'Die Stem', the national anthem of South Africa under white rule. The apparent aim of these three anthems was to emphasise the broadness of the Dutch-speaking family of nations. All it managed to achieve was total confusion. Diksmuide on Pilgrimage Day is the only place in the world where 'Die Stem' is still sung. As a result – and not surprisingly – almost nobody knew the words. I was one of the few who were able to join in with the chorus of *'Ons vir jou Suid-Afrika'*. My French-speaking neighbour maintained a stony and dignified silence.

To the sound of trumpets, a party of standard bearers marched past, whilst a group of young girls in virginal white dresses danced across a stage. This was followed by reminders of the First World War, including the reading of poems and letters from Flemish soldiers who had fought at the front. I looked around me and found it impossible to imagine the horrors that had taken place here 85 years ago. Farmers in the area still regularly find bits of metal and bones in their fields – victims of the 'Great War Between Nations'.

Suddenly, there was an air of unrest around the Tower of Peace. The Chairman of the IJzer Pilgrimage Committee, Lionel Vandenberghe, an idealistic academic from Antwerp, had mounted the podium and his appearance had been greeted with catcalls and whistling by a group of 'pilgrims', each wearing a yellow scarf.

All around us were symbols of unity and reconciliation. During the mass we had sung 'Give peace in our time, O Lord' and had prayed 'Dear Lord, do not let your princely people of the Old Netherlands be consumed by hate, division and shame.' The Tower itself was decked with slogans reading 'what hate destroys, love rebuilds.' Vandenberghe appealed for 'silence, serenity and contemplation', but his appeal fell on deaf ears. Unmoved by the spirit of the place, his yellow scarfed opponents – who had now closed ranks to form a single group – continued to try and boo him off the platform.

I decided to leave the press box, to see if I could get a better view of what was going on. A little further along, in a reserved part of the tribune, sat politicians from the Volksunie and the CVP. The section of the tribune immediately behind them was packed with supporters and also several officials of the Flemish Block. The Blockers began to edge forward and had soon worked their way into the area reserved for the political guests. The Volksunie politicians soon found themselves surrounded by hordes of Block hard-liners, who were aided by the Block's own so-called 'security' service, *Voorpost* (Outpost).

Pushing and shoving inevitably resulted and the situation looked like getting out of hand. It seemed as if the Block, *Voorpost*, *Were Di*, the Nationalist Students Union, the Flemish Nationalist Youth Movement, even the Block's own uniformed brass band, were all getting ready to storm the IJzer Tower. I recognised some of the faces from the articles I had already written on the Block and it was obvious that they were all intent on a showdown.

Matters quickly reached boiling point. The Block politicians began to blow on whistles, while members of the Youth Movement began to bang drums and chant slogans. A number of the more radical nationalists broke through the security barriers and made a rush for the Tower, in a kind of modern day re-enactment of the storming of the Bastille. In their path stood a group of Flemish veterans, who scattered in confusion. I then realised that the next person in their line of advance was me! By this time I had moved close to the Tower and had a good view of the Block militants as they came forward. They screamed, they swore, some were even foaming at the mouth. It was not a pretty sight, but it was instantly clear that this rabble intended to let nothing stand in the way of their occupation of the IJzer Tower. Following the wise example of the veterans, I, too, began to fall back, but found my retreat blocked by a line of muscular men, who had taken up position on the steps of the podium. This was the Pilgrimage Committee's protection team and they were obviously determined to defend the Tower at all costs.

I hesitated. What should I do? Join the line of defenders? Or just make a run for it? My instinct for survival got the better of me: I made a run for it. Besides, it would have been too much of an historical irony if I, a Hollander of all people, had been crushed to death between two rival wings of the Flemish Movement. Although it would, perhaps, have been a fitting and symbolic end to the ideal of the Greater Dutch Nation.

Luck was on my side and I managed to scramble to safety. I turned to watch the clash between the two opposing groups and saw that the security team on the steps were comfortably holding their ground. Robbed of their prize, the angry Blockers returned to the spectator's gallery, where they continued a stream of ugly chants. The other guests, many with tears in their eyes, looked on in astonishment and disgust at this desecration of the IJzer legacy. When tempers had cooled a little, there was an attempt to sing the 'Flemish Lion'. But even then the Block supporters maintained their cries of 'Split up Belgium'.

So ended my day in Diksmuide. Shaken but otherwise unharmed, I left the memorial enclosure and drove back to the office. News of the 'storming' had already reached my colleagues. I sat down at my desk and saw the editor approaching. 'Did you have a nice time?' he enquired. 'At least you saw something worth seeing. If you're a good boy, we'll let you go again next year...'

The next year turned out to be a far more relaxed affair. The nationalist militants of the Flemish Block had decided to boycott the IJzer Pilgrimage and consequently did not turn up. All was quiet and the ceremony would be able to follow its usual course. Like the year before, I had driven to Diksmuide early in the morning. I sat thinking about the story I was planning to write. A detailed story, rich in history and deep in insight. A story unmarred by internal disunity and confrontation. A story with no risk that I might get crushed to a pulp by rival groups! I began to think that I might actually enjoy my afternoon. To kill the time until the ceremony, I turned on the radio and tuned it to the BBC World Service. To my surprise, I heard the British national anthem. The news that followed it was even more amazing: 'This morning Lady Diana, the Princess of Wales, died...' I could hardly believe what I was hearing. Britain's most popular royal had been killed in a car crash in Paris.

From a professional point of view, I knew immediately what this meant. No space for my detailed story, nor for my rich history, still less for my deep insights. For the first time in many years, the IJzer Pilgrimage would be forced off the front page of every Belgian newspaper. I had come to Diksmuide as a journalist. Events in Paris had reduced me to the status of a tourist.

After this, I never returned to the IJzer Pilgrimage, but followed its progress – or rather its decline – in the press. Each year there were fewer and fewer pilgrims, and each year their average age rose steadily. The appeals for reconciliation continued. There was even an apology for the collaboration which had taken place during the Second World War. The IJzer Tower was still a symbol, but for me it had lost much of its mystique. I no longer saw a sinister and threatening structure at the centre of a Flemish separatist conspiracy, but rather a monument to the victims of the Great War and a permanent call for world peace. With a little creative imagination, I even came to see it as an emblem of pacifism.

Having left the Holy Cross of Flanders behind me, I did not really expect to have much further involvement with the other great Flemish symbols. 'All for Flanders, Flanders for Christ' was simply a relic of the past. I knew exactly what it meant and I knew how to differentiate between its fact and its fiction.

Notwithstanding my expectations, I was soon destined to come into contact with another important part of this world of symbols and symbolism: the freemasons. Freemasonry was a closed book, as far as I was concerned. All I knew were the horror stories I had been told as a child. Namely, that the masons were a secret society, where members were chosen by lot to commit ritual suicide. This was enough to scare the pants off an impressionable 10-year-old. To add to my confusion, I couldn't understand why these suicidal maniacs should be called 'masons'. Were they all members of the building trade union, perhaps?

My first contact with freemasonry in Belgium occurred almost by chance. A member of the Flemish Liberal Democrat Party – the VLD – invited me to lunch. In itself, this was nothing strange: after all, he was a politician and I was a political journalist. Even so, I was slightly puzzled why a man I hardly knew should ring up and offer me a free dinner. We met a few days later at a restaurant on the Fish Market in Brussels and began chatting about politics in Belgium and the Netherlands. All very ordinary and all just what you would expect. Until, that is, he asked quietly: 'Have you ever been interested in the Lodge?' I spluttered into my coffee and managed to reply that the subject certainly interested me, although it was something I knew little about. 'Then why not join our lodge and learn some more?' he continued smoothly. 'We are looking for some good young members.' He looked at me earnestly, one might even say hopefully, but I kept my reply as neutral as possible. 'I'm not really the kind of person who goes in for secret societies', I answered. I added that the requirement to attend lodge meetings would be difficult for someone in my profession and also that I wasn't too keen on the initiation rite. This involves the new member being led blindfold into a darkened room, where he has to answer questions put by the existing members of the lodge. The initiate is then led outside, whilst the lodge decides whether or not to accept him. If the decision is favourable, he is taken back inside and the blindfold is removed, so that he can meet his new colleagues. If the decision is negative, he is simply put back on the street, without ever having had the chance to see – or identify – his interrogators. 'I find it all rather spooky', I told my disappointed host. 'To be honest, I'd prefer not to get involved.'

Nevertheless, this strange encounter had awakened my curiosity and from then on I tried to keep a closer watch on the activities of the masons' network. For the first time in many years, the number of masons in the federal government – known from the respective colours of the political parties as the 'Purple-Green' Coalition – was relatively high. Almost a third of the ministerial posts were in the hands of lodge members, including

Louis Michel, Luc Van den Bossche, Laurette Onkelinx, André Flahaut, Rik Daems and Secretary of State Pierre Chevalier. The subject remains, however, something of a taboo. Whenever I ask a masons-related question, I am almost invariably met with blank looks and stony silence. 'No comment' or 'that is not relevant' are the most common replies. This reluctance is hard to understand, particularly at the beginning of the 21st century, when the old antagonisms no longer have the power to sway the emotions as they once did. What is the point of an anticlerical organisation, now that there are hardly any clerics left? There is even talk of an 'open dialogue' between the church and freemasonry. In March 1997, for example, Cardinal Danneels gave a speech to the *La Fraternité* Lodge of Hervé Hasquin of the Francophone Liberal Party, an ex-minister in the Brussels Regional Government and later Minister-President of the French Community. According to the church authorities, the Cardinal spoke on the 'value and meaning of sacred symbols'.

Indeed, it is noticeable how both the Church and the masons rely heavily on more or less the same kind of symbols and language. Danneels – who the Vatican sees as a bridge to the modern age – and a number of the more progressive masons have both been arguing for a 'frank and free exchange of views' between their respective organisations. It is also remarkable how both religious and freemason considerations were involved in the negotiations which eventually led to the forming of the 1999 federal government. The first tentative moves towards a 'Purple' Coalition between the 'red' socialist party and the 'blue' liberal party were made by politicians active in the masons' network. In the *De Morgen* newspaper on 30 March 1999, the liberal politician Karel De Gucht – an ardent and open advocate of freemasonry – made known that various politicians in the socialist and liberal parties had been discussing the possibility of a 'purple' government as early as the autumn of 1998. Amongst those involved were the Ghent socialist Luc Van den Bossche (the then Minister of Home Affairs), Tuur Van Wallendael (member of the Flemish regional parliament) and Fred Erdman (Chairman of the Socialist Party). Coincidentally or not, all three were members of the Lodge although Van den Bossche has not been particularly active during the past 10 years. The talks came to an end in December 1998, when the leading Flemish socialist, Louis Tobback, let it be known that he was not in favour of a 'purple experiment'. He thought that any such experiment was more likely to lead to 'black and blue' than to 'purple', and he remained firmly convinced that it was not possible to govern Flanders without Catholic support. Moreover, within the existing 'Rome-Red' Coalition between the socialists and the Christian-Democrats Tobback was anxious to maintain good relations with the powerful Catholic trade union, the ACV. Add to this the fact that Tobback – like other leading politicians such as Johan Vande Lanotte, Marc Verwilghen, Herman De Croo, Guy Verhofstadt and Frank Vandenbroucke – is not a mason, and it is easy to understand why he ordered the talks to be torpedoed. 'It is clear evidence of the political poverty in our land', wrote a disgruntled Karel De Gucht, 'that such a promising initiative should be smothered at birth.'

In these talks, the freemasons in the liberal VLD and the socialist SP had been trying to recreate at a national level the same 'purple' success that had already been achieved at provincial level (Limburg) and in some of the larger cities (notably Ghent). In Limburg, it was Willy Claes of the SP –also a prominent member of the *Tijl Uilenspiegel* Lodge in Hasselt – who had been the driving force behind the 'purple' coalition. His political successor, Steve Stevaert, is also a mason. In East Flanders, it was the socialist governor, Herman Balthazar – a member of the *De Zwijger* Lodge – who was the main architect of 'purple' alliances in cities such as Ghent, Aalst and Eeklo. 'Purple' was seen as the only way to break the Catholic stranglehold on power that had dominated the political landscape for the last 50 years.

After the national and regional elections on 13 June 1999, there were many freemasons in both the socialist and liberal parties who were anxious to try and form new 'purple' majorities in Brussels and Bruges. Others in the VLD and SP were less sure. The socialist SP had ruled jointly for many years with the CVP and was reluctant to break this traditional link. In the liberal VLD – even after their electoral triumph on 13 June – there were many who argued that an alliance with the CVP would create a more 'natural majority' than a partnership with either the socialists or the 'green' ecological parties.

In French-speaking Wallonia, the move towards a 'purple' coalition progressed more rapidly. The French Christian-Democratic Party lost heavily on 13 June and the liberals and the socialists had already made a pre-election agreement to drop their former partner. Both had had enough of the Christian Democrats, whose power was out of all proportion to its electoral strength. Moreover, the social and economic differences between the Gaullist liberals and the privatising socialists were no longer as great as they had once been and both were anxious to share power without the limitations of a traditional Christian-Democrat agenda. Once again freemasonry was on hand to smooth the pathway towards the new alliance: liberal Chairman Louis Michel and socialist top man Philippe Busquin are both lodge members, the latter at the appropriately named *Les Amis Discrets* – Discreet Friends – in Nijvel. This 'purple' coalition was expanded by the addition of the Ecolo Party – the main winner of new seats in the Walloon elections – thereby creating a model that would be employed elsewhere throughout the country to form 'purple-green' majorities at national, regional and municipal levels.

The frequency with which the masons play an important role in the politics of Belgium is striking, particularly in comparison with neighbouring countries, where the influence of the Lodge is much less strongly felt. This even applies with regard to Great Britain – the cradle of freemasonry, where there are still more than 350,000 accredited members. The term 'freemason' also comes from England and is a contraction of 'freestone mason' – the name given to the old independent craftsmen who built the great cathedrals of Europe.

During this medieval period it was important that the secrets of the trade should be preserved. As a result, every new apprentice to the mason's guild had to undergo a strict initiation ceremony –just like the freemasons of today. Modern freemasonry has its origins in religion. This is made clear by many of the most important masonic symbols and metaphors. Life is seen as the construction of a perfect building – the Temple – and each person is a 'rough stone', which needs to be shaped so that it can take its place in the finished structure. To this end, the mason makes symbolic use of a compass and a set square to determine our 'right relationship' to God, who in masonic terminology is referred to as the 'Supreme Architect of the Universe'. Little wonder that Cardinal Danneels had little trouble in finding points of common contact for his 'free dialogue' with the *La Fraternité* Lodge in 1997!

Originally, there was no conflict between the Church and the new society of 'free masons'. Freemasonry was given a formal organisation – and tacit official sanction – with the founding of the Grand Lodge in London in 1717. The Grand Lodge is still seen as the 'Mother of all Lodges' and its decision still determines whether or not other lodges in the world are recognised as 'regular' or 'irregular'. The main criterion for this decision is the lodge's acceptance of the god-figure, the Supreme Architect of the Universe. If the lodge accepts the Supreme Architect, it will be recognised by the Grand Lodge as 'regular'. If the lodge rejects the Supreme Architect, it will not be recognised by the Grand Lodge and will be labelled as 'irregular'.

In the course of the centuries, the freemasonry movement in Europe has become divided along 'regular' and 'irregular' lines. There is an Anglo-Saxon grouping of largely 'regular' lodges, counterbalanced by a mainly 'irregular' Mediterranean wing. Most of the lodges in the Netherlands (6,000 members) are 'regular' and are hard to distinguish from other Protestant church organisations. Even the term 'freemason' has become neutral to the point of meaninglessness. The Lodge has no political agenda in the Netherlands. A number of prominent liberals have been members of the masons – such as Professor P.J.Oud (1886-1968), founder of the VVD – but freemasonry as a movement has never played a significant role in the politics of The Hague.

By contrast, most of the Belgian lodges (20,000 members) are 'irregular', a fact tied up with the origins and development of freemasonry in Belgium. In 1830 most of the freemasons were loyal to the Orange (Dutch) cause and were more concerned with their activities in the 'wet room' – as their drinking chambers were known – than with the growing movement for an independent Belgian nation. This was to change dramatically after the Belgian Revolution of 1830. The Belgian masons saw the new king, Leopold I, as their natural figurehead and when the lodge the 'Great East' of Belgium was founded on 23 February 1833, it was assumed that Leopold would be the first Grand Master. It was not to be. In spite of a brief flirtation with freemasonry – as a young man he was a member of a lodge in Switzerland –, Leopold now saw himself as a representative of Unionism, the alliance between Catholics and liberals which lay at the very foundation of the new Belgian state. This unifying role was incompatible with a position as Grand Master of the Great East and so he turned the offer down. Instead the position went to the Chairman of the Senate, Baron Goswin de Stassart who had been a prefect in The Hague under Napoleon.

The first cracks in the uneasy Catholic-liberal alliance soon began to appear and it was not long before the freemasons came into conflict with the Church. In the first instance, the dispute centred on the control of education. Under pressure from the Ultramontanes, the educational system of the new Belgian nation was very firmly Catholic. No account was taken of the wishes or feelings of other believers and non-believers (Protestants, freethinkers, etc.). In political terms, this pushed the Flemish Protestants and the liberal-freethinking-freemasonry grouping into each other's arms – with the Catholic Church as the clear and common enemy. To counteract the Roman influence in education, on 20 November 1834 the freemasons set up the VUB – the Free University of Brussels. Even to this day the VUB and its French-speaking counterpart, the ULB, remain centres of Belgian freemasonry – anyone wishing to make a career in the Free University and in its associated hospital is almost obliged to join the Lodge.

There followed a period of uneasy truce, but following the declaration of papal infallibility in 1870 the break between the Church and freemasonry became final. The Catholic establishment seemed all-powerful and freemasonry became the last refuge of liberal resistance. The traditional position of the masons that 'the lodges should not become involved in religious or political issues' was scrapped from the statutes. In 1872 even the concept of the Supreme Architect of the Universe was rejected. The Great East now stood foursquare as the enemy of the Church – and vice versa. The forces of clericalism were now openly opposed by the equally potent forces of anticlericalism.

These developments inevitably led Belgian freemasonry in the direction of atheism. As a result, the lodges not only offered a natural home for liberal politicians and thinkers, but also for many prominent socialists, such as Emile Vandervelde and Camille Huysmans. Many reminders of the freemasonry of this period can still be seen today, particularly in Brussels. One of the city's main parks – between the Palace and the House of the Nation – was laid out in the shape of a compass and a set square. Numerous streets and squares were named after leading masons, such as the soldiers Auguste Belliard and Jean Meiser, or the politicians André Fontainas, Charles de Brouckère, Jules Anspach, August Reyers, Emile Jacqmain and Louis Schmidt.

During the two world wars of the 20th century, the conflict between the Church and the Lodge was temporarily set aside in the cause of national unity. However, in the postwar years the struggle was once again resumed, reaching a climax in the so-called 'Battle for the Schools' in the 1950's. The socialist-liberal government of Prime Minister Van Acker (1954-1958) launched a fierce attack against the Catholic monopoly in education. This provoked an equally fierce clerical reaction and Belgian society very quickly became divided along sectarian lines. Once again, the power of the Church proved to be too great and Van Acker's 'purple' coalition – consisting mainly of freemasons – was voted out of office: for the rest of the century either the liberals or the socialists would be forced to work with the Catholic CVP, if the country was to be governed.

These political developments were reflected in a number of radical changes within the freemasonry movement itself. The Great East remained strongly anticlerical and as an 'irregular' lodge was cut off from the mainstream of 'regular' mason activity. This was particularly damaging for contacts with the United States, where the 'regular' lodges had millions of influential members, including several recent Presidents: Franklin D.Roosevelt (1933-45), Harry S.Truman (1945-1953), Lyndon B.Johnson (1963-1969), Gerald Ford (1974-77) and George Bush Snr. (1989-1993). For many sectors of the Belgian economy – notably the diamond trade in Antwerp – the bridge to the American market, via the Lodge, was of great importance. However, this bridge could only be used through 'regular' channels. As a result, many Belgian freemasons decided to withdraw from the 'irregular' Great East and on 4 December 1959 they set up the Grand Lodge of Belgium. The Grand Lodge returned to many of the basic principles of the masonic tradition, including non-activity in politics and the reinstatement of the Supreme Architect of the Universe. This led to the Grand Lodge being recognised as 'regular', following an inspection visit from London in 1965. Unfortunately, many of the lodge's members were more concerned with business contacts than with masonic principles. The 'regular' rules were hardly followed at all, resulting in a break with London and a reclassification as an 'irregular' lodge in 1979.

This was not to the liking of a number of masonic purists, who consequently founded the Regular Grand Lodge of Belgium on 15 June 1979. The majority of the new lodge's members were military personnel from NATO, but a number of existing Flemish lodges also decided to join the new movement, including *Les Disciples de Salomon* in Leuven and *De Wijngaardenrank* in Aarschot where one of the members was the politician Jos Daems, father of Rik Daems, a minister in the first Verhofstadt government. Pierre Chevalier is another of the few politicians to belong to a 'regular' lodge. The Regular Grand Lodge (1,500 members) continues to be recognised by London. The Great East (10,000 members) and the Grand Lodge (4,000 members) remain 'irregular'.

In principle, the freemasons are an all-male society, but in the course of time a number of mixed lodges or even all-women lodges have developed. The first of these was the *Droit Humain*, a mixed lodge founded in 1911, amongst whose present-day members is Els Witte, the former rector of the Free University of Brussels. It was not until 1981 that the first lodge exclusively for women was founded: the Women's Grand Lodge, with the Socialist politician Anne-Marie Lizin as one of its most prominent figures.

In general, socialist politicians belong to the Great East, whilst their liberal counterparts tend to be members of the Grand Lodge. For example, Socialist leader André Cools, who was murdered in 1991, was a member of the Great East, through his affiliation with the *L'Incorruptible* Lodge in Seraing. But there is no hard and fast rule. Luc Van den Bossche and Eric Derycke (both socialists) belong to the Grand Lodge. So, too, for many years, did Karel Van Miert. On the other hand, liberals such as Karel De Gucht and Ward Beysen are members of the Great East, respectively at the *Ontwaken* Lodge in Aalst and the *De Geuzen* Lodge in Antwerp. In other words, the society of freemasons is not just one organisation but many different organisations; there is not just one lodge, but several lodges. It is this that makes Belgian freemasonry such a colourful tapestry.

Conflicts within lodges or between lodges occur regularly. However, there are some actions that are frowned on by all sides. No socialist or liberal leader would ever dare to put himself forward as the 'spokesman of freemasonry'. This would be regarded by all masons as a flagrant misuse of the Lodge for political purposes. Freemasonry has no need of a pope-like figurehead.

The writer Andries Van den Abeele once told me: 'No fights are more fiercely fought than the fights between freemasons.' In 1991 he published a book on the subject, called 'The Children of Hiram'. In it he wrote: 'Whoever breaks the lodge's code of honour, is likely to find himself called before a masonic court.' This masonic court would then pass judgement on the member who had 'gone astray'. If he was pronounced guilty, he could be suspended or even expelled from the lodge: 'put to sleep', as masonic terminology so quaintly puts it.

By constantly trying to seek a balance in the precarious Belgian social and political system, between right and left, Catholic and liberal, freemasonry itself has become an important element in the making of social and political appointments. This is perhaps most noticeable in the judiciary. If the judge has a Catholic background, then it is almost certain his deputy will be a liberal or a socialist – and probably a freemason as well! This same division applies equally in the world of politics. Promising Catholics turn to the christian democrats for support and advancement, whereas promising freethinkers look to the Socialists or Liberals. In the latter case membership of the freemasons can be a distinct advantage, since quite often the 'kingmakers' of both Socialists and Liberals can be found amongst the lists of local lodge members.

In the past, a socialist who wanted a job in the Antwerp judicial system had little option but to seek the help of 'brother' Fred Erdman. Similarly, a liberal who wanted a key post in Ghent was obliged to ask the 'advice' of 'brother' Geert Versnick, Member of Parliament and one of Guy Verhofstadt's right hand men. This system of political appointments permeates every level of Belgian society and applies equally to top positions in the civil and diplomatic services. The Catholic/freethinking divide can even be found in the exalted halls of the royal court. The Secretary of the King's Cabinet is Jacques van Ypersele de Strihou, a French-speaking Christian-Democrat, whereas the Grand Marshall, diplomat Jan Willems, is a socialist freemason. The trend towards the use of more objective criteria to decide judicial and administrative appointments will eventually diminish the influence of this kind of political horse trading. It will, however, take many, many years: the system is far more deeply rooted than most outside observers could ever imagine.

The links between politics and freemasonry are used by the majority of politicians to promote their own careers. As Andries Van den Abeele once put it: 'Politicians generally need the Lodge more than the Lodge needs them. The truly dedicated freemasons have little time and even less respect for politicians who seek to use the Lodge to further their own political career plan.' In this respect, it should be noted that the politicians only form a small minority of lodge members. The majority comes from the ranks of the civil service or the state education system. Education has always been a key area of interest for the masons and even today there is a very clear *Kulturkampf* in Flanders between the Catholic establishment and those who wish to see their dominance broken. And this is a struggle in which the Lodge is in a strong position to help. The cabinet offices of the past Flemish Ministers of Education Luc Van den Bossche and Eddy Baldewijns – Socialist Member of Parliament and also member of the Great East in Hasselt – both contained freemason officials who 'regulated' appointments within the local education system.

In the Wetstraat – at the very heart of central government – the presence of freemasonry is less strongly felt. However, very occasionally the influence of the compass and the set square can be seen in action. One such occasion was on 19 October 1995, when Willy Claes was forced to defend himself in parliament against charges of corruption. At the time he was also Secretary-General of NATO and wished to make use of his parliamentary immunity from prosecution. His barrister, Van den Heuvel, suffered a mild stroke during the first part of the proceedings and was unable to make a final plea on his client's behalf. Consequently, Claes was obliged to make the closing plea himself. The sitting was held behind closed doors, but a number of MP's later told me what happened. Claes appealed directly to the Lower House in unmistakably masonic terms: 'I address myself directly to those of you who have also known dark days, in the hope that you will once again help me towards the light... I am certain that my plea will not be in vain.' Beforehand several freemason MP's had also telephoned known or suspected masons in the House, with the request that they should stand by 'brother Willy Claes'.

It was an impressive show of strength but it was not enough. Of the 150 MP's present, 97 voted that the matter should be referred to the High Court, 52 voted against and 1 abstained. Claes' own socialist parties were only good for 42 votes, so it is clear that the influence of the Lodge secured him at least 10 votes from other political parties. The gap, however, had been too great for even the masons to bridge. Claes lost his parliamentary immunity and the next day he was forced to resign as Secretary-General of NATO.

The most heated public incident between the Christian-Democrats and the freemasons occurred on 8 May 1998, during an open parliamentary debate on the report of a Committee of Inquiry into the murky world of cults and sects. The Committee had drawn up a list of 189 suspect groups, ranging from the Church of Satan to Opus Dei, and from Abrasax to the Charismatic Movement which had many followers in the royal court during the reign of King Boudewijn. The Chairman of the Committee of Inquiry was Serge Moureaux, a French-speaking socialist MP and also a freemason. The motion to accept the report was proposed by 'brother' Antoine Duquesne, then a Liberal Member of Parliament and later Minister of the Interior. The official Opposition spokesman, Luc Willems of the CVP, gave a lacklustre performance and the members of his party seemed equally uninspired. Most of them sat reading their newspapers. All this changed when the list of 'sects' was read out, and it was found to include almost all the mainstream religious groups! The subsequent debate was bitter and acrimonious in the extreme. The leader of the CVP grouping in the Lower House, Paul Tant, accused Moureaux of 'a lodge operation'. Moureaux replied that he was being persecuted by 'sectarian and integrationalist forces'. The report was passed, but in a typical Belgian compromise it was agreed that the list of sects should be left for 'further consideration and amendment'.

Freemasons always claim that the Lodge has little influence on day-to-day politics. However, a story recently told to me by a

Flemish research student would seem to suggest otherwise. She presented herself at the cabinet of Minister of Labour Laurette Onkelinx, a French-speaking socialist and also a mason. My researcher friend hoped to discuss some of her findings with the Minister, but first had to get past her cabinet secretary. Their conversation went something like this:

Cabinet secretary: 'Are you French-speaking?'

Researcher: 'No, I am Flemish.'

Cabinet secretary: 'Are you a member of the socialist movement?'

Researcher: 'No, I don't belong to any political party.'

Cabinet secretary: 'Are you a member of the Lodge, perhaps?'

Researcher: 'No, of course not.'

Cabinet secretary: 'My dear young lady, what on earth are you doing here?'

My writings on the subject of freemasonry had a strange follow-up. Without asking, I was sent some information literature by the Prelate of Opus Dei. If anything, this organisation was even more unknown to me than freemasonry had been. I had heard all the usual stories of black masses and religious conspiracies and had come to associate Opus Dei with Catholic fundamentalism at its worst. I was almost ashamed to open the envelope, but, like a good journalist, curiosity finally got the better of me. The contents turned out to be a summary of recent editions of the *Osservatore Romano*, the official newspaper of the Vatican, in which the good works of the Catholic Church and of its Pope were given full and somewhat exaggerated coverage. Further envelopes continued to arrive and gradually they began to get thicker and thicker. Some contained material about the founder of Opus Dei, the Spanish priest Josémaría Escrivá. Others invited me to attend meetings. Should I go? 'What in the name of all that's holy would a good Protestant find to interest him at a meeting of Catholic fundamentalists?' asked my spiritual conscience. 'What have you got to lose?' replied my professional instinct. Professional instinct won.

After my encounters with the IJzer Tower and the world of freemasonry, I was now hot on the trail of another of Flanders' great mystical symbols. Would I find black masses and sacrificial virgins: the Belgian Parliament had labelled Opus Dei as one of the 189 suspect sects? Or would I find serious old men in raincoats discussing the finer points of Catholic theology? It was to answer these questions that I set out one misty Saturday morning to attend an Opus Dei meeting at the Congress Building in Brussels.

The purpose of the meeting was to celebrate the 100th anniversary of the birth of Josémaría Escrivá (20 April 1902), the founder of the movement. One of Escrivá's French biographers gave an exhaustive summary of the Spanish priest's life and work, which was followed by an equally lengthy documentary film on the same subject. Escrivá had founded Opus Dei in 1928 as a lay organisation, which sought to worship God through the ritual performance of mundane, everyday tasks. Originally, the movement was neither large-scale nor spectacular: it was for ordinary people doing ordinary jobs. According to his followers, Escrivá wanted to 'show his passionate love for the world' by enclosing it in a web of ordinary deeds, performed through faith. In other words, Opus Dei attempted to combine Christian spirituality with secular labour. Bishop Leonard of Namur, a tall man with a loud voice, gave the meeting a philosophical framework with an impenetrable speech about 'Christian materialism'.

I sat quietly in the corner of the hall, keeping a sharp look out for the slightest sign of political conspiracy or satanic wickedness. I was to be sadly disappointed. There was not a single politician or public figure amongst the 300 or so people present. The majority were old ladies who were long past their pension age. There were also a big number of young people, but nearly all of them spoke Italian, Spanish or Polish. It was difficult to imagine this mixed gathering as a hotbed of religious perversion, let alone as the nerve centre for political conspiracy and manipulation.

It was clear that almost all of those present were deeply religious and totally committed to their beliefs. After talking to these men and women for 10 minutes, all mystery surrounding Opus Dei fell away: there was nothing sinister or machiavellian here. On the contrary, they were gentle and friendly and kind: just ordinary, nice people, trying to worship their God in their own way.

The documentary was instructive and showed a lively and humorous Escriva – not the sour and embittered cleric I had been expecting. He had travelled the world and had died in 1975. In 1928, he had begun with just three members, but by 1984 Opus Dei had acquired an international following some 84,000 strong; 48,700 of whom live in Europe, 300 in Belgium. It suddenly struck me that Opus Dei had something in common with both the Flemish movement and freemasonry: all three are desperately in search of younger members.

This is no easy task. In modern times Flanders has become demystified. As a consequence, it has also become more ordinary, perhaps even a little more boring. Yet it is undeniable that mysticism and symbolism make life more interesting, warmer, more lively, more spiritual. People are desperately searching for values they can cling onto in an increasingly cold and lonely world.

During the meeting, the followers of Opus Dei had been particularly excited. In 1992 Josémaría Escrivá had been beatified by the Pope and in 2002 he would be made a saint. An old lady came up to me and held out a brochure with the invitation 'Come to Rome for the canonisation of Josémaría Escrivá'. Apparently, I had a choice of making my trip to Rome by bus, train or plane. 'There are some very good all-in packages', added the lady helpfully. I declined politely. My brother-in-law, a fervent anti-papist, would have excommunicated me.

However, my dealings with Saint Josémaría were not quite yet at an end. A year later I received an invitation to attend a solemn mass in honour of his canonisation at the Our Lady of Zavel Church in Brussels. As with my previous venture into the world of Opus Dei, I was still curious to see whether or not any prominent politicians would turn up. Once again, I was destined to be disappointed. There was the same collection of Spaniards, Poles, Italians and Africans, mainly young families. However, just as I was about to try and slip quietly out the back door, I suddenly saw a face that I did vaguely recognise. The lady in question sat four rows in front of me and I eventually remembered that she had recently been made a baroness by the King, in recognition of her work as the head of a charitable religious foundation in Antwerp. With growing horror, I also recalled that she had been to see me once or twice, to try and get me to write an article about her 'good works', as she called it. I hoped to God, which was appropriate in the circumstances, that she wouldn't see me. I had come here to recognise others, not to be recognised myself! If the story got out that I was attending arcane Catholic masses, my credibility would be ruined. There were many politicians who would have been only too happy to see me labelled as an Opus Dei freak. 'Now we know what your secret agenda is,

Eppink', I could almost hear them saying. I had to avoid being seen at all costs, but how? I moved to a seat behind the tallest man in the church, in the hope that he might give me some cover. But I knew that when the baroness returned from the altar after taking communion I would be in her direct line of sight. What could I do? The only viable hiding place seemed to be in one of the confessional boxes, but not even my pragmatic Protestant soul could stoop to such desecration. Sweat began to break out on my brow and I realised that there was only one solution: in the time- honoured tradition of cowards through the ages, I decided to make a run for it! The whole church turned to look as I raced for the exit, but thankfully all they saw was a clean pair of heels and the back of my head. I was safe, at last!

Was I over-reacting? To me, both freemasonry and Opus Dei smacked of secrecy. I would never have felt at home in either of them although I had had the opportunity to join both. A real Belgian would probably not have missed that opportunity and would have joined both, seeing them as just another way of getting on in the world.

BELGIFICATION

In the space of a few short years, I have travelled across the length and breadth of Belgium, usually to visit towns and villages where I have been invited to give a talk or make a speech. Flanders has a finely woven network of social and cultural organisations – and they are all in desperate need of speakers. As a result, I think that I have probably seen the inside of every cultural venue in the land. One week I would be a guest in a fashionable Brussels restaurant, the next at a bar in downtown Antwerp. On Friday evening my hosts might be a historical society in Roeselare and on Saturday a woman's association in Lanaken. Sometimes I would speak in a castle, sometimes in a small and draughty parish hall – usually bearing an evocative and emotive-sounding name, such as the 'Christ the King'.

Public speaking in Flanders can be a time-consuming business. If I ever had the choice, my preference was to arrive, do my talk and then go straight home. However, things were seldom that simple. Audiences in Flanders expect a lot. They are not happy with just a speech, no matter how witty and amusing: they demand personal commitment – and punctuality. 'You will arrive on time, won't you?' was the most common comment after I had accepted an invitation. 'I'll do my best', I replied, trying to convey that West Flanders or Limburg (or wherever else it might be) was not exactly just around the corner. 'We're counting on you to be here in time for the aperitif and we would like you to stay the whole evening. The food is very good – honestly!'

There was no escape. Like a good boy, I arrived in time for the aperitif and duly shook hands with everyone in the room. As always, the atmosphere was relaxed but expectant. Experience had taught me that the best moment to give my talk was after the main course. By then, the wine would be flowing freely and everyone would be in a good mood. If I was going to get a laugh, that would be the time. I had long since noticed that the Flemish sense of humour is very different to that of the average Dutchman. The Flemings like cool asides, veiled allusions, sarcastic remarks. They find the Dutch sense of humour too blunt, too lacking in subtlety, almost offensive. Hollanders love to see people being tricked or made a fool of. For them humour has to be laid on with a trowel: thick, hot and steamy, preferably with plenty of sex. This type of comedy is guaranteed to fail with a Flemish public. It's not that they don't understand it: they just don't like it.

The average Flemish audience is suspicious, always reserving its judgement for later. Before the beginning of each talk, I can see them all saying to themselves: 'Who the hell does this Hollander think he is and what's he got to say that's going to interest us?' When they discover that I am actually on the same wavelength, you can almost see them visibly relax. The smiles and the laughter soon follow. Sometimes I almost feel like a cabaret star – or at least a shrewd political satirist.

The end of my talk seldom meant the end of my evening. 'You will stay for a drink afterwards, won't you?' Usually I did and usually it was fun. In general, the Flemish public is warm, sympathetic and kind. Often it was midnight before I made my way home – having once again shaken every hand in the room before

I left. Driving along the brightly lit motorways of Flanders, I imagined myself to be a kind of a popular entertainer who had brightened the evening with the same old songs and the same old jokes, but who no longer really knew why he did it.

Why did I do it? God only knows. Certainly on most evenings I was reluctant to leave the comfort of my home, setting off for a cold hall in a remote village, armed only with a sketchy (and often inaccurate) plan provided by my hosts. I could usually manage to get to the right general area but I could seldom find the right address. If I was lucky there might be a petrol station open where I could ask the way. But even then, there always seemed to be road works, or missing signs or malfunctioning traffic lights to lead me astray. It was as if I was perpetually jinxed – a Dutch albatross loose on the streets of Flanders. Often I arrived only at the very last moment, nervous and out of breath. But by the end of the evening, I usually left with a satisfied feeling. In most cases, a grateful public had enjoyed my discussion of the cultural differences between Holland and Flanders; had laughed at the old stereotypes and familiar clichés, irrespective of whether they were still true or not. As so often in life, it is not 'how things are' which is important, but 'how you think things are.'

Wherever I went, there was always one particular question which kept cropping up time after time: 'How has life in Belgium changed you?'

This is not an easy question to answer, requiring as it does a certain degree of critical self-examination. A person develops because of his changing relationship with his social environment and because of his personal experiences through the years. To that extent, Belgium must have changed me. I was certainly no longer that 'young Protestant lad from the Netherlands', who knew nothing of Belgium and who tried to keep Belgium at arm's length. But how had Belgium changed me and why? Would I have been a different person if I had gone to some other country instead of Belgium? Who might I have become then? As I said, these are not easy questions to answer.

One of the first things that struck me when I began to compare in particular Flanders and the Netherlands is that they are two countries separated by a common language. This is not unusual in Europe. The Germans and the Austrians also share the same language but have very different national characters. The Germans see the Austrians as *klein, fein und niedlich*. The Austrians see the Germans as interfering know-it-alls. A common language is often quoted as one of the most important factors in helping to create a common culture. Well, not if Germany and Austria are anything to go by. Moreover, similar differences in identity can also exist within the same country. Take Italy. The citizens of Milan and Naples both speak the same language, and yet they think of themselves as being totally different from each other. Much the same thing is true of Flanders and the Netherlands.

Paradoxically, there are sometimes greater similarities between nations which speak different languages than between nations which speak the same language. The Dutch and the Germans, for example, have much more in common than most Hollanders would like to admit. Both societies have the same legalistic Protestant foundations, which results in a methodical and systematic approach to all life's little problems. Perhaps the only real difference lies in humour. 'A Dutchman is a German with a sense of humour.' 'A German is a Dutchman with a lobotomy.'

The same can also be said of the Italians and the Belgians. The language is different, but their mental programming is remarkably similar. They both live in countries which are socially and politically complex, where a high degree of 'creativity' is required to survive and prosper. In Belgium and Italy, the quickest way is never the most obvious one. They are masters of the back door and the detour – but they always get what they want!

Perhaps this is what makes the European experiment so interesting. We all live in a melting pot of different languages and cultures and yet it is perfectly possible to bridge these differences, if only we try to meet each other halfway. Europe demands empathy; it forces you to put yourself in the other person's position. Its very diversity is its great strength.

As a Dutchman in Flanders, I spoke the same language as my new neighbours, but I didn't always understand them. Not every word has the same meaning or the same emphasis. The same language does not mean the same way of thinking or the same way of looking at problems. On the contrary, the same language can often lead to misunderstandings, disappointments and rejection. You think that you are making yourself clear and yet the other person shrugs his shoulders or gives you a blank stare. You become suspicious. Perhaps he doesn't want to understand me. Perhaps he doesn't like me and just wants to make me look a fool.

After much reflection, I am now convinced that a Dutchman who comes to live in Belgium will never be the same Dutchman ever again. Belgium reforms you. Belgium deforms you – but in the nicest possible way! Your old habits and your old customs will gradually slip away and before you know it you will be doing things the Belgian way. You have no choice – it is simply the nature of Belgian society: you adjust, you compromise or you go under.

As a rule, the Dutch are an outspoken race. We have an opinion about everything, from bullfighting in Spain to the fate of the Indians in the Amazon rain forests. And not only do we have an opinion: we have to let the whole world know about it – and the louder the better. Occasionally, I watch televised debates on Dutch politics and am struck by the fact that nobody seems to be listening. Everyone is keen to express his own point of view, but nobody wants to hear what the other man has to say. And the harder you shout, the more it seems that your opinion is the right one.

In my 'pre-Belgian' days I would have fully understood and sympathised with this way of doing things. I would probably even have joined in. Not any more. Because now I have become a semi Belgian myself!

Now I would just put forward a few vague ideas and listen to what kind of response they get.

I would speak calmly and quietly, without shouting.

I would let the other man have his say, without interruption.

I would offer an opinion, but would withdraw it just as quickly, if it became clear that the majority was in favour of a different opinion.

I would argue on points of principle, but would also have a reserve set of alternative principles ready, just in case the first set are not too well received.

Does this mean that I have betrayed my Protestant heritage? Would I be a disappointment to my teachers at the Bible School and to the famous Professor I.A.Diepenhorst of the Free University in Amsterdam? Certainly, there are a lot of Hollanders who would say that I have become a hypocrite. A Fleming would say that I have become sensible, because I now avoid making unnecessary trouble. 'You wormed your way out of that well' is a compliment in Belgium. It is a half-insult in the Netherlands.

That being said, a Protestant upbringing is something that you never lose altogether. It is a part of you and it will always remain a part of you. The desire to always be on time. The desire to do a job properly. The desire to plan ahead. The desire to apportion blame, where blame is due. All these things are ingrained in the genes of the Dutch people, whether they like it or not and whether they are churchgoers or not (and most of them now are not). Holland is a Calvinist land, but without a Calvin.

So what has Belgium changed in me? Above all, Belgium has helped me to put things in their proper perspective; to see that there is not just one universal truth, but a whole range of different truths; to understand that no one person is always right, but that lots of people are sometimes a little bit right. The Flemish are as much conditioned by their Catholic past as the Dutch are conditioned by their Protestant one. The Flemish seldom reveal their true feelings, because it is always useful to keep an ace or two up your sleeve. They are seldom outspoken or controversial, because they understand the need to get along with everyone. Who knows when you might need somebody's help?

A Fleming likes to portray himself as a respecter of authority and a supporter of the existing social and political structure. Yet at the same time he is always thinking: 'How on earth can I get out of this?' He is a born deserter, and a born survivor. Between 1940 and 1945 it was often said: 'There is more chance of living out the war as a Fleming than winning it as a Dutchman.' The same is probably still true today.

In Holland, the Protestant clergy set standards which are too high for the average man and woman. They tell their 'brothers and sisters' how they are supposed to behave in an ideal world, and are then constantly disappointed when the 'brothers and sisters' fail to live up to the mark. In Belgium, the Catholic priests have a far better understanding of man's frailty and weakness. To this extent, Catholicism is more in keeping with human nature than its Protestant rival. For the Catholics, guilt is not eternal and hereditary, but temporary and relative. Its purpose is forgiveness, not retribution. Penance should therefore be constructive, not punitive. It is a view of the world which makes life more bearable. It is a view of the world which I sometimes envied – and still do.

When I arrived in Belgium, I found myself in a kind of no-man's-land between these two different mentalities. Not surprisingly, this led to tension and confusion. My instinctive Protestant reaction was to reject and to condemn. A Dutchman abroad is always quick to say: 'In Holland we do things differently.' What he means, of course, is: 'In Holland we do things better.' Or to put it another way: 'What a mess this place is!'

I tried to avoid this knee-jerk reaction to my new home. I wanted to give myself time to get to know Belgium. I wanted to see what was different and why it was different: only then would I pass judgement. Why do the Belgians always beat about the bush, instead of just saying 'no'? Why are Belgian plumbers always late, even though they have promised faithfully to be on time? What makes a Belgian driver reverse along a motorway, risking all our lives, just because he has missed his turning? It would have been easy to jump to the obvious conclusions: the Belgians are scared to say what they think, fail to live up to their commitments and have no respect for the law.

After more mature reflection, I came to see things differently. The Belgians do not like to offend people directly, but prefer to keep their options open. Whilst in Holland an appointment is something set in stone, in Belgium an appointment is a purely temporary arrangement, which can be changed if the circumstances require it. Perhaps my plumber is always late because he has to go and help someone whose need is greater than my own. Is this so unreasonable? As for the law, this has always been subject to 'flexible' interpretation in Belgium. But what else can you expect from a country that has been permanently occupied for the past 500 years? When you have been used to dodging Spanish laws, Austrian laws, French laws, Dutch laws and most recently German laws, it is only to be expected that people will continue to try and dodge Flemish laws and Belgian laws. Particularly as most Belgians still regard the Belgian central government as a form of foreign occupation!

Personally, I am still inclined not to break the law, for the simple reason that it is forbidden – and therefore wrong. This is a very 'un-Belgian' way of thinking. A Belgian will nearly always break the law, unless he feels that there is a reasonable chance that he might get caught. Someone who breaks the speed limit in the Netherlands is almost certain to be condemned within his immediate social circle: 'Shame on you; you're a menace on the road!' In Belgium a speeding driver can count on sympathy and understanding from his friends: 'Bad luck; the only time you ever see a policeman is when you don't want one!'

At first glance, the Belgians seem to attach great importance to social and economic position. A Belgian will always address his boss as 'Sir' or 'Mr. Director'. However, there is a huge difference between appearing to conform and actually conforming. Having paid lip service to the hierarchy, most Belgians do exactly what they like – not what they are told. This leads to complex structures, whose only common factor is that they are hardly structures at all. In these circumstances, work becomes more a question of improvisation than planning and 'doing your own thing' is the order of the day.

In the Netherlands, the concept of a social hierarchy is either laughed at or ignored. A manager will call his employees by their first name and will try and treat everybody just the same. It is a kind of 'all for one, one for all' philosophy gone mad. There is so much discussion and debate that there is hardly any time to do any work. The net result of all this social equality is delay. In the Netherlands it takes decades before new road, rail or waterway projects are finally completed – not because they take so long to build, but simply because they need to go through so many different stages of the 'consultation process'. Everybody, however humble, has to have his say. Or at least think that he has had his say. Because in the final analysis, it is always the politicians in The Hague who decide. None of the local residents were in favour of the notorious Betuwe railway, but it still came, in spite of their protests.

Even so, the question of presentation is all important. The use of power – whether in the business world or the economic world – has to be camouflaged with fine rhetoric. In the Netherlands, you would never say: 'I have decided.' This sounds too authoritarian and 'authoritarian' is a dirty word. It is far better to say: 'we have decided.' This makes it sound like a collective process, even though it is nothing of the kind. It appears as though everyone is in agreement, but in reality the boss is doing exactly what he wants. He is simply getting his employees to rubber-stamp his decision: a decision which they will then feel honour-bound to keep. Because in Holland, a deal is a deal.

A good example of this kind of attitude was the well-publicised transfer of the Philips Company from Eindhoven to Amsterdam. The President of the company was Cor Boonstra, a friendly and likeable man who everybody knew as Cor. However, when he decided to relocate his factory and offices 100 kilometres down the road, good old Cor gave his staff a simple choice: move or be sacked. Most moved. Cor might be on first name terms with everybody, but he was still the boss – and his word was law.

Another striking difference between the Netherlands and Belgium is the position of women. In the past, both Holland and Belgium were male countries, in which the top men did business with each other, like members of the same exclusive club. During the course of the 20th century, the Netherlands was transformed into a female society, based on the model of the Scandinavian countries. Belgium in general – and Flanders in particular – has managed to resist this trend. Much of the Flemish establishment is still male-dominated, although most women have a regular job.

The voting patterns of men and women have also begun to differ. In the old days, a woman would usually vote the same way as her husband. Not any more. Electoral research has shown that nowadays men are more concerned with matters such as taxation, employment and transport, whereas women are more interested in education, health care – and how a politician looks. Women are more inclined to ask: 'Is he a nice man?' Most men couldn't care less. In short, men concentrate on arguments and women concentrate on sentiment.

Yet in our new and emancipated society, the modern man also has to be able to show his softer side. During the last 50 years women have become more masculine: they now want babies *and* a career. As a consequence, men have had to become more feminine: they are kinder, more sympathetic, less certain that they are always right. We are now living in a world where the relations in society are regulated by the kind of language that used only to be reserved for the office of the marriage guidance counsellor.

It is even starting to creep into politics. After a sharp exchange of views in the Dutch Parliament, Prime-Minister Kok and Foreign Minister Van Aartsen apologised to each other like a married couple after a row:

'We have had a talk to clear the air and will now move forward together, fully confident in each other', said Kok.

'I intend to make a personal investment in our new relationship', added Van Aartsen.

The language of the therapist has become the language of government.

To put it another way, the Dutch woman has become more macho, or should that be macha? And the Dutch man has become more of a sweetie. It all sounds fine in theory, but it can lead to certain practical problems. In particular, the differences between the sexes can sometimes become very blurred. The man of the house is supposed to be tender and kind, but also hard and domineering, when the occasion demands. He is supposed to be a caring soul, sensitive to his partner's every need, but also a man of decision and action. If he goes out to the pub every night, picks his nose and farts in bed, he's a male chauvinist pig. If he does the washing up, reads Woman's Own and changes the nappies, he's a limp-wristed wimp. In short, your average Dutch man doesn't know whether he is coming or going. His life is a permanent piece of play-acting, part comedy and part tragedy. Little wonder that most therapy groups in the Netherlands contain more men than women.

In Flanders a degree of feminisation has also taken place, under the influence of the general emancipation movement which swept Northern Europe in the last decades of the 20th century. Even so, in Flanders there is still more scope for a woman to be a woman. If you hold open a door for a Flemish woman, you will be given a polite smile. If you hold open a door for a Dutch woman, you will be told: 'I can do that myself, thank you!' This kind of militant feminism is still rare in Flanders, where women prefer to use their feminine charms to get their husbands to do things for them: not browbeat them into submission, as is so often the case in Holland.

If the truth be known, both men and women would probably prefer a return to the days of clearer sexual distinctions. Sadly, political correctness has made this a taboo subject. A couple of years ago Hans Hillen – a member of the Dutch christian democratic party CDA – gave his thoughts on the man-woman situation in Dutch politics to *Opzij* Magazine. At that time, there were 50 female MP's out of a total of 150 parliamentary seats: an all-time record. Hillen was not impressed. He complained at the number of 'pit pussies' in the Lower House – an unflattering reference to the scantily-dressed young ladies who hang around the Formula 1 pit lanes. 'I don't know any funwomen in politics', he went on. 'Most of them are humourless fanatics, driven only by ambition and the desire to be right. If you have a disagreement with a man, you can usually sort it out later in the bar over a few beers. Not with a woman. They always have to have the last word.' Not surprisingly, the 'pit pussies' of The Hague were furious. The CDA leadership was quick to distance itself from Hillen and soon afterwards he left parliament: probably to be replaced by a young and ambitious woman! Yet whatever the rights and wrongs of Hillen's position, it is indisputable that he gave expression to the genuine social frustration of the Dutch male. For notwithstanding the outward symbols of success – good job, nice house, fast car – the average white, heterosexual man in the Netherlands is not a happy chap. He is allowed to pay taxes, but for the rest he is supposed to keep his mouth shut. He is held to be responsible for racial and sexual discrimination, he earns a 'socially unacceptable' amount of money and his car pollutes the environment. The way things are going, before long he will probably be blamed for all the evils of mankind, ranging from Third World debt, right through to the white slave trade. His only hope is to attach himself to some kind of minority group – in Holland minority groups are always in the right.

Happily, Belgium has no need of a Hans Hillen. In Belgium all such matters are taken with a large pinch of salt. Hairsplitters and nit-pickers – male or female – have never been popular with the Belgians. They know better than any other race that no one person has a monopoly on the truth and that there is no such thing as an absolute set of principles. As a result, everyone is free to do as he pleases, as long as he doesn't interfere with anyone else. In short, Belgium is the land of live and let live.

Many of my fellow-Dutchmen have a problem with this concept. I am frequently asked how it was possible that I – the product of a Christian-Protestant education – could contemplate working for liberal and socialist politicians and writing for catholic and left-liberal newspapers as I did, during the various different stages of my career. My answer has always been: 'I serve many flags, because I am a man of principle.' The Hollander will shake his head in disgust at such shameless 'opportunism'. The Belgian will smile and wink his silent approval. Because this is the way things have always been done in Belgium. A Belgian is his own boss and he only does as much or as little as he wants. The influence of priests, government ministers and neighbours is minimal. Until now it has always been possible to find a Belgian solution for every Belgian problem. It is a simple system but it works beautifully – at least for the time being! That's why Belgians feel at home in a Europe which requires empathy, mutual understanding and ultimate compromise. Belgians manage to keep together six governments, six parliaments and three language communities at the same time. That turns a Belgian into a 'European par excellence'.

PHOTO CREDITS

Belga: photo 13

Kristof Ghyselinck: photos 5, 6, 7, 16, 18, 19, 20, 21 and 22

Eric Peustjens, © Sofam Belgium: photos 10 and 11

Photo News: photos 8 (D. Geeraerts), 9, 12 (K. Ibourki), 14 (N. Vereecken), 17 (D. Gys)

Private collection: photos 1, 2, 3 and 25

Fernand Proot: photo 15